AROUND THE WORLD IN THE MIDDLE SEAT

Around the World in the Middle Seat

How I Saw the World
(and Survived!)
as a Group Travel Leader

Joyce Brooks

Around the World
in the Middle Seat

How I Saw The World
(and Survived!)
as a Group Travel Leader

Published by
The Intrepid Traveler
P.O. Box 531
Branford, CT 06405

Copyright © 2002 by Joyce Brooks
First Printing, Printed in Canada
Book Jacket: George Foster, Foster & Foster, Inc.
Photographs from Joyce Brooks Collection
Library of Congress Control Number: 2001088546
ISBN: 1-887140-39-5

Publisher's Cataloging-in-Publication Data, prepared by Sanford Berman

Brooks, Joyce.
    Around the world in the middle seat; how I saw the world (and survived!) as a group travel leader. Branford, CT: The Intrepid Traveler, copyright 2002.
    Illustrated with 35 photos, 1 map, and 1 news clipping.
    PARTIAL CONTENTS: When nature calls. -Baggage blues. -So you want to be a group leader? - Places visited.
    1. Women travelers--Personal narratives. 2. Tour guides--Personal narratives. 3. Tour guides--Vocational guidance. 4. Tourist trade--Personal narratives. 5. Package tours--Personal narratives. 6. Travel--Personal narratives. I. Title. II. Title: In the middle seat around the world. III. Title: How I saw the world (and survived!) as a group travel leader. IV. Title: Group travel leader. V. The Intrepid Traveler.

910.4

To

My husband, Keith, who was always with me
through the good and bad times

and

All my Frequent Followers, for without them
I would not have acquired the knowledge and experience
to write this book.

ACKNOWLEDGMENTS

To my daughter, Heidi Frock, and stepdaughter, Karon Wheeless, for their efforts in proofreading the manuscript and their special encouragements to keep me writing.

To my son, Corky Cootes, who with patience and knowledge saved me when numerous computer disasters occured and always came to the rescue when I needed him.

To my publishers, Kelly Monaghan and Sally Scanlon of The Intrepid Traveler, who had faith in me to fulfill my lifelong dream of having a book published.

TABLE OF CONTENTS

BROOKESMITH GIRL LEAVES MONDAY ON ALL-EXPENSE TRIP TO NEW YORK CITY

Miss Joyce Connaway, 16-year-old daughter of Mr. and Mrs. Ira Connaway of Brookesmith, will leave Love Field, Dallas, Monday on an expense-paid plane trip to New York and Washington by American Airlines.

About a month ago she was announced as winner of girls' division of the third annual rural life essay contest sponsored by Farm and Ranch-Southern Agriculturist, with a prize of the expense-paid trip and $100 in cash.

At Nashville, Tenn., Miss Connaway will meet Harlan Blount of Decaturville, Tenn., winner of the boys' division of the contest, and Mrs. Milbrey Cullom, associate editor of Farm and Ranch-Southern Agriculturist, who will accompany them on the trip to New York and Washington.

Subject for essays entered in the contest was how to achieve better living on the farm. The contest was open to rural high school youth.

When asked how she felt about winning the contest, the tall, brown-eyed Brookesmith farm girl said, "It's just wonderful, because all my life I have wanted to see New York City. But I never knew I would be paid to go."

Her mother said, "I worked on her from November last year until March—three days before the contest closed—before she would enter."

For the past three years Miss Connaway has lettered on the Brookesmith basketball team at forward. After graduation next year, she plans to enter Howard Payne College and later a career in journalism.

During her trip in New York City, the contest winners will stay at the Waldorf-Astoria Hotel, and take in all the sights of that metropolis. Later, they will visit historic spots in the nation's capital.

READY FOR TRIP—Miss Joyce Connaway of Brookesmith is pictured here in the ensemble she will wear when she boards an airliner at Dallas Monday for an all-expense trip of five days to New York and Washington. (Jimmy McDonald Photo).

Mr. Waisam had my picture taken and sent it to the Samsonite Company.

I got my first taste of travel at sixteen. I entered a writing contest — and won!

PROLOGUE

Have you ever been trapped in the middle seat in coach for fourteen hours? No fun! My husband, Keith, prefers the window seat and wants me to sit beside him, so being the good wife that I am, I have to take the middle seat on a plane that has the three-seat configuration. You'll find me next to the big fat man. Or the fidgety lady who is constantly digging in her bag, turning the light on and off. Or the mother with the screaming nine-month old child. If I'm really lucky, there's a three-year-old behind me constantly kicking the back of the seat. Or a little old man with a bladder problem who catches hold of my head each time he leaves his seat, which is frequently. Sometimes the person in front of me reclines so far back I feel like the middle of an Oreo cookie, only not as sweet. I never have room to eat the "gourmet" airline food, which may not be such a bad thing. Recently I was served what the airline called "dinner." It consisted of a "Hot Pocket" (some smashed up vegetables and some alleged chicken, all totally inedible), a package of chips, and one cookie. Take it from a country girl, that's *not* "dinner"!

In the past twenty-five years, Keith and I have flown thousands of miles and usually the flight to and from the destination was the only unpleasant and bad part of a trip. But it was certainly worth every inconvenience and all the dreadful food to see and to do everything that I have experienced during that period of time. We have visited over one hundred countries, and led over two hundred group trips, including forty cruises. We also made many trips on our own. How I did this without being independently wealthy (and I certainly do not qualify) is what this book is all about.

But let's start at the beginning. I was born during the Depression on a farm and ranch in Central Texas. There was no television and there were no close neighbors to occupy my free time. When I wasn't helping Daddy with the cattle or sheep, which I liked, or working in the fields gathering corn or picking cotton, which I detested, I read. As I devoured books on faraway places, I thought, "If I could ever see Paris, the wild animals in Africa, and the Taj Mahal in India, my life would be complete." Well, I have been there, done that (plus much more) and I certainly am not ready to call life quits. I also dreamed of writing and publishing my own book, and here it is.

I got my first taste of travel at sixteen. I entered a contest sponsored by *Farm and Ranch* magazine with an essay entitled "Achieving Better Living on the Farm." I certainly wanted to achieve a better life than chopping and picking cotton! To my total astonishment, I won first prize in the girls' division, an all expenses paid trip to New York City and Washington, DC, plus $100 cash. With the prize money, I bought a new suit, shoes, purse, hat and gloves (everything the well-dressed lady wore in 1950) plus two pieces of the latest hot-pink Samsonite luggage. The country girl was ready for the big city.

It was a traumatic morning when my folks accompanied me to Love Field in Dallas to catch the four-propeller American Airline plane (this was before the days of jets). Mother was crying and moaning that something would happen to me in those big cities and I would never return. Daddy told me to go and have a damn good time. My little brother, Delbert, was complaining that he never got to go anywhere. Up to then, I had been to the same places he had — down to the Texas Gulf coast. I had never been on a plane in my life, and here I was boarding that monster machine all by myself. Needless to say, I was apprehensive. I had wanted to see the world, and this was my big chance to start, and I was not going to let fear get in the way. I flew to Nashville where I joined the boy winner and our lady chaperone and mailed a letter I had written on the plane.

June 5, 1950

Dear Mother, Daddy and Delbert:

We are not far from Memphis now. The ride is wonderful. I am not a bit sick. Every once in a while it swerves up and down and kinda makes your stomach feel funny. Otherwise, you don't even know you are up in the air. We had the biggest breakfast you ever saw — eggs, 2 pieces of ham, half grapefruit, 2 muffins with nuts and raisins in them, milk or coffee. I ate most of mine and it is still with me. It is so funny to look out the windows. As you said, Mother, it makes you feel like an angel. The houses look just like miniature scale models and the fields are so pretty. I can't even describe it. One minute you will be riding over clouds and can't see a thing below, then it will clear up again. Now the sun is beaming down on us. I am just right in temperature. I know I would be too hot in anything wool. We just crossed what looked like the Mississippi River. I don't know where we are at present. The hostesses are very nice.

Don't worry about me a bit, for I know I will have a wonderful time. I will try to mail this at Nashville, so you will know I have met the woman chaperone and all is OK.

Love, Joyce

In New York I had a private room in the Waldorf Astoria Hotel. As this country bumpkin looked out that eighteenth-story window at the mass of yellow cabs, she was overwhelmed. But that little taste managed to fuel my desire to see the world. We took in all the sights of the Big Apple, including the United Nations where we starred on a "Voice of America" radio show. At night we went to Broadway. What a thrill to see Jean Arthur and Boris Karloff in "Peter Pan" and Mary Martin in "South Pacific." In Washington I had my picture taken with Lyndon Johnson, then the Senator from Texas. This gal was hooked on travel!

Let's fast-forward through a life that included graduating from Texas Woman's University in Denton, Texas, working as a journalist, publicist and fundraiser, marrying and giving birth to two wonderful children, Heidi and Corky, and getting divorced in 1974. After seventeen years, my husband decided he no longer wanted to be married to me and, at the time, I thought my world had come to an end. Here I was, forty years old, divorced with two children, ages seven and ten. At least I had a good job as a fundraiser for a public television station in Austin. I still had not ventured out of the United States and had seen very little of it. Needless to say, traveling around the world seemed impossible, although it was still a lovely dream.

Then a miracle came my way. Two weeks after my divorce was final, I met Keith Brooks on a blind date and, just like in the romance novels, it was love at first sight. We were married four months later and my whole outlook on life began to change. Keith enjoyed traveling. We took one trip abroad each year, and I studied all the guidebooks and made all our travel plans. One trip a year was great, but my itchy feet were not sufficiently scratched.

At age forty-five, I decided I wanted a career change from public television fund raising, and since travel had always been my prime interest, I went to work briefly for a travel agency. Shortly after I started, I called on an Austin bank with a small travel club to solicit their business, and the president said, "I'm not doing anything in travel right now, 'cause I just fired the little girl that was handling the program." He explained that she had taken a group to a Dallas Cowboys football game and had engaged in rather inappropriate relations with a couple of the male customers, hardly the image the bank wanted to project. He offered me the job.

"I don't know anything about banking. I can hardly keep my checkbook straight," I said.

"You just handle the travel program, the bank's publicity, and customer relations, and leave the banking up to the rest of the employees," he said with a smile.

I seized the job without a second's thought. It was the start of my career escorting people around the world.

Successful travel programs have to start small and grow slowly. It takes lots of patience and effort to gain the customer's confidence. I began by offering one- and two-day bus trips. Soon the program grew to include four local banks, then other statewide banks in the company's network. After ten years of intense effort, I was organizing and leading about a trip a month all around the world and had an exceptionally faithful following.

In 1990, the bank was acquired by a larger holding company and conditions were changing. Keith wanted to move back to his ranch, which he had worked prior to our marriage and where we had built a small house a few years before. So I retired from the bank and we moved a hundred miles to the small community of Evant, Texas. We added on to the house and became country residents.

I had retired from the bank, but not from travel. Out in the country I installed a fax machine, got an 800 number, and notified all my FF's (frequent followers) that I was setting up Joyce Brooks Tours. I invited them to come go with me. And they did.

After five years of active travel with my own business, one day Keith asked, "Can we go anywhere without forty people?"

I thought about it. Keith had been so supportive all these years, looking after the luggage and being my helpmate during trips. And I was a little tired, too. So I replied, "OK, I'll quit." And I did — for two days.

Collette Tours, a wholesale travel company that I had been booking with for several years, found out I was going to close up shop and asked me to be a Texas Sales Representative. As we had seen most of the world, but not all of Texas, I agreed. For two and a half years Keith and I drove from the Texas Panhandle to the Rio Grande Valley, from El Paso to Wichita Falls. I called on banks, travel agents, and individual groups, helping them set up tours.

In 1999, I decided it was time to unpack the suitcases for good and get to work on that book I'd always dreamed of writing. So I retired one more time and now I have the leisure to reflect on my many marvelous memories and extraordinary adventures.

Everything in this book actually happened. Some names have been omitted for reasons that should be obvious. The legends and the numbers were told to me by local guides and therefore may vary from things you may have read, but I accepted their word as fact. Also, I have recorded my personal impressions of areas visited and they, too, may differ from the "official" version. Many things have changed through the years in the destinations described here, but this was the way it was when I was there. I want to share with you these experiences and the knowledge derived from them. So grab an aisle seat and come along with me.

Dream Destination #1: Paris

1

DREAMS DO COME TRUE

When I was a girl, three magical places haunted my dreams of travel. The Taj Mahal, Paris, and the game preserves of Africa. In my imagination I could be an Indian princess who inspired the world's most beautiful building. I could be a mysterious artist strolling down the Champs Elysee. I could be a fearless hunter stalking lions in the veldt by the light of the moon. I never grew up to be any of those things, of course, but, once I started living my dreams in the travel business, I got to go to every one of those places and have a terrific time being plain old Joyce Brooks.

The Taj Mahal in India is the first place I can remember dreaming of seeing. I saw it in 1980 on an around-the-world trip made possible with the travel agent perks and discounts I received as a travel industry insider. Keith and I were accompanied by the husband and wife owners of the agency where I worked.

The Taj is probably the most celebrated and most beautiful building in the world. Many people think it is a palace, but it is in fact a mausoleum, a tomb, built by Shah Jahan in 1630 in memory of his beloved wife, Mumtaz Mahal. He sure owed her something — she bore him fourteen children!

Even after seeing so many pictures over the years, I was unprepared for the brilliant colors of the millions of inlaid jewels in its creamy white marble. As we were walking around the grounds, we met an Indian family who were also there as tourists. They were all dressed up — mother in her colorful sari, father in his Nehru jacket, and the children in regular western attire. I asked if I could take a picture and they agreed. It was a very hot day, and as a thank you token I gave each of them a "Wet One" moistened towelette. They had never seen anything like that and I showed them how they could cool off by wiping their faces, arms, and hands. Later I saw the smallest boy, about six, had his dried-out towelette folded in his shirt pocket like a handkerchief.

Although seeing the Taj Mahal was literally a dream come true, my favorite part of India was our visit to Srinagar in the Kashmir Valley. Our guide met us at the airport with two private cars. As we drove away, our driver turned on a siren.

"Why do you have a siren?" I asked.

"You are VIPs," he said with a big smile. "I have saved for ten years to have a siren on my car, and when I was informed that I would be your driver, I went to Delhi to get it — it cost me 550 rupees (about $70)," he explained.

I could not figure out why he thought we were "VIPs," but just sat back and tried to hold on as he raced through the streets with the horn honking and the siren blasting.

We arrived at Dal Lake where we boarded a water taxi called a shikara, with a fancy covering over half of it to protect passengers from the intense sun. A ride along the lake revealed houses on stilts, some floating houses, and even floating gardens — piles of dirt on a board with plants growing.

Srinagar revolves around this expanse of blue water, bustling with activity. We arrived at a houseboat moored at the edge of the idyllic lake, cradled a mile above sea level by the snow-capped Himalayas. The name of our houseboat was the "Union Jack" and a British flag was flying from the roof. Bright colorful awnings and flower baskets welcomed us.

Wealthy British citizens owned the houseboats during the colonial era. When India gained independence, most owners left the houseboats to their Indian managers. Even though the houseboat had no means of propulsion, we had a captain. His wife did all the cooking and his two sons served as houseboys. They lived on a smaller boat tied to the back of the houseboat. Staying with them was the captain's 101-year-old father, who had been the original captain during British rule. He had been awarded ownership by the former English proprietor. When we visited the elder gentleman, he was lying on a thin straw mat. He seemed very pleased that we had come to see him. I then discovered that his daughter-in-law had been cooking all our delicious meals on a small hibachi stove — I have no idea how she managed.

The houseboat had a large sitting and dining area, two bedrooms, and two baths. The furniture was exquisitely hand-carved walnut. I have never received such service. The two houseboys were there to wait on us hand and foot.

Keith and I set aside 5 o'clock each day as a special time just for us, an opportunity to relax from our busy schedules, discuss the day's activities, and have our one drink of the day. It was a ritual we brought to Srinagar. To my surprise, Number One Houseboy could mix the best Vodka Gimlet I have ever tasted! Apparently the British had anticipated my favorite drink.

On the open top deck, you could relax and absorb the tranquility and beauty all around — the clear, reflective lake and the high snow-capped mountains in the distance. I loved to watch the local people float by in their small flat-bottomed boats, maneuvered by means of a long pole. Some larger boats carried merchants with their food and supplies and others served as taxis. Frequently we would see people dipping up the sea grass into their boat to feed to their sacred cows.

The top deck was best at night. The lake took on a totally different appearance with twinkling lights from the shikaras and the near-by shore buildings sparkling on the water. The gentle breeze rocked the houseboat and you could easily believe this was truly the most peaceful and scenic place in the world.

I had heard of a wildlife refuge near Srinagar and I asked our tour company in the US to book a tour for us. What I didn't know was that the Dachigam Wildlife Sanctuary had been a hunting lodge for the Maharajah of Jammu and Kashmir and later served as a retreat for high government officials, much like Camp David in the United States.

When our guide picked us up at the Srinagar Airport, he commented on how difficult it had been to get the permit for us to go to Dachigam. When we arrived at the Sanctuary entrance, there were guardhouses and armed soldiers about. Our guide showed our permit papers, and we were admitted. I then found out that up until that day, only the Indian Prime Ministers and their guests were allowed to come there and, as far as our guide knew, Vice-President Nelson Rockefeller was the only American who had been a visitor there. Now I realized why our driver thought we were "VIPs." When the request came from the US, they apparently thought we must be high officials and went ahead and granted the permit.

The guesthouse was not open to us, so we peeked through the windows. It resembled a hunting lodge with heavy ornate furniture and trophy heads of tigers and deer mounted on the walls. The gardens were dazzling with many blooming flowers, trees, and fountains. On the lush green lawn we had our picnic. Number One Houseboy laid out a large Oriental rug as our dining table. He then served us roast chicken, potatoes, fruit, and wine. Quite a production.

The only wildlife we saw were some deer and a small bear in cages nearby. We were told that the tiger is almost extinct in this area and, of course, we couldn't see any in this populated region. But we were honored to get to visit a place of such esteem and for one time in our lives to be "VIPs."

As we drove back to the city, our driver had the siren blasting and was driving so fast that village children and chickens scurried from the road as we raced by.

"Stop going so fast," I admonished the driver, "you're going to kill us!"

"No fear," he said, as he turned all the way around to talk to me while driving. "Mohammed will take care of us."

I responded: "Mohammed may be taking care of you, but he is not taking care of us, so slow down."

He did reduce the speed some, but left the siren screaming.

Unfortunately, the Kashmir area of India is currently in the grip of a civil war and unsafe for travel. What a waste to mar this delicate beauty. Reports are that lakes and streams are being polluted, forests plundered, and wildlife sanctuaries denuded of flora and fauna as a result of marauding militias, struggling natives, and government neglect. Such is the chaos of war. I even read that at Dachigam military forces have been accused of slaughtering the rare Kashmir stag, an endangered species of red deer. I pray for peace in Kashmir, for this paradise was one of my favorite places in the entire world.

ë ë ë ë

"The first time I saw Paris" my feet did not touch the ground the entire time. Even though I have now been there many times, it still is my favorite city and at night, I think, the most impressive.

Our first trip was in 1976 before I started group travel work so it was just the two of us. I was new to travel planning, but studied all the books on Europe and, in those days before faxes and e-mail, made our hotel reservations by mail with a return self-addressed international stamped envelope. I was looking for the most economical way and found a charter flight roundtrip to London. Imagine my surprise when after the overnight flight came the announcement that we were landing in Paris and then the same plane would continue to London! We could have booked to Paris where we had wanted to be in the first place, but since our luggage would go on to London we had to go too. We arrived in London about 10 a.m. and rented a car so we could drive to Dover to catch the channel ferry back to France.

It took about two hours to cross the English Channel on the ferry. (In 1999 we took the Chunnel Train and made it in about twenty minutes!) On the ferry I discovered that men and women used the same restroom, quite an eye-opener for this Baptist-reared central Texas gal, but I found out that it was very common in France.

We reached Calais around 8 p.m., dead tired. We tried to get a taxi but none were available. So off we trudged, dragging our suitcases the two miles into town to our hotel. We ordered dinner, but were too exhausted to eat; after being without sleep for about forty-eight hours, we fell into bed around eleven and died.

The next morning we rented a French car and drove through the lovely farming country to Paris enjoying the quaint villages along the way. We were amused as we went through a hamlet when we saw a little boy running down the street hitting a little girl (I assume it was his sister) on the head with a baguette, the traditional long loaf of French bread. We stopped at a little French grocery and purchased cheese, bread, wine and fresh cherries with honey. What a great picnic!

I had selected a hotel downtown, right across from the Louvre. It was around five in the afternoon when we arrived in Paris, and you can imagine the traffic. Unable to read the signs and not knowing where we were going, we finally found the hotel, parked our little car, and did not retrieve it until we were ready to leave the city — at around 5 a.m. to avoid traffic.

We walked all over Paris and I was in heaven. We took tours of the city and out to Versailles to see how old King Louis XIV lived. Our first stop in Paris was the Grand Louvre, a must for every tourist. As a visitor, it is practically impossible to see all the collections, which range from Egyptian antiquities, to masterpieces from every epoch, to the French crown jewels. I was disappointed, however, when I saw the Mona Lisa. Here was this little painting measuring only thirty-one by twenty-one inches! I was prepared for something much larger. Still, I was glad I did get to see the famous lady smiling back at me.

The magnificent statue of winged victory and the many other Louvre treasures made up for my "Mona" disappointment. The Louvre is now graced with an imposing glass pyramid at the entrance, designed by I. M. Pei. I liked the wonderful old building as it was, and personally think this new modern addition detracts from its aura — but, again, no one asked me before it was erected and I am sure many people like it.

We did discover things to be rather expensive. Like most tourists, we took a stroll on the Champs Elysees where we stopped at a sidewalk café for a drink. I ordered wine — the cheapest and best thing to order in France. Keith doesn't drink wine, so he looked at the drink menu and ordered a Margarita. Wrong thing to order in Paris. Not only did it cost $14, it was not fit to drink!

Maybe that's why one of my favorite things to do in Paris is to go to the top floor of Le Samaritaine Department Store just a few blocks from the Louvre. There, for free, you can have just as good of a view of the city as from the costly observation decks of the Eiffel Tower. I suggest you go there for lunch and request a table by the window with a river view. This is where Parisian shoppers lunch. The menu is good and, thanks to daily specials, not too expensive. You may have a hard time finding English-speaking waiters, as this restaurant and its observation deck are rarely frequented by tourists. It is one of the locals' best-kept secrets. After lunch, take the elevator to the top floor and there you can see the rooftops and gardens of this fabulous city. You have a complete view of Paris, in all directions. It will certainly be worth the visit and the price is right.

& & & &

Wildlife in its natural habitat is our favorite sight to see and was one of my three top travel dreams. So, when I had the chance, I organized not one but two group safari trips to Africa — one to Kenya in 1984 and another to Tanzania in 1997.

Our eight-day safari in Kenya was part of an exhausting twenty-six-day trip from "Cape to Cairo." I do not recommend covering this much territory in such a short time. It is better to go to one area at a time, so you can physically and mentally enjoy it to the fullest.

The lovely lodges located in the wilderness are one of the most pleasant surprises of an African safari. The only lodge we stayed in that I would not recommend is Treetops, which I found highly overrated. Treetops gained fame when Princess Elizabeth was a guest in 1951. While there she received word of of her father's death and at that moment became the Queen of England.

A "big game hunter with a big gun" met us at the entrance. Personally the only thing that impressed me was his big belly. He was to protect us from wild animals on our walk of about one quarter mile up to Treetops. There was no wildlife to be seen in the blazing heat of midday.

Treetops is a three-story building with bars over the windows (to keep out the animals, I was told) and little cubby holes for rooms. I felt like I was in jail. In front of the building was a water hole. Since we arrived during a drought, they had to fill the hole from the hose to keep a moist mud puddle. A bell is rung during the night for you wake and see the wild animals as they come down to drink. During the night, we were awakened once to see one old cape buffalo at the water hole. The only thing of interest we saw there was a white and black colobus monkey that I dubbed a "skunk monk." (Years later we were staying at a B&B in eastern Canada on the Bay of Fundy and Keith noticed a black and white fur rug in the sitting room. He asked the hostess if that was from a colobus monkey, and she was startled. She said he was the first person to correctly identify the rug that she had obtained while working in the Peace Corps in Africa.)

My favorite resting place in Kenya was William Holden's famous Mount Kenya Safari Club. This place has class. The club covers one hundred acres of gardens, mountain streams, an enormous heated swimming pool, and a nine-hole golf course. I kept looking around for the many famous people who have stayed there such as Sir Winston Churchill and Clark Gable but, after all, they were there many years before our visit. Each couple was assigned a "William Holden Cottage" where a cheerful fire glowed in the corner fireplace and fresh flowers adorned the rooms. Cookies and coffee awaited us on the coffee table. After driving over dusty, bumpy roads, we thought we had reached heaven. Dinner that night was a dress-up affair and the multi-course meal was a delight.

The view from our window was the massive bulk of Mt. Kenya, rising over 17,000 feet from the agricultural plains. Once the mountain was higher, but as it is a giant extinct volcano, the rim has long since fallen away, leaving the eroded plugs as twin snow-capped peaks. The only thing we did not like about the Mt. Kenya Safari Club was the briefness of our visit.

From there we went to the Samburu National Reserve where we were awarded views of all kinds of wildlife — elephant, giraffe, zebra, wildebeest (millions of them), wart hogs, cape buffalo, and all types of gazelles.

Perhaps the most awesome sight was at Lake Naivasha, the highest of the Rift Valley lakes, where two million flamingos make their home. As you approach the lake, you see a rim of pink all around it. At the water's edge, it is solid flamingos, and numerous other birds as well. Obviously, you need to watch where you step and the beach area can be appreciated best if you hold your nose.

One morning in the Serengeti National Park we came upon a small hill that was dotted with mother lions and their cubs. There must have been twenty or more adults and many more babies. The mothers were just resting peacefully and the cubs were tossing and playing with each other. I was amazed at how close we got to the lions in our Land Rover. They knew they are protected; we drove within a few feet of them and they just yawned in our face. It is a sight I will always remember.

We both wanted to see Tanzania, so I signed up for a Collette Tour in 1997. I promoted the trip vigorously, but had no takers, so we decided to take the trip alone and enjoy ourselves without any tour leader responsibilities. Things didn't work out that way. Three days prior to departure, a man from the Collette Tour Guide Department called me. The guide scheduled for the tour had injured his back, and a replacement guide would not have time to get a visa or the required shots. I would have to be the tour guide.

I panicked. I explained that I was going to Tanzania because I had not been there before. He said that I didn't have to worry; the drivers were the local guides. All I had to do was take care of the people, the luggage, the tips — and on and on — which he assured me I knew how to do.

As we were to be traveling alone, Keith and I were flying on frequent flyer miles and could only get tickets to Nairobi, Kenya, instead of Arusha, in Tanzania, where the tour started. So I made arrangements with the local tour operator to drive us the hundred miles to Arusha. The other members of the tour had arrived in Arusha the night before.

When I walked into the hotel lobby in Arusha, I immediately noticed a woman loudly complaining to the lady at the tour desk.

"Collette Tours is certainly going to hear about this and they had better do something about it!" she screamed.

I wanted to turn around and walk out. But knew I would have to face the music sooner or later, so approached them and introduced myself as the "Collette Tour Guide."

At this point, the group's spokeswoman, Terry, walked up and began to explain to me the many problems they had encountered. Terry was a very reasonable woman, widely traveled, and because of her I was able to keep peace with the group during the tour. The major problems when I showed up seemed to be: (1) when they arrived in Arusha, there was no Collette tour guide to meet them, just the local operators. I had faxed the hotel asking them to put in each person's key packet a copy of a letter stating when I would arrive. The copy machine was broken and the hotel staff never mentioned that I had attempted to make contact. (2) The hotel was not the one listed in the brochure. Back in Wisconsin, their Collette representative had told them they would have a view of Mt. Kilimanjaro and the only view from this hotel is a parking lot. (3) Now they find out that their tour guide had never been to Tanzania and was not even an official Collette tour guide. Reasons enough to be upset.

Late that afternoon, I threw a cocktail party for the group — it always helps to put a drink in their hand! — and told them that although I was not familiar with Tanzania, I was definitely experienced in handling groups, and I was going to work very hard to see that they had a very enjoyable tour. Everyone except the first complaining lady seemed willing to give it a try.

My next stop was the gift shop where I bought a "Guide to Tanzania." I stayed up late each night boning up on the area we were to visit the next day. I worked harder than I ever had in my life to make things as smooth and pleasant as possible for the group. The incredible sightings of wildlife and the luxurious lodges along the way helped. By the end of the tour, everyone was happy, and to this day we are close friends with the members of the safari.

On one game drive, we approached a watering hole with hundreds of zebras milling about on one side. Did you know they make a barking sound just like a dog? The zebras were lining up to drink, and were very organized — just like at the post office where you have to take a number. About ten would go to the waterhole and drink, and then return to the herd and ten more would come up. All the time they seemed to be frightened.

"Why are the zebras acting this way?" I inquired.

"Look on the other side of the watering hole."

Our guide pointed out three female lions sitting in the brush ready to pounce. We waited there for a while and our guide decided there was not going to be any action so he drove on. Later that afternoon, when we came back by that same route, the zebras were all gone, and on the side where the zebras had been, there was a pride of three females and one male. Each lion had a piece of a zebra and was in the process of eating it. It was quite an emotional feeling, but one must realize that this is just part of the natural food chain in the wild. The female lions do all the hunting and work together to surround the prey and make the kill. Old Papa Lion just sits back and waits until dinner is provided, then he helps himself to the first serving. The female lions need Women's Lib.

Another time we were driving along the road in the Serengeti and noticed a mother giraffe and baby acting nervous. In among the trees, a group of fourteen female lions slowly surrounded her. One would come closer, then stop. Then others would circle around. This pattern went on for about fifteen minutes, with the mother giraffe pacing back and forth. Finally, the giraffe made a run for it and to our joy was able to escape with her little one clumsily galloping close behind. Then the entire pride of fourteen females, several cubs and old Papa Lion came up and rested under a shade tree. Lunch would have to wait.

A great place to view wildlife in Tanzania is the Ngorongoro Crater, the largest intact crater in the world. The volcano that formed it has been inactive for several million years, leaving the floor of 160 square kilometers as a very fertile grazing area for about thirty thousand animals from the smallest gazelle — the foot-high dik-dik — to the mighty elephant. The close quarters provide unsurpassed wildlife viewing, as if you had just stepped into a Garden of Eden.

The Ngorongoro CraterLodge is perched on the rim of the crater, 7,500 feet above sea level. From the private deck of your hotel room you can watch, through binoculars, the animals milling around the numerous water holes.

We entered the crater in a Land Rover and descended about three hundred feet from the rim. As far as the eye could see were lines of zebras and wildebeests. They roam together and were going single file across the crater. We also saw ostrich, buffalo, elephant, eland, warthog, jackal, hyena, lion and cheetah, and — in the distance — two rare black rhino. Both Kenya and Tanzania have had problems with the poaching of rhinos for their horn, which is in high demand in Asian countries as an aphrodisiac. Now the governments have clamped down and they are protecting the rhino and trying to rebuild the herds.

There were many birds, but the most unusual was the "Secretary Bird." This creature stands on long skinny legs about four feet high and has a crested head with spike-type feathers sticking out resembling pencils or pens behind a secretary's ear. It was like being tuned into the Discovery Channel without having to adjust the set. If you can only go to one country on an African safari, I recommend Tanzania for the sheer abundance of wildlife.

Every day on an African safari is a new drama, with plenty of magnificent animals roaming in the wild and the tall and colorful Masai people with their bead neckpieces and earlobes draped down almost to their shoulders. For so many places in the world, one visit is enough, but I could never get my fill of Africa.

Dream Destination #2: The Taj Mahal in India

Dream Destination #3: On Safari in Africa

The Welcome Wagon, Irian Jaya style

The Berlin Wall is no more

2

WELCOME TO MY COUNTRY

As we traveled from one nation to another, sometimes we encountered immigration and custom difficulties. In Europe, even back in the '80's and '90's, it was very easy to go from one country to another, and now of course, with the European Community fully integrated, it is a breeze. In many other places, however, we experienced a long wait in line upon arrival at a destination. Usually only one or two immigration officials were on duty and it was a very slow process. And just like at the grocery store or at the bank, I always select the slowest line.

In 1984, during my early days as a tour leader, I was leading a group from Capetown, South Africa, to Zimbabwe, to Kenya, and on to Cairo, Egypt. I didn't have a tour guide who stayed with us for the entire trip and I learned the hard way the importance of having a courier traveling with you for the duration of the tour to get you through sticky situations, especially if you do not speak the language. On this trip, we had a different local guide in each country, which meant that we had to clear immigration and customs on our own before we met the local representative outside the baggage claim areas.

When I planned the trip, I was advised that you could not go directly from South Africa to Kenya, due to the tense political storm swirling around South Africa's apartheid policy. So I deliberately routed us from South Africa to Zimbabwe to see Victoria Falls, then on to Kenya. When we arrived in Nairobi, I rushed ahead of everyone through immigration to collect baggage and look for our new tour guide. After a period of time, my group had not made an appearance. I went back up to the immigration area, where they were being detained. I could see them on the other side of the immigration counters.

"Joyce, they won't let us in," they screamed in desperation.

I was informed that the group could not enter Kenya because their passports indicated they had come from South Africa. (Seems that the agent failed to notice anything wrong when he had admitted me.)

"If you will check the passports and airline tickets, you will see that we came from Harare, Zimbabwe," I pointed out.

"Makes no difference, you were in South Africa, and we cannot admit you to Kenya," the official stated emphatically.

I took my sternest position, and said, "We have paid a local company a very large sum of money for twenty people to take an eight-day safari. If you will not admit us, then refund our money and immediately provide airline tickets back to the United States."

The immigration officials looked at each other and agreed they had to check with their supervisor. In a few minutes they returned and said with a smile, "We will be glad to make this exception and welcome to our country our friends from the United States." They quickly began stamping everyone's passport and away we went to the baggage area.

After a very dusty safari, the Nairobi Hilton looked wonderful to us. I was washing my hair when our local guide called.

"Does your group have yellow fever shots?" she asked. "They are required now before entering Egypt from Kenya."

Before we left the U.S. I had checked carefully, and yellow fever shots were not necessary.

"Just get your group together and I will pick you up and take you to the clinic to get the shots," she added.

I wasn't about to back my group into a Nairobi needle. Besides, even if we had been exposed in Africa, it was too late for a shot now. So I called my tour organizer in the States, asking what we should do in this situation. He said he would check on it and let me know.

That night, a telegram was slipped under my door. It stated: "Yes, now yellow fever shots are needed to get into Egypt as there has been an outbreak of the disease in Kenya. Agree you should not get shots there. Suggest when you arrive in Cairo, state you are VIPs from Texas and have diplomatic immunity."

I nearly died. If he thought I could pull that off, he was crazy. I decided not to worry the others, so I didn't say a word about our dilemma.

Just as we had trouble getting into Kenya, we had trouble getting out. I had twenty passengers and twenty bags to check. We were flying to Cairo via Air Egypt (NEVER fly them if you can avoid it). As always, I checked the baggage as a group. The Air Egypt representative said there would be a $780 overweight charge. I nearly came unglued!

"We have been flying all over Africa with the same luggage and no mention of overweight charges," I replied firmly.

He wouldn't budge. It was getting close to takeoff, and he could see that I was not backing down either, so at the last minute he agreed to settle for $300. I had no choice at this point, so I paid the man and asked for a receipt. The receipt just had cash indicated, with no amount listed, a minor point I did not notice until I was airborne.

Every seat was full and my people were scattered throughout the plane. The passengers were mostly Eqyptian men, wearing long flowing robes and a heavy body odor. Both the restrooms on the plane were out of order, so I was thankful it was not a long flight. A box lunch of something unidentifiable was handed out. I gave mine to the man sitting next to me (yes, I was in the middle seat).

When we landed in Cairo, I told my group to wait outside the building and let me find our local guide. Inside, he came running up to me.

"Is it true that you don't have yellow fever shots?"

"That is correct. So it is up to you to get us through immigration or you can refund the money for our eight-day tour, complete with the Nile cruise, which comes to several thousand dollars," I said sternly. (If it had worked in Kenya, I might as well try it again, I thought.)

"Wait here. I will be right back." Shortly he returned and said, "Have your passengers file in with that group that is just arriving from Greece. If the custom officials ask where you came from, just say Greece. Yellow fever shots are not required if you are coming from Greece."

"Just a minute," I said, "our landing cards say we embarked at Nairobi."

"Makes no difference. They can't read English," he replied.

I returned to my group, sweltering outside in the hot Egyptian sun, and told them to join the people just arriving and, if they were asked where they were coming from, to just say "Greece." Bless their hearts, they did not ask a single question, but just followed me right in. We proceeded to the immigration desk where they stamped our passports and arrival cards without comment. I had gone through first without a problem, and stood behind the counter holding my breath as each one came through successfully. Welcome to Egypt!

The Air Egypt saga continued. Back home, the more I thought about that guy getting $300 out of me, the more upset I became. So I wrote the Egyptian Embassy in Washington, recounting my story of the luggage charges. I heard nothing from the Embassy, but about three months later I received a letter from the Air Egypt clerk informing me that he was in trouble because of my letter. It seems he had turned in only $100 of my $300 to his boss and pocketed the rest. Now he was about to lose his job and wanted me to write a letter saying I had made a mistake about the amount he had extorted from me and that it was really only $100. He went on to say that he had a wife and children to support and he might lose his job. I wasn't about to lie and since I felt that I wasn't the first person he had ripped off, I didn't respond in any way. What happened to him, I do not know.

&a &a &a &a

In 1980, ten years prior to the fall of the Berlin Wall, we took a tour of "East Berlin." The tour bus picked us up at our hotel in West Berlin and we drove to "Checkpoint Charlie." An East German lady officer, who looked like a Communist official straight out of a James Bond film, boarded our bus. She was very sturdily built and I thought that if she ever smiled her face would surely crack. She took her own good time, stopping at each tourist on the bus (and there were about forty). She would collect the passport, then study each picture and each person about two times, before advancing to the next. After this long process, she took the passports and returned to her little guard stand where she remained for about thirty minutes. Then she came out and motioned for the driver to pass through. She still had our passports, which did not give us a very comforting feeling.

We picked up our local guide who had been thoroughly trained in promoting the Communist way of life. We saw many new buildings, and many bombed-out ruins left from the war. When we stopped, we were not allowed to go anywhere without the guide. At lunchtime, the room at the restaurant where we dined was locked while we ate. We found out that East Berliners could not come west legally until they were sixty-five years of age — then they could leave. I guess the thinking was that they have served the work force by then and the government didn't want to be saddled with old age expenses. Of course today, Germany is reunited and people can travel freely throughout the city of Berlin.

When we returned to "Checkpoint Charlie," our "friendly little lady" boarded the bus and, with passports in hand, approached each person, checked each passport and face, and then returned the document. She left the bus and we thought we were through, but then our bus drove over to another area. Several men came out with mirrors on wheels that they rolled under the bus to see if anyone was clinging underneath to make his or her way to freedom. Our driver explained that many times someone would crawl under the bus when it is parked and try to ride his or her way across the border. Checking out all OK, we then drove over to West Berlin, and were certainly glad to be there.

Keith and I returned to Berlin in August of 1992. Once the city's biggest tourist attraction, the Berlin Wall was now gone. It was dismantled and pieces were being offered for sale. I even have a small piece I bought at a souvenir stand, the only thing remaining at the Checkpoint Charlie site. It was good to see that terrible barrier removed, but I am also glad that I had the opportunity to see how people were forced to live during the Communist era. It makes me appreciate my freedom so much more.

ð ð ð ð

My group of fifty-six had a pleasant Caribbean cruise that departed from San Juan with ports of call in Palm Island (Princess Cruises' private island), Martinique, St. Maarten, and St. Thomas before returning to San Juan. As Puerto Rico is part of the U.S. Commonwealth, we went through customs there prior to boarding our plane for the mainland. We had been reminded before disembarking the ship not to bring any food or plants into the United States.

One of my ladies was unable to walk the long distance at the airport, so I was pushing her in a wheelchair as we arrived at security. I put our hand luggage on the x-ray belt and rolled her through the security gate. As our bags came through the x-ray machine, the officer said: "Don't you know you can't bring food products into the U.S."

"Oh, yes sir," I replied.

"Then what are you doing with this apple and orange?" he snarled as he took them out of my little lady's bag and threw them into the garbage can behind him. "I will not take any further action this time, but let this be a lesson to you."

"Oh, yes, sir," I said meekly. I collected our bags and as I was wheeling the silent lady down to the gate, I was furious.

"What were you doing with that fruit in your bag?" I demanded. "You could have created a lot of trouble for me."

"At least he didn't get the chicken leg," she replied.

And as it happened, our plane was delayed and, as the rest of us sat in the gate area hungry and waiting, she was happily munching on her chicken leg.

ð ð ð ð

Twenty passengers flew with me from Austin to Miami where we connected to SAETA Airlines for a flight to Quito, Ecuador, where we were to stay for a few days before continuing to the Galapagos Islands.

In all my years and miles of flying, I have never experienced such great food and service in coach class as on SAETA, the Ecuadorian national airline. We were wined and dined all the way from Miami to Quito — about a four-hour flight. While waiting on board prior to departure, we were served champagne and orange juice. Then we were presented with booties that came up to our knees so we could remove your shoes and still protect your feet in comfort. Candy was handed out before lift-off. There was not one word about "fasten your seat belt," life vest and oxygen instructions, or any of that stuff that usually comes with take-off. As soon as we were airborne, (not thirty or more minutes later as on other flights) here came the cart with all kinds of complimentary alcoholic beverages and soft drinks, accompanied with first cold and then hot hors d'oeuvres. The flight attendants were constantly replenishing our drinks.

Oriental chicken salad was the next offering. Then a menu presented a selection from three entrees. Three other dishes, along with a choice of wine, accompanied the main course. This was topped off with Grand Marnier cake with ice cream. The climax was Ecuadorian coffee and liqueurs. All was served in crystal glasses and on china plates with linen tray cloths and napkins. I almost forgot to mention, hot towels were handed out before and after dining.

For someone who always rides in the middle seat in coach class and is lucky to get a Coke and pretzels on a flight, this was outstanding. The return flight offered similar epicurean delights. So fly SAETA, if for no other reason than for the food and drink!

We arrived at Quito quite stuffed and feeling no pain. All went well through immigration and customs. We collected our baggage and were welcomed by our local guide, Cecelia. When we were ready to depart the airport, as "mother hen," I counted my "chickens" and noticed one was missing. Just then Mary, the lost chick, came up to us.

"Where have you been?" I asked.

"When I stepped off the plane, my heart started racing. I guess the altitude got me and I just sat down on the plane steps for a while to catch my breath. I just now came in and saw you over here." Quito is 9,250 feet above sea level, so after all the food and drink, her condition was understandable.

The next day Mary approached me. "My roommate said that you had your passport and entry card stamped last night when you came in. When I walked through that area, there was no one there, so I just joined you."

Great! Now I had an illegal entry on my hands. I did not know the penalty for this, but was sure we would be in big trouble when we tried to leave and she did not have her entry card stamped. Cecelia said we would have to wait until the evening to go to the Immigration Office at the airport, as customs officials are there only when the planes arrive, which for some reason is always at night.

At 8:30 p.m., Mary, Cecelia, and I took a taxi from the hotel out to the airport. I had told Mary to bring plenty of money, for there was no telling what this was going to cost. We entered the Immigration Office and found four uniformed men. One (obviously the Numero Uno) was stretched out on the couch dictating something to a man at a desk with a very old typewriter. He was typing with one finger of each hand, and not going too speedily with those. The other two men were just standing around.

Cecelia pleaded our case, explaining that there had been no official available last night when Mary had come through the customs area, and could they please stamp her passport and entry card. Silence — no one said a word after the request. Then the one on the couch grunted something and Cecelia turned to me. "He says, no."

"Then we go to higher authority," I stated.

Cecelia and one of the men left. I had already told Cecelia that we would pay whatever was necessary to straighten this out.

After a while, they returned. Cecelia was smiling. "They agreed to stamp her card and passport, but it will cost $10."

I nearly leaped with joy — I had told Mary to be prepared to pay as much as $100. Mary had given me her money, and quickly I handed over the $10, and — stamp, stamp — all was completed and we left immediately. As we passed the Immigration Office, I noticed that Numero Uno was still reclining on the couch.

The cab to the airport had cost 2000 centavos. There were about ten cabs lined up waiting for the international flights to arrive. We inquired how much to go back to the hotel, and were quoted 3000 centavos. When we asked about the difference in price, we were told: "We can get more from the foreigners arriving than from locals in the city." Makes sense to me.

ॐ ॐ ॐ ॐ

Keith and I always took one big trip a year before I entered the travel game. In 1977 we planned an extensive trip to Bora Bora, New Zealand, and Australia. I always studied all the travel guides and planned our itinerary in detail, then went to a travel agent to book the trip. I was very green in travel at this time, and when I picked up all our tickets and documents from the agent and was walking out the door, she asked: "You have your visa?"

I thought it was strange that she should be concerned whether or not I had my credit card, but replied, "Yes," and walked out. Dumb me. This was a costly learning experience.

We went to Bora Bora and all through the North and South islands of New Zealand. The tour concluded at Christchurch on the South Island. On a Sunday afternoon, we arrived at the Christchurch Airport and presented our tickets to Quantas Airlines for our flight to Melbourne, Australia. Upon checking our passports, the agent queried, "Where are your visas for Australia?"

Naturally, we did not have them, since I did not even know what they were in the first place. But I found out. A visa is a permit issued by a country's consular office for travel in that country for a specified length of time. It must be stamped in or attached to your passport before you are permitted to fly there.

As this was late Sunday, we had to wait until Monday morning and buy an airline ticket to Auckland on the North Island, where the Australian Visa Office was located. We took a cab to the office, only to see a large sign: "Visas require one week for processing." Well, Joyce had to do some tall talking to somehow convince them to issue us one right away. Then we needed two color photos for the application. (Now I always travel with extra photos, but I didn't then). Off we ran to the nearest photo shop. You should see those pictures — totally stressed out and not very happy campers. We took our ugly photos back to the Visa Office where for double the fee, our Australian visas were issued. Then we returned to the airport, purchased *another* ticket to Melbourne (as our original one was from Christchurch), and arrived there over twenty-four hours late and missing one day of our tour. All this cost us over $600 (plus losing one day in Melbourne) and a lot of stress and trouble.

But I learned my lesson. Now I know that a visa is not a credit card and I certainly check to see if one is needed for any country I plan to visit.

&a &a &a &a

Iguacu Falls, on the border between Brazil and Argentina, is a favorite destination. Keith and I had been there twice with groups so, in 1998, while traveling in nearby Paraguay with my brother Delbert and his wife Wanda, we decided to take them to see the famous falls.

Iguacu Falls are 8,100 feet wide and drop 200 feet. Compare that to Niagara Falls which are 2,500 wide on the wider Canadian side and drop a maximum of 192 feet on the American side. You can hear the roar and see the mist of Iguacu Falls as far as fifteen miles away, so it is quite an awesome sight.

After our stay at an *estancia*, a large estate ranch, in Paraguay, our itinerary called for us to drive from Asuncion to Iguacu Falls. Our hotel would be on the Argentina side, with scheduled tours over to the Brazil side. When I asked our U.S. tour operator if we needed a visa for Brazil (as I am now checking this little detail), I was advised that it was not necessary for just the day's visit.

Two days before departure, I contacted the land tour operator in Buenos Aires to reconfirm our arrangements, and he said that we did in fact need a visa because we were American. It seems only U.S. and Canadian residents are required to have a visa for the one-day visit. Our man said that since we did not have time to obtain a Brazilian visa, we would have to take the long route, staying in Argentina all the way, making the car trip five hours longer and costing $75 more. He would arrange all our Falls' tours to originate on the Argentina side. As there seemed to be no other alternative, I consented.

When we arrived in Paraguay, our guide, Pedro, said: "Do you really want to make that long drive around to get to Iguacu Falls?"

"No, but what else can we do?"

"Leave it to me," he said with a grin. The night before we were to drive to the Falls, he announced he had a friend who could get us across the border without a visa, but we had to leave at 4 a.m.

Very early the next morning, Pedro and another man picked us up at our Asuncion hotel. I noticed it was a different van than the one we had been using previously. After about three hours, we arrived at Cuidad Del Este, on the Paraguay-Brazil border, which Pedro called the "Hong Kong of South America." Later I read that the *Wall Street Journal* referred to the site as "15,000 shops jammed into twenty blocks", and a "chaos of mass consumption that turned over thirteen billion U.S. dollars annually in dubious merchandise."

Well, I can tell you — I have never seen such a mess in my life. People were running everywhere carrying big shopping bags, boys were knocking on the van windows hawking their merchandise, and vanloads of people were coming and going — it was unbelievable. Pedro explained that the Brazilian people flock to this so-called "duty free" place to buy merchandise with their currency that has a higher value than Paraguayan money. Traffic was four lanes deep as we crept along. Suddenly we pulled over to the side, and Pedro said, "OK, unload everything and get into that car parked in front of us. I will move your bags."

There stood a nice looking young man in a tour operator's uniform indicating that we should get into his car, which I noted had a Brazilian license plate.

"We are not going anywhere without you, Pedro," I protested.

"Sorry, but this is the only way this will work — we will be right behind you."

So into the car the four of us climbed, and the man (still don't know his name) asked for our passports, which we handed over. This is what I guess you call "blind faith." We stopped at the Paraguay Immigration Exit Office. He jumped out, went inside, and shortly returned, passports in hand. Then we drove about a mile and stopped at the Brazil Immigration Entrance Office. Again, the driver left us in the car and, in no time, returned and handed us our passports all stamped for entry into Brazil. At the Brazil-Argentina border we were just waved through. As we rode along in silence, I looked back and to my relief, saw Pedro and friend right behind us. The total distance covered during this operation was just about fifteen miles and took less than thirty minutes. When we arrived at the hotel in Argentina, I asked Pedro what we owed our "angel" that had smuggled us in and out of Brazil without a visa. "Oh, $10 should be OK."

We would have had to pay $75 extra for a long and tiring journey that would have gotten us to the Falls very late, and here we were arriving at noontime for only $10. I was amazed. Later, when we asked Pedro about it, he laughed abd said, "You just have to know the right people."

Needless to say, Pedro got a very nice tip, and it was certainly earned. We hated to say good-bye to him, but he was just our guide for Paraguay. Someone else would show us the sights of Iguacu Falls.

The hotel room had a panoramic view of the thundering cascade. Our tours led us on walkways up close enough to feel on our faces the spray of many of the twenty-two separate waterfalls. The only mishap was the loss of the cap that matched my purse. It blew off into the raging river and is probably now floating in the Atlantic.

A long way from DFW, in many senses of the phrase

Getting to Iguacu Falls took some doing

Sometimes you wonder if the wait . . .

. . . is worth it.

WHEN NATURE CALLS

3

Many tour guides tell the old joke: "You can use our International Restroom on the bus. When you enter you are 'Russian,' while you are in there 'European' and when you depart you are 'Finnish.'"

In a foreign country, the first problem is what to call it. Here in the United States, we refer to the "bathroom" or "restroom." Outside the U.S., if you ask for a bathroom they think you want to take a bath. Ask for a restroom and you'll get a restaurant.

In the United States, we use euphemisms such as pit stops, using the facilities, potty break, rest break, go to the john, gotta pee, tee tee or — in proper company — relieve yourself. Men sometimes call it the latrine, go to the can, or take a leak. Kids just scream, "I've got to go!" Then there are the cutesy places such as the seafood restaurant that uses "Buoys" and Gulls." None of this translates very well.

In France it is called the "loo" which I always thought was something you skipped to, and in England they say "the lavatory," which to me is a basin for washing your hands. In Europe you see a sign for the "WC" (standing for Water Closet). I first thought it referred to "Women's Can" until I saw men going to the same place. Why it is named Water Closet is beyond me, since most of the time there is not enough water there to flush the things.

Women have more trouble when it comes to restrooms than men and the more remote the area, the bigger the problem. When I am reincarnated, I want to come back as a man or a pigeon, because they can go ANYWHERE!

I have learned after many years of travel that the best reference worldwide is "The Toilet." That conjures up in my mind the two-holer back of the house we had when I was a young child complete with the Sears and Roebuck catalogue, spiders, and wasps. Something about my Southern lady upbringing makes it difficult to say, "Where's the toilet?" It also helps to know the country's word for men and women, or you could get easily misguided.

🐦 🐦 🐦 🐦

When you find the place, the trouble has just begun. First, it may not be the traditional fixture, as we know it. If it is a commode, it may have one of several diverse types of tanks — up high on the wall, behind the wall, or on the ceiling. The next problem is where to flush. I have spent a lot of time just looking for the flush lever. It may be on top of the commode, a string suspended from the ceiling, a button on the wall, a knob on the floor. And in public places, you just hope that, once you've located the flush mechanism, it will operate. In some areas, a bucket of water with a dipper on the floor nearby substitutes for the flush. Or, if there was never a flush to begin with, you might find a water faucet running into a container next to the fixture. This can be spilling over, producing a wet floor, which can be slippery and inconvenient when you have to pull down your slacks. Sometimes the first rule is to roll up your pant legs or hold up your skirt. (All my observations, obviously, are from the woman's perspective, and not that of the envied man or pigeon.)

At one place in rural Argentina, a woman attendant handed you a bucket and showed you where to go fill it with water before going into the stall and doing your business. You then poured the water into the commode and hoped everything went down the drain. Afterwards you returned the bucket to her for the next customer. Very organized.

Of course, all this assumes there is a commode present. In many Asian and some French countries, you will find a porcelain fixture in the floor with two places marked for your feet. These fixtures are correctly referred to as "squatters." This position does not set too good with U.S. travelers, especially older ladies who have difficulty getting up after the job is completed. Some "squatters" do come equipped with a flush, but stand back — for usually the water comes with such force that it covers the floor and you. This may serve a purpose by washing the floor, as not everyone hits the intended hole. Other facilities of this type have the traditional bucket of water and dipper, some nothing — the latter is bad news.

I guess the worst I have encountered was a place in India where the toilet was just a hut with a dirt floor and a hole in the ground. Facing this situation could make you realize that you did not have to go after all. While I was gagging and holding my nose as I used the hut, my husband was leisurely standing with a group of men in front of a "peeing wall." This was literally a wall with a trench in front of it and men just stand up there out in the open enjoying their freedom, and I guess, the view. I later discovered the advantage of the Indian ladies' long skirts. When they felt the urge, they just squatted down with the skirt all around them. Sure seemed better than the stinky huts.

In France, and in many luxury hotels all over the world, the bathroom comes equipped with a commode plus a bidet. I have been told that a bidet is for feminine hygiene purposes, but can be used as a foot washer also. There was even a bidet in the ladies restroom in a French café — guess it was for a "nooner."

On safari in Tanzania, we were staying at the luxurious Serengeti Lodge. It is such a shock to travel over horrible dirt roads with deep chug holes for hours and arrive at a lovely hotel in the middle of nowhere. Here we had a large bedroom with an equally large bathroom complete with commode and bidet. The lodge obtained its electricity from a generator, and the lights were turned off at 11 p.m. and did not come back on until 6 a.m. I have never experienced such complete darkness. I had the uneasiness of knowing that I could not turn on a light. We had a flashlight that I kept by my side. During the night, Keith did not want to disturb me for the flashlight, so he started feeling his way to the bathroom. The first cold porcelain fixture he touched, he used. He did not attempt to flush so I would not awaken. The next morning we discovered he had used the bidet, so I guess it can serve several purposes.

In Singapore, there is a sign in each public restroom stall: "$100 fine for failure to flush after using." I wondered who policed this process, but I certainly made sure I complied.

All cruise ships have a suction flush. If you happen to be sitting when you pull the handle, you have to hold on to avoid being sucked down the drain. The noise is a very loud "Whoosh," so you can easily keep track of your neighbor's activity. Another thing about cruise ship bathrooms (other than being so small that you can usually take a shower while sitting on the commode) is that there is a step up of about three or four inches at the threshold. Many bruised and broken toes have resulted from ramming a foot into the board as you go to the bathroom in the dark of night. I guess the barrier is there in case the shower overflows, but you have to remember to step high when you enter.

We in the United States take something as mundane as toilet tissue for granted. Not so when you travel. In the first place, ladies should never enter a foreign public restroom without Kleenex in their pocket or purse for, as a rule, toilet paper is never furnished. If you are lucky enough to have toilet tissue in the stall, you probably would rather use the Kleenex anyway, as the tissue may resemble a paper sack. I believe Russia wins the prize for the worst toilet tissue, as I have encountered some there rougher than a brown paper sack.

≈ ≈ ≈ ≈

Traveling over the years with groups that were always primarily female, I have found that the bathroom situation has presented plenty of challenges. When a bus makes a "rest stop," there usually is just one men's and one women's facility, and frequently, it is a "one-holer." This creates a long line for the ladies. While we are standing in line, the men are in and out very quickly. I then have one of the men guard the door, so the ladies can use the men's restroom. Well, I can tell you, men's restrooms are not as clean as women's. But it is a means of expediting the process, although some ladies refuse to enter a men's room, regardless how long they have to wait.

I guess the most elaborate public ladies' restroom I have ever visited is at the Shoji Tabuchi Theatre in Branson, Missouri. It is called the "Powder Room" and its design is reminiscent of a 1920s New Orleans courtyard. Granite and onyx pedestal sinks adorned with fresh flower arrangements and individual gold leaf mirrors fill an entire wall. Magnificent chandeliers and original marble fireplaces add accents to the gold leafed wall coverings. And this is no one-holer. There must be forty or more individual stalls. Attendants are standing around to offer you hand lotion and perfume. The LADIES sign is made of stained and jeweled glass. I was told that the men's room had a pool table as its center of attraction.

Another surprise in the facilities was in Rheims, France. Right off the city square is a public "toilet" which is totally free (many European restrooms charge). Three attendants stood on duty. When one person departed a stall, an attendant went in and wiped off the toilet seat with a disinfectant before the next person entered. Never have I seen that, nor is it a job I am seeking. I have traveled with my own Lysol can, but to have someone clean the seat for you right before you enter the stall was mind-boggling.

In the baby changing area they had a separate sink, lots of fresh towels, and even stuffed toys to distract the child while the operation was performed. As we left the ladies' room, I glanced next door to the Men's. It had a glass front door and you could see all the action inside (of course, I did not stare very long), but I thought that was rather unusual. I guess the men could check to see if it was too crowded before entering.

As I mentioned, foreign places usually charge for admittance to public facilities. In Hungary, I didn't happen to have the correct local currency. The large lady in charge refused to let me in — she was not interested in my American money. I had to go back out and wait until Keith appeared to get the correct local coins.

At the Paris railway station, you had to pay the attendant 2.6 francs (about 50 cents). She then gave you a token to put in a slot to open the gate to the restroom. My token would not work. I had to get back in line where I had purchased it. She gave me 2.6 francs back and then I gave it back to her to obtain another token. I never understood why she could not just exchange the token without the money transfer. Also, why not make it two francs or three francs, instead of 2.6? But of course, I am not running the pay toilets in France (thank goodness).

Another funny occasion was in London. Keith and I were shopping (or rather looking, as everything is so expensive) in the city's most famous department store, Harrods, and I needed to go to the restroom. I was directed to the "Luxury Wash Rooms." There was an attendant sitting by the door.

Rules for entry were posted on a sign: "To use the 'Luxury Wash Room' you must either: (1) Present a Harrods' Charge Card, (2) Show a just purchased receipt of a minimum of 100 Pounds (nearly $200) or (3) Be pregnant."

Since I did not qualify on any of these counts, I asked what was needed for me to enter. The attendant did not seem to know what to do, but finally said I could enter for one pound (worth nearly $2.00 at the time — the cost of elimination is going up). I was in a pretty bad state, so gave her the money. She then tried to put the coin in the machine, and it was out of order. I guess the pained look on my face elicited her pity, so she handed me back the one-pound coin and told me to go on in. I offered to give her the pound, but she said she could not take it, for it had to go into the machine. Inside, everything was very nice, but not up to Shoji Tabuchi's standards and not worth $2!

At Lake Como, Italy, a public restroom was totally automatic. When you stood up in the stall upon completion of your business, it flushed. We now have many of these in the U.S., but the first time I experienced this automatic flush it scared me to death. I thought someone must be in the stall with me. Anyway, at Lake Como, not only did the potty flush by itself, the water at the sink came on when you held your hands under it, and then something I had not seen before — the paper towels were automatically dispensed when you held your hands by them. Another restroom in that area of Italy had two faucets above the commode, one red and the other blue. I wondered if this meant you could have hot or cold flushes.

We encountered an unusual "toilet" place in Portugal. Outside the facility, we paid our fee to a man who issued us about three inches of toilet paper (sure hoped we did not have a big job ahead of us). When we entered the place, there was a television set high on the wall, which could be viewed from all of the stalls. A travelogue about the country played continuously. So you could do two things at once — take care of your physical needs and learn about Portugal's tourist attractions. A unique way to publicize your country.

Our trip around the world brought us to Nepal, a lofty mountain kingdom tucked away in the Himalayas. One day our guide took us for a tour to see the countryside around Katmandu. It reminded me of the stories of Shangri-la, surrounded by high snowy mountains and lush green vegetation. Our van was the only vehicle on the road. The native people walk everywhere. We watched as they stood in knee-deep water planting rice along the lower mountain slopes. The road came to an end, and when our guide asked if we would like to walk about a mile through the foothills to see a cheese factory we agreed. The cheese factory was a brand new building, outfitted with stainless steel cheese-making equipment. It had been a gift from the Danish government. There was only one problem — it was one mile from the nearest road, making it hard to ship products. On top of that, they had no cows. So this new facility remained closed and unused, and had never produced anything.

Before we started the trek back, Dolly and I needed to go to the bathroom. We had been waiting, thinking there would be a place at the cheese factory. As it was locked, the guide told us to go around back. "Around back" was a small mound of earth. We got behind it, and as one watched for intruders, the other went. I was first and just as Dolly was rising and adjusting her clothes, two boys around six years of age appeared out of nowhere. We had no idea where they had been hiding. They seemed very friendly. I gave them some candy, but they wanted a pen. Said they needed it for school, so we found a couple of pens in our purses to give them. They seemed happy and we went on our merry way back down the mountain.

We were on safari in Kenya when we stopped at a service station, but the only similarity to our service stations was that it sold gas. Behind the building was one "restroom." Inside a room about four feet square was a concrete floor that slanted down to a hole about six inches across. That was it. One look and I decided quickly that I did not have to go. One of my passengers said she was so desperate she would try it.

"I'll stand here and guard the door," I said, as the door did not have a lock.

After a few minutes, I heard a cry: "Joyce, I have slipped down and can't get up."

In my rush to help her, I pushed the door in too quickly, sending her sliding all the way across the very slick and filthy floor. Slipping and sliding, I finally managed to get my arms around her and drag her outside. There she stood, her slacks and panties around her ankles and we did not even want to think about the condition of her rear end.

"Stay right there. I have some Wet Ones in the van."

As I rushed to the vehicle, the others said, "Why is Inez standing there with her pants down?"

We managed to wipe her up rather well, and that night she said she soaked in a tub of disinfectant. As far as I know, she never had any repercussions except enduring a very embarrassing situation. I gave my shoes a good Lysol spraying.

On a Cunard Vistafjord cruise around the British Isles, we took a launch from the ship for about forty-five minutes to Glengariff, Ireland. Where we disembarked from the boats there were no restroom facilities of any type and there were no lavatory facilities on the buses we were to board. We were instructed to go to the waiting motor coaches to take us around the "Ring of Kerry."

One of our men pulled Keith to the side and said he had been constipated and had taken some medicine earlier and it was now having effect. Keith pointed out there were no facilities here and advised the man to head for the nearby bushes. Poor thing, he didn't make it in time. He had on a "London Fog" raincoat that had to be left in the brush. Keith donated his handkerchief to the effort, but it was not enough. Finally they got him cleaned up as best they could and came to the bus I had waiting for them. The man and his wife were sitting behind us, and the odor was rather overwhelming. Finally at the next stop we found washrooms with water, and he was able to clean up fairly well. As we were in the British Isles, he later purchased a new London Fog raincoat.

During a Cunard Princess Cruise around the Canary Islands, we made a port call at Agadir, Morocco on the northwest corner of Africa. From here we took a full-day bus tour to "The Oasis of Tafraoute." The nine-hour excursion was via an old rickety bus without a restroom. We drove through stark countryside with small Berber villages dramatically abutting the pink granite of the Anti-Atlas Mountains. Occasionally there would be a small green area with a palm tree or two that sprang up from underground springs, just like those oases you have seen in the movies. We had been driving without stopping for over three hours when we entered an almond grove, all in beautiful full bloom. The bus stopped in the middle of the road and I assumed this was a "photo op" time. Just then our guide yelled out (there was no microphone on the bus) "PeePee Stop!"

Everyone just looked at each other, and thought, well, why not. So the ladies took one side of the almond patch and the men the other side. Those almond trees have very skinny trunks and don't provide much privacy but when you gotta go, you do it. Once again I wished I were a man with one of those handy things to have on a picnic. We continued on to our lunch stop, and believe me, the restroom was so bad there, I really preferred the almond grove — it certainly smelled better.

🦆 🦆 🦆 🦆

Bus travel has produced a lot of "bathroom humor." When I started the travel program at the bank, my first bus trip was to a Cowboys football game in Dallas. I had been told to have beer and cold drinks available on the bus for the customers. Having no idea how much to buy for forty-four people, and not being a beer drinker myself, I purchased what I thought was plenty. Well, on the return trip home, we ran out of beer. This offense, I found out, rates right up there with murder one. When we returned to the bank parking lot, one of the men said to me as he exited the coach, "Joyce, it was a pretty good trip, but you certainly don't know how much beer to buy!"

The next trip, I was going to be sure I did not commit this same crime, so I had an ample supply of beer, which was consumed happily by the travelers. Upon our return, as we were unloading, everyone got off the bus but the man who had complained on the previous trip. As I started to board to look for him, he came out of the bus restroom, with the front of his pants all wet. With a red face, he said: "You had enough beer this time." I just smiled and made no comment.

Attending the Kentucky Derby festivities, we were on a motor coach city tour of Louisville. We were at a stoplight and, when it turned green, our driver started to cross the intersection. From the side street came a car speeding through the red light. To avoid hitting the offender, our driver slammed on the brakes with such force that the two people sitting in the front seat were thrown over the rail. I ran up to see if they were injured, and luckily, they were just shaken up a bit. As I was checking on everyone else, out from the bus lavatory came a gentleman, pants soaking wet — "Whaaaat happened?" he cried.

In many European motor coaches, the lavatory is in the middle of the bus by a center door, instead of in the rear as on most American buses. The particular coach we took on our trip through Germany had a television set right above the restroom door. Because we made numerous rest stops, this room was not used for several days into the trip. One day as we drove along, a man decided he needed to use it. The other bus passengers ganged up and when he came out, they all clapped their hands and said "Good job!"

He looked bewildered. We pointed up to the TV screen and said, "We saw the whole show." It took some time before he was convinced that he really was not on candid camera while in the restroom.

In traveling all over the world, I have encountered many different and bizarre things in ladies' restrooms. But, ironically, one of the most unusual signs was found in a nice office building complex in Austin, Texas, my home territory. Posted on the wall over the commode was a sign that stated: "PLEASE Do Not 'pee' on the seat and clean-up after Yourselves! THANK YOU."

I saw an article in *USA Today* that reported a survey of travelers' opinions on toilets around the world. The United States was way out in front as the best, followed by Western Europe, the former Soviet Union, and the Middle East, with China coming in last. I guess I would have to go along with that, but there can be good and bad situations, regardless of the country. My best advice — take your own Kleenex, Wet Ones, and Purell Hand Sanitizer. And a small can of Lysol for those terrible places. Then you will be ready for whatever you may encounter.

That's me, on the job, waiting for the next emergency

CALL 911
OR JOYCE

Thank God! I escorted over two hundred group tours from 1981 to 1999, and no one died. This is exceptional when you consider that my clientele had an average age of sixty and many were over eighty. Someone once said to me: "Joyce, you have experienced every emergency except childbirth, and if it ever occurred with this group, it would be the second miracle birth of the ages."

I certainly did have plenty of emergencies to take care of, including some harrowing experiences and a few visits to hospital emergency rooms.

There were incidents like the one at SeaWorld in San Antonio when a lady sat down on a concrete platform by a street light and fire ants instantly covered her feet and her legs. She was in terrible pain. We rushed her to the first aid tent for treatment. Because we were able to get help quickly, she did not have any bad effects, just pain and itching from the bites.

Falling accidents were my biggest problem. On one trip to Costa Rica, I had seven people out of forty-four hit the ground. I called them the "Domino Bunch," because they just seemed to topple over like lined-up dominoes, but this was a hardy group, and they bounced right up with no serious injury inflicted.

In Ireland, Arlene stumbled over a step in the hotel restaurant. We installed her in the back of the bus with ice packs on her ankle. When she returned home, her doctor pronounced the ankle broken. So she ended up with a cast for several weeks.

Joe was observing the Indian ruins at Montezuma National Monument in Arizona when he somehow fell over a three-foot rock wall, breaking his leg. A visit to the emergency room produced a temporary cast that would last until he could get to his son who was an orthopedic surgeon.

Another fall occurred in Montreal, Canada. A gentleman just stepped off the curb and fell down, cutting his face and breaking his eyeglasses. So it was off to the emergency room again. Since they have socialized medicine in Canada, if you are not part of the program, they could care less about seeing you. After waiting hours, I approached the registration desk and explained that we needed to see the doctor and would gladly pay for the service. A nurse looked at my patient and said, "He is not bad enough to see a doctor. Come in here, and I will clean him up and put a bandage on."

We had just arrived at the airport in Las Vegas. I instructed the group to board the waiting bus for transfer to the hotel. Somehow, one lady missed the bus step and cut a long gash in her shin. Off to the emergency room one more time! She required several stitches. The doctor said she should not walk on it for a week. He provided crutches, but we needed a wheelchair. The Riveria Hotel where we were staying did not furnish one, so I had to locate a rental company. After several phone calls, I did get a wheelchair delivered to the hotel. Then there was the hassle with the bus company, filing all the proper papers on the accident and procuring a statement from the doctor. Most of the time during my three-day trip to Vegas was involved with this one incident.

On the bright side, I saved money, since I didn't have time to play the slots.

રત્ન રત્ન રત્ન રત્ન

We were at the Jack Tar Village Resort in Jamaica. This resort is "all inclusive," meaning that all food, drink and recreation are included in the purchase price. The open bar was a big favorite. One of my lady passengers, about forty years old and a registered nurse, took a special liking to this feature. On the second day, one of my tour members asked me if I had noticed that this particular person was a little high, but I thought, "This is her vacation, so let her have her fun." Early in the morning on the fourth day of the seven-day trip, the front desk called me.

"We have one of your passengers who has passed out and we think she should go to the hospital." I rushed over there, and found her out like a light. I instructed the man traveling with her to help me get her into the taxi that the hotel had summoned.

For a real experience, you should go to the emergency room at Montego Bay, Jamaica. It was packed with mothers and screaming kids — no air conditioning in about 100-degree temperature, plus about one hundredd percent humidity. Our patient was still totally unconscious (I kept checking her pulse to make sure she was alive). When we finally did see the doctor, he diagnosed her condition as an "alcoholic coma." He gave her a shot which revived her and advised us to take her back to the hotel, keep her in bed and give her lots of tea with sugar to prevent her from getting the "DT's." Her body would need sugar to compensate for all the alcohol in her system.

"She should not drink anything with alcohol for at least seven days until her body has flushed out all the poison, or she might go into a coma again and die," the doctor warned.

When we returned to the hotel and installed her in bed, I called her companion aside.

"It is your duty to watch her and see that she does not take another drink. Getting a corpse back to the U.S. is a very difficult and costly operation, and you'd have to cover the the expense," I stated emphatically.

I instructed all the hotel bartenders to refuse to serve her if she ordered a drink. I dutifully took her tea with lots of sugar, and by the next day, she said she was feeling much better and would go out to the beach. With all of us closely watching her, she did not take a drink at the hotel. On the flight home, I sat near her to make sure she did not order a mixed drink or a beer during the flight. The last time I saw her was when we arrived in Austin. She headed for the airport bar and was drinking a beer. I just walked on out — she was not my responsibility any more.

I never heard anything from her, but did receive a very nice thank you note from the gentleman with her expressing his appreciation for all I had done on her behalf.

≋ ≋ ≋ ≋

We stopped at Old North Church, which dates back to 1723, during a city tour of Boston, Massachusetts. This church is famous because on April 18, 1775, the sexton hung two lanterns from its steeple to signal that the British were launching their raid by sea. With this information, Paul Revere made his historic ride proclaiming, "The British are coming! The British are coming!"

We sat in the uncomfortable box pews that have plaques engraved with the names of the original owners. Physically sitting in the same place where our forefathers worshipped made me feel like I was part of our nation's history. With spirits high, my group departed the church, which is located on an incline. Somehow, when Loraine stepped off the curb, she fell and injured her hand and her foot.

Loraine's husband and I accompanied her to the nearest hospital in a taxi. I had encountered many nightmare ordeals at emergency rooms, and was prepared for another bad time. The people at Boston General could not have been nicer. Everything was handled quickly and professionally. They immediately put Loraine into an examining room while her husband and I filled out the necessary papers, giving them her Medicare card. A doctor arrived, x-rayed the foot, and confirmed she needed a cast. This was quickly applied and, in no time, we were on our way back to finish the tour. The ordeal was not so great for Loraine, but I can say that it was my "best emergency room visit."

A few days later the thank you note arrived. *"We especially appreciate the many extras you did when I took my tumble. You went far beyond the call by accompanying me to the hospital, getting wheelchairs, and providing extra services to make it possible for me to move around with the group. Following additional x-rays of both hand and foot, I am now in a great big hard-soled shoe. Even though both are still sore, I am doing fine and am truly grateful to you."*

ea ea ea ea

This tour of San Francisco, Napa Valley, Tahoe, and Yosemite Park was custom-designed for my group of forty-three. I did not have a tour company guide, just a local one at each place.

In San Francisco, on the morning we were to leave by train for Napa Valley, I received a call that Kermit was sick. I rushed to his room and realized right away that he needed a doctor. The hotel provided a doctor in an amazingly short time and he said Kermit needed to get to a hospital immediately. Why he did not call an ambulance, I do not know. Anyway, Kermit, his wife, Virginia, and I crammed into a cab bound for St. Mary's Hospital. I thought we would never get there and had horrors of his dying before we made it. Upon arrival, they whisked Kermit into the emergency room. I sent Virginia with him and I proceeded to take care of the registration. When I saw him again, he was hooked up with all kinds of wires. The diagnosis was that his blood pressure was way too high and his heartbeat was irregular. They kept him in intensive care.

I brought Virginia back to the hotel to get her packed up and the hotel helped us find a place for her to stay near the hospital. I hated to leave them, but I had to continue on with the rest of the tour group, as I was the only guide. Fortunately, in a few days Kermit was feeling much better and was able to fly home and enjoy life and travel for several more years.

ea ea ea ea

You would think that a little weekend bus trip down to Corpus Christi, about two hundred miles from Austin, would be no problem. Not so. I was at a disadvantage because Keith was unable to go with me, so I had to handle all the drinks, luggage, and people myself. The first thing to go wrong was the special tour of the newly-opened Corpus Christi Aquarium. Apparently, the volunteer docents had not had time to be trained properly, and as I had snorkeled for years and observed the ocean's inhabitants, I knew more about sea life than they did. However, they did not appreciate my explaining to my group various things they had missed.

The Greyhound Dog Races were next on the schedule. This was a very nice facility and our seats were right on the finish line. I just cannot get excited about a bunch of dogs chasing a mechanical rabbit around the racecourse. Someone said that the winning dog is always the last one to "pee" before the race, because this made him lighter. I don't know how true this was, but I did follow this rule and broke even at the end of the day on my $1 bets on each of the races.

That evening, as I was alone, I just wanted to have room service and go to bed. I was exhausted with all the pressures of the day and I had been up since 5 am. I had just settled down to sleep when the fire alarm went off. This was all I needed — a hotel fire. I called the front desk and they said it was a false alarm, so I returned to bed. Instantly, there was a loud knock on my door. When I opened it, there stood one of my travelers, a rather large lady. She had on a long flowery nightgown, large colored curlers in her hair, big fuzzy slippers on her feet and in her arms were her huge purse, plus all the clothes from her suitcase. "Where are the stairs?" she screamed.

It took all I could muster to not burst out laughing at the sight of her. She looked like something from a comic strip. All my people were running around in the hall in a panic. I explained that it was a false alarm, sent them all back to their rooms, and returned to my bed. Just then a siren screamed from outside. The phone rang.

"There's a fire truck out front. What should we do?" one of my ladies screamed into the phone.

Another check with the front desk advised that every time the fire alarm goes off, the fire department is alerted and responds regardless. I then had to go to all the rooms and comfort everyone, assuring them that all was OK. About one hour later I finally was able to get back to my bed.

The next morning I was eating my breakfast in the room when Mr. A called and said that his wife was throwing up and could not stop. As soon as I arrived at their room, I could see she was in bad shape. I had the hotel call EMS who arrived quickly. They said she had to go to the hospital, so I gathered her purse and a change of clothes and climbed in the back of the ambulance with her and the attendant. Her husband rode in the front. As the ambulance sped along, the medic hooked her up to the oxygen and then she started throwing up again. I was holding the tray for her while the he was trying to insert the IV needle. Just then we slid around a corner. His needle slipped, and blood went all over the floor of the ambulance. The medic finally got the needle in correctly and we arrived at the emergency entrance. During this episode, I realized why I had chosen travel over nursing as a profession. As they wheeled her into the hospital emergency room, I took Mr. A in to get all the registration forms signed.

After examining Mrs. A, the doctor said she needed tests to determine the cause of her condition. I had to get the group ready to leave the hotel at ten, so I rushed back, went to their room, packed up everything and put it in hotel storage. I was just able to get the luggage checked and hotel accounts settled in time to depart with the group.

Mrs. A had to stay in the hospital in Corpus Christi for several days, and I never did hear what was wrong with her, but do know that she recovered and is doing fine.

る る る る

This was just a little evening trip down to San Antonio, eighty miles south of Austin, to see the opera "Carmen." I had a busload of forty-four. We were scheduled to depart from the Austin Bank at 4 p.m., drive to San Antonio, and let the group out at the River Walk where they could have dinner and then meet me at the Arneson River Theater. This outdoor venue has grass-covered terraced seats on one side of the river and a stage on the other.

Everything started off badly. At departure time, all the customers were seated on the bus ready to go except my boss, who was the bank president, and his wife. I am a stickler for on being on time, and people who travel with me know this and are usually very early or certainly on time. As fifteen minutes passed, I became more upset. Many of the passengers had made dinner reservations, so I made a decision to leave without my boss and his wife, which in retrospect, was not the best move.

We had gone about forty miles when a car came streaking and honking past us — the two late passengers. When our bus stopped at the River Walk in San Antonio to unload everyone, they pulled up right behind us. The president's wife jumped out and admonished me thoroughly for running off and leaving them. For several months, I had to suffer penance at work for this deed. Today, I am pleased to say, the president and his wife are my very good friends.

Around 7 p.m., the sky opened and we had a genuine Texas down pour. True to Texas weather, it stopped in about forty-five minutes. The theater people said that the show would go on, but would just start about thirty minutes later. As the grass seats were soaked, they put folding chairs up on top of the grass terraces, making the seats higher and very precarious. After safely seating my group, Keith and I took two seats at the very back under a tree. All during "Carmen," the tree was dripping water on us.

At intermission, Sunny, one of my ladies, was getting up from her folding chair when she caught her shoe heel in the leg of the chair and took a hard fall face first. I was sitting at the back, battling the drippy tree and the worms that were also falling from the branches, when I noticed the commotion about halfway down the theatre. I rushed over and helped put Sunny on a stretcher that had just appeared. The theater had called an ambulance and I sent her and her husband on to the hospital. With all that occurred this evening, I cannot tell you a thing about "Carmen."

Afterwards, we stopped by the hospital to see Sunny. She would have to stay overnight, but doctors indicated that there was no serious damage. With the opera starting late, a longer intermission than scheduled due to the accident, and then going by the hospital, we finally made it home about 4 a.m.

ε&. ε&. ε&. ε&.

Tikal, in Guatemala, boasts the oldest known Mayan ruins in the world. Artifacts dating back to 292 A.D. have been found there. Historians believe this area had over 50,000 inhabitants during the Classic era from 300 to 900 A.D. Although many of the structures are crumbling, many have been restored and the basic foundations have survived throughout the ages. Temple I, also called the Temple of the Giant Jaguar, rises 145 feet over the east side of the main plaza. Very few of my group cared to venture up the forty-eight steep steps to the top of the temple. The weather was hot and humid, another reason not to try it.

One of my gentlemen, Wells, age eighty-four, climbed up the steps with us and then continued to walk up and down on many of the other structures. I commented on how well he was doing for his age. When we started the walk down to the bus parking lot, (about three quarters of a mile) Wells' leg muscles cramped up and he was unable to walk. Keith and Larry, one of my younger male tour members, wanted to make an arm seat and carry him down. Being full of pride plus a doctor himself, he refused to be carried. He insisted on making it on his own, even though it was very slow and painful. I realized that this was going to take a while, and knew the rest of the group was sitting in the hot bus waiting for us. I told our local guide to take the others to the restaurant for lunch and have the bus return for us. We finally made it down with Wells in about an hour and I did convince him to stay in his room for the rest of the evening and had dinner sent to him. The next day, he seemed OK.

When I returned home, I received a card: *"You took the time, you cared, you gave so much when you didn't have to. . .thank you."* Signed: Wells and Eloise. Nice things like that make it all worthwhile.

ε&. ε&. ε&. ε&.

For our farewell night in Ireland we were guests for a medieval banquet at Bunratty Castle. The castle dates back many centuries, but was rebuilt to its present state in 1353 (sometime back when you consider that Columbus discovered America in 1492). Bunratty is touted as Ireland's most authentic medieval castle and houses the priceless Lord Gort collection of furniture and many objects of art dating from before 1650.

The current medieval banquet is a tourist attraction, and there were many other guests other than my group there that night. I was asked to select one of my couples to reign as King and Queen for the evening. This would entail being crowned in a special pre-dinner ceremony, then leading the rest of the patrons to the dining hall. The King and Queen would sit at the front table and be served first as befits royalty. I selected Conrad and Kathleen, as I knew Conrad would make a fine king, and he indeed proved an excellent choice. I had their camera and was all poised to take pictures of the coronation when right behind me I heard what I thought must be someone falling down. I turned around and there was Dottie (one of my most frequent travelers) lying out cold on the floor. She is a very small lady, and we picked her up and stretched her out on a nearby bench. I rejoiced when I felt a pulse. A nurse in the crowd came up to assist and, with the aid of wet cloths, we were able to revive her. I looked over to her husband, Monty, and he was as white as a sheet.

Dottie had not felt well all day, and when the rest of us went to the pub for lunch, she said she did not want anything to eat. Therefore, she had not had any food all day. When we arrived at the castle we were immediately served warm mead, a very strong wine drink popular in medieval times. Apparently, it was too much for her on an empty stomach, and she passed out. I had our driver take her and Monty back to the hotel. In the process, I missed the coronation, and part of the banquet. Next day we flew home, and she was weak, but OK. But she certainly gave all of us a scare.

If you have been to the Grand Canyon in Arizona, as far as I am concerned, don't bother going to Copper Canyon, Mexico. Perhaps my opinion is clouded by the circumstances of our trip.

First mistake, we took a bus all the way from Austin, Texas, to Los Mochis, Mexico, a distance of over twelve hundred miles without a decent roadside restroom after you cross the Rio Grande. I had forty-six people — every bus seat was full, even the back seat, where I usually kept the drink cooler. To add to this, Frances and Claude were on the back seat. She had her foot in a cast and was on crutches. She wanted to make this trip so badly that she came on crutches. She never complained or caused any problem the whole trip, and I know it was difficult for her.

When we had to make road rest stops, I stood at the entrance of whatever was designated as the restroom and dispensed toilet tissue when the ladies went in and Wet Ones when they came out.

It took six days to make the trip to where we would board the train to Copper Canyon. This highly publicized tour did not measure up to my expectations. This was in 1988, and I know now there are some private trains that make the trip much more comfortable and enjoyable. The train takes a dramatic route from Los Mochis on the Pacific Coast at sea level to up to six thousand feet in the mountains. The track is four hundred miles long from Los Mochis to Chihuahua.

The food on the train we took was served on ancient Melamac plastic dishes. They were cracked and you could see black lines all over each piece. I imagined that I could see the germs nestled on each dish, too. I suddenly was not hungry. When the train stopped at villages along the way, the local children would run up with buckets to take the garbage from the train. (I certainly contributed to their cause, as I did not eat any of the food that was served.)

We stopped for two nights at a hotel on the rim of the canyon. The canyon is impressively deep and wide but, to me, does not have the brilliant colors of the Grand Canyon.

I have been all over the world, but the poverty and conditions of the Tarahumara Indians who live in caves in the canyon upset me more than anything I have seen. The ladies sit in the sun by the railroad track and weave belts and baskets to sell to the tourists. The tribe is so depleted that there is a lot of inter-family marriage, resulting in many lethargic children. Some of the children looked sick and did not run and play as normal children would.

Reboarding the train, we continued to Chihuahua City where our bus met us for the drive back to Austin. After ten days in Mexico, everyone except Keith and me had "Montezuma's Revenge." We were taking an antibiotic and did not get sick. But the bus ride back was one from hell. We had to stop frequently for people to run to the terrible restrooms. One lady threw up all over herself and the bus seat. I had an extra shirt in my bag and we were able to clean her up so she could make the trip home.

I know many people who have taken the Copper Canyon trip and thought it was great, and maybe under other circumstances, I might agree. But, for now, this was the worst trip I ever took.

&⪼ &⪼ &⪼ &⪼

It is said that altitude sickness is the worst sickness in the world. I have not experienced it personally, but sympathize with my people who have. We flew to La Paz, Bolivia, situated 13,000 above sea level. Keith and I had obtained some altitude sickness pills from our travel clinic doctor and I know they helped. Keith had experienced some bad headaches a few years earlier when we were in Machu Picchu, Peru at 12,000 feet. This time, after taking our medication, he had a slight headache and that was all. My only reaction was some shortness of breath in climbing stairs.

Others in my group were not so lucky. After an overnight flight, we went to our hotel in La Paz. Our guide advised us to rest and to request that oxygen be brought to our room if we had difficulty breathing. Dorothy, a much traveled lady in my group, was having trouble, and we advised her not try to go on the afternoon city tour. As we were driving around the city sights, two members had to rush off the coach to vomit. By next morning, everyone was doing fairly well except Dorothy. We encouraged her to stay in her room and breathe the oxygen and not go on the day's tour.

The third morning, we were transferring to Lake Titicaca, at 12,600 feet the highest navigable lake in the world. Poor Dorothy. She and her oxygen tank came along, but she was sick the whole time. She could not keep anything on her stomach and was still having trouble breathing. Nothing we could do seemed to help her. Finally, after four days of sickness, she conceded that she couldn't make it to Machu Picchu; she needed to return home to lower ground. Our wonderful Collette Guide, Bruce, arranged her flight back to the U.S., which was not a simple task in this remote area. By the time she got to Miami she was already feeling much better, just weak from not eating. I hated that she had to leave, for she wanted to see Machu Picchu so much. That was the real reason she had booked the tour.

ɜ**ʌ** ɜ**ʌ** ɜ**ʌ** ɜ**ʌ**

I had taken groups to the Jack Tar Resort in the Bahamas and Jamaica. Both of these resorts are great. So when Jack Tar announced a trip to their all-inclusive resort in the Dominican Republic at a very attractive rate, I presented it to my customers. It sounded like a great deal and sixty people signed up.

When we arrived at the resort, there were numerous complications. Some of the rooms did not even have a bed. There was no air conditioning — a must for Texans especially in this hot and sticky tropical area. Ceiling fans did help stir a little breeze. We had been promised sea-view rooms but the hotel was back in the dense foliage and the only way to get a sea view was to walk a quarter of a mile through the brush. On top of that, the swimming pool was dirty. These things did not make for happy campers. Finally I got everyone settled down to accept the conditions and hoped they would start trying to enjoy the seven-day holiday.

On the fourth day, I noticed fewer and fewer of my people showing up at meals. I went to check and they had a bad case of diarrhea. I went from room to room dispensing Pepto Bismo tablets, until I had to run to the bathroom myself. Some found the that best thing when the pain hit you was to run for the sea and dive in. This worked fine, but was not too pleasant for anyone swimming downstream. By the end of the trip, everyone had the bug. We were one sick group when we finally boarded the charter plane headed back to Texas. As we took off, one of my crew cried: "Goodbye Shits!" And those were my sentiments exactly.

🐌 🐌 🐌 🐌

Since I had a lot of repeaters on my trips, it was probably to be expected that some folks would have more than one problem on more than one trip. But no one seemed quite as jinxed as Mrs. G, a sweet little lady who traveled with me numerous times. It got to the point that whenever she signed up for one of my tours I immediately started crossing my fingers.

Once she showed up at the Airport in Austin, for a cruise/tour of the British Isles without her passport. I told her to take a cab and retrieve it immediately. She lived quite a distance from the airport, but she made it to her house and obtained the passport. On the trip back to the airport, the taxi ran out of gas. It was time for the plane to leave, and no Mrs. G. I advised American Airlines, and they said they could put her on a later flight. So I booked that for her and then boarded my plane. I was worried the entire flight that one little lady alone would have trouble when she arrived in London.

We landed at Heathrow Airport around 8 a.m. and transferred to the posh Ritz Hotel where we were to stay for three days prior to the cruise. Naturally, at this time of the day, they did not have the rooms ready. My people were literally falling asleep in the lounge chairs. Finally, by around 11 a.m., everyone had a room but Keith and me. I was waiting at the reception desk, and to my surprise, in walks Mrs. G, happy as a lark. She had met a man on the plane from London, and told him of her plight. He had his car at the airport, so he brought her to the Ritz Hotel.

We sailed from Southampton with stops at Glengarrif and Dublin, Ireland, the Isle of Man, the Isle of Skye, the Orkney Islands, Invergordon and Edinburgh, Scotland, Hamburg, Germany, and back to Southampton, where we took a bus to London to catch the plane home. After breakfast the last day of the cruise, everyone was instructed to go through immigration formalities on the ship before disembarking. Keith and I went through first and then stood at the entrance to make sure all my people cleared. It was nearly time to leave the ship and two were missing — Mrs. G and her roommate, who was also my mother. I sent Keith down to their room to see what was delaying them. He came right back and said that Mrs. G was unable to walk. I rushed to her room. When I saw her, she was just like a Raggedy Ann doll, limp as a dishrag.

"What's wrong?" I asked my mother.

She explained that as last night was our final night on board, Mrs. G had celebrated with two martinis. Then she couldn't get to sleep, so she took a Valium tablet. It's a wonder she was still alive. I knew we had to get her off the ship, so I obtained a wheelchair, and Keith lifted her in it. We had to tie her in with a dress sash to keep her from sliding out. Then we pushed her up to go through immigration and off the ship to the bus. When we reached the airport she still could not walk. I was able once again to obtain a wheelchair, and we managed to get her on the plane. After the eight-hour flight back to DFW, she was recovered enough to walk by herself. So miraculously, she arrived home safely.

Mrs. G joined another tour that began in Amsterdam for the Tulip Festival, then continued by motor coach through Belgium and France to Basel, Switzerland where we boarded a riverboat for a five-day Rhine River cruise.

To begin with, upon arrival at the airport we were using the moving sidewalk that takes you to the baggage claim area. My mother was talking to someone and did not realize that she was coming to the end of the walkway. When she reached the end, she was immediately thrown forward, falling and breaking her glasses. Several others of the group also fell in a domino effect. No one was injured and, fortunately, Mother had an extra pair of glasses to make the tour. But it was an omen of problems to come.

We reached Basel and were getting settled on the ship for our Rhine cruise. It had been a long and tiring day. I was getting ready for bed when Mrs. G knocked on my door. She said that she was very sick and needed to see a doctor. There was no doctor on this small vessel. The ship's purser called the Basel hospital and then a cab for us to make the trip. It was now around 9 p.m. and we were to sail at midnight. I told Mrs. G to exchange money for some Swiss Francs and we caught our taxi. It was dark and beginning to rain.

"City Hospital," I instructed.

As we drove along, the cabby started talking cheerfully in broken English. "City Hall, hundred years old," he said pointing into the pitch darkness where we could see nothing except an occasional street light.

"No tour," I said, "just get us to the hospital as soon as possible."

We went up and down old cobbled streets and I had no idea where we were going. Finally we came up to a solid steel gate that automatically opened. I thought of those James Bond films where he is taken through an automatic steel door to some hideout. But this did indeed take us up to the hospital entrance. Was I glad to get here! I paid the man and took Mrs. G inside.

"Doctor," I said. We were led to a small curtained waiting room. None of the nurses could speak English. Oh my, I thought. We probably won't be able to communicate with the doctor, either.

Then entered this nice-looking young man. "What is our problem?" he said in perfect English and with a big smile. I wanted to hug him. He had attended medical school at the Mayo Clinic in Rochester, New York.

After an examination, he made his diagnosis: shingles. Mrs. G had a band of clear blisters that went under her arms and circled half of her upper body. When I saw her severe condition, I was glad we had come to the doctor. He wrote out a prescription.

"Where will we get it filled this time of the night?" I asked.

"Here is the address of an all-night laboratory" (their word for pharmacy).

We paid the hospital and asked them to call us a cab. As we were standing at the entrance waiting, a taxi drove up. The door opened and out fell a woman I could only assume was a "lady of the evening" due to her dress and makeup. As she fell, the contents of her purse spilled all over the sidewalk. She had been brutally assaulted and was bleeding at the nose and mouth. No one from the hospital made any attempt to come to her aid. I retrieved the contents of her purse and then helped her up and into the hospital. Finally a nurse did come up and take her off my hands.

After that emotional incident, I returned to the cab and gave the pharmacy address to the driver. By now it was raining hard as we went bouncing through the dark cobbled streets of Basel. When the cab stopped, all I could see in the darkness seemed to be a house.

"Are you sure this is the right place?"

"This is the address," he replied.

I couldn't see a sign or anything. What was I getting into now? I ran through the rain and rang the doorbell. At the side of the building, (that I could not see because it was dark) was a window. A light came on and the window opened. Without saying a word, I handed over the prescription. Within a few minutes, the prescription was filled, I paid them, and we were on our way back to the ship. We made it at 11:45 p.m., just fifteen minutes before sailing time. Keith was about to have a fit. I assured him that I had the ship personnel promise not to sail without us.

With the medication, Mrs. G was able to enjoy the remainder of the trip. But the experience did not help my blood pressure.

ðŸ ðŸ ðŸ ðŸ

On the fourth night of a cruise around the Hawaiian Islands aboard the S.S. Constitution, the first seating group was standing in line to enter the dining room. From the front of the line I heard a scream and saw people gathering around someone. I looked to see a little lady holding her bloody hand. Then, to my horror, I saw she belonged to me.

Ruth had been standing at the head of the line with her hand resting on the doorframe by one of the hinges. When they opened the dining room doors, her finger was caught and thoroughly mashed. I grabbed a napkin from one of the tables, wrapped it around her hand and proceeded to the ship doctor's office. The doctor examined her, said she would need stitches, and told her to get up on the patient table. As she started to lie down on the examining table, she let out a painful cry.

"Is your finger hurting that much?" I asked.

"No, it's my ribs. The first night on the ship, I had to go to the pot. I did not want to turn the light on and wake my roommate. When I entered the bathroom, I fell over that darn board across the door. I reached to catch myself on the shower wall, only to find out it was a curtain, not a wall, and fell into the shower and hurt my ribs."

"Why didn't you tell me about this before now?"

"I was afraid you would send me home and this is the only big trip I have ever taken." She was eighty-seven years old.

After taking three stitches on her finger, the doctor x-rayed her and confirmed that she had a cracked rib. He said she was to take it easy and provided a wheelchair for her.

So, over an hour later, I wheeled her into the dining room where we got to eat at the second seating instead of the first. I managed to get her through the remainder of the cruise and airports in a wheelchair. Sadly, a few months later I heard she had passed away. I am glad that I at least helped her have some pleasure in her last days.

༺ ༺ ༺ ༺

American Hawaiian Cruises for a brief time offered cruises of the Tahitian Islands. We were on the S.S. Liberte for the second cruise of the program.

Once on board, I was pleased at the size of the cabins. If you have taken a cruise, you know the rooms don't look like the ones on television's "Love Boat." As a rule, standard rooms are very small. But these rooms were large and we even had a king size bed, instead of those little old narrow single things usually found on cruise ships. I always wondered how they could call it the "Love Boat" with those tiny twin beds.

We had an enchanting cruise of the strikingly beautiful Polynesia Islands. The landscapes, the foliage, and the people were breathtakingly lovely. The snorkeling in these crystal clear aqua waters was wonderful.

Ports of call included such paradises as Rangiroa, Hauhine, Raiatea, Moorea, and Bora Bora. I consider Bora Bora to be one of the most beautiful places in the world.

Rangiroa is an atoll enclosing a large lagoon measuring about fourteen miles by forty miles. The ship had to wait until high tide before it could enter at a break in the landmass. The lagoon, which was formed by the rim of an extinct volcano, offered the best snorkeling we ever experienced. Totally untouched by pollution or tourists, everything was pristine and beautiful. This was the first cruise ship to stop here, and the natives were just as curious about us as we were about them, and they had shells for sale at a very inexpensive price. Later we heard that the ship company decided to eliminate this port of call, due to the difficulty of maneuvering the large ship into the cut at just the precise moment of high tide.

I was beginning to think this was the most perfect tour I had ever escorted. We had outstanding scenery, great accommodations and food, unique sea and village activity, and all were having a good time. And, since these islands were not accustomed to cruise ships, everyone was eager to see us and very friendly. But all good things must come to an end.

We were returning by launch to the ship after an exciting day at Raiatea. As Opal stepped from the small tender to the ship's ladder, she caught her ankle between the rocking launch and the side of the ship.

Bad news. We went immediately to the ship's doctor. I believe I knew more about medicine than he. He was too young to have ever graduated from medical school. There was no x-ray equipment on board, so he arranged for the ship's local operators to take us to a doctor. They provided Opal with crutches and we carefully helped her back on the launch. On shore, our transportation turned out to be a pickup driven by the local representative. With him was his twelve-year-old daughter, the only one who spoke English.

We managed to get Opal in the cab of the truck with them, and I climbed into the open back. Off we raced through the village to a long wooden building that had been built by the U.S. Navy during World War II. This was the hospital. There were no screens on the windows or doors. We were escorted into a room with a huge x-ray machine, also left by the troops over forty years ago.

The doctor appeared, and I thought I was on the set of *South Pacific*. He looked just like the French doctor in the film. In fact, he was French. I imagined he had left France to escape some problem, just like in the movie. He took an x-ray and said that her ankle was only cracked. He just put a sock on it and dismissed us. I asked if we could take the x-ray films with us to the ship and he obliged. So off we drove, with me in the back of the pickup holding the large x-ray sheets flapping in the wind much to the amazement of the locals.

Back on the ship, I had the purser make an announcement to see if there was an orthopedic doctor on board. Our great luck produced a doctor from Chicago and he even had his medical kit with him. He looked at the x-rays and said that the ankle was definitely broken. (Maybe that was why the island doctor was there – he was not a good doctor.) Our Chicago doctor managed to wrap the ankle securely so as not to do any damage until she could get home and have it properly set. We kept Opal in a wheelchair or on crutches for the remaining two days of the trip. Back home, she did have it set in a cast. Her doctor said that she would have had permanent damage had it not been properly wrapped. If we had taken the advice of the French doctor, she would have been in big trouble.

દે દે દે દે

Since casino gambling is not available in Texas, all trips I scheduled to gaming destinations usually were filled quickly. Once, when a gambling ship announced day trips out of Port Isabel, Texas, I combined the day cruise with a tour to the Texas Valley along the Rio Grande and a side trip to Mexico for shopping.

The cruise ship was an old tub that had been refitted for gambling. There was one deck for slot and video poker machines and gaming tables, and one for a restaurant, bar, and small lounge where they had a very poor excuse for entertainment. The eight hour cruise was scheduled to travel the required three miles out to sea where gambling would be legal and sail around all day and then return. As a seasickness precaution, I took a Dramamine pill.

At the three-mile limit, they opened the casino and everyone flocked in to grab a slot machine or a seat at a gaming table. I sat down at a video poker machine and was doing OK, at least pretty well staying even. I noticed that the water seemed rougher, but I just concentrated on my poker screen. After about an hour or so, I suddenly realized that I was the only one in the casino except the employees.

"Where'd everyone go?" I asked.

"They all were getting seasick and went on the outside deck."

I decided I had better check on things. I cashed out of my poker machine and had five quarters left. On the way out, I put those quarters in a slot machine and hit a jackpot of $300! I was so excited, I ran up the stairs to find Keith and tell him the good news.

Outside, the deck was covered with people sprawled everywhere, some leaning over the side. It was a total mess. I found Keith stretched out in a deck chair. His face was green. I showed him my winnings and he was too sick to even care. I checked around with the rest of the people, and all they wanted me to do was get the captain to turn the boat around and go home. The captain said he was obligated to stay out at least six hours, but he would return two hours early.

As the ship approached the dock, someone said, "I have never seen anything that looks as good as that dry land." The group was not too happy with the gambling trip, and I did not dare tell them I had won $300 while they were throwing up.

🐛 🐛 🐛 🐛

During my tenure as a group leader, I was very fortunate to remain healthy. I never missed a scheduled tour in my nineteen years on the job. But I did have to leave during one.

We travel to all these exotic places with all kinds of insects and what have you, but the only bug problem I ever had was when a brown recluse spider bit me in my home in Texas. This happened about ten days prior to a U.S. National Parks tour. I made four visits to the Scott and White Hospital emergency room, and right before we left, I was given an extra strength antibiotic, as the other medication did not seem to be working. The second day of the trip I broke out in a terrible rash and began running a fever. We were at the Grand Canyon in Arizona. I lay in the bed in pain while everyone walked around the rim of the canyon, enjoying one of the most spectacular vistas in the world. The only thing that made this bearable was that I had been here before and had already seen the beautiful views. Fortunately, I had an excellent Collette Tour Guide to take care of everything, for I certainly was in no condition to help.

We went on to Zion National Park, and at this point I knew I had to see a doctor. This remote area of Utah is not the ideal place to seek medical attention. I went to the park emergency clinic. The two attendants there had never heard of a brown recluse spider and had no idea how to treat its bite, so they gave me some pain-killers and charged me $110!

By the fourth day, in Salt Lake City, I knew I could not go on and after talking to the doctor back in Texas, it became clear that I was having a reaction to the medication. Collette Tours quickly arranged flights for Keith and me to return home, where it was confirmed that I did have a medication reaction and after a few days, I was OK. I received a get-well card signed by the entire group from Yellowstone National Park.

In all these years, there was just one time I had to send Keith home. We had two busloads plus our van (ninety-four people) for a Cunard Princess Cruise sailing from Galveston. The day before departure, Keith had root canal work. That night, he was in pain and I called the dentist, telling him we were leaving the next day. He prescribed some pain pills and said Keith could go on the cruise and would be fine in a day or two.

We sailed from Galveston and the next morning Keith woke up with his jaw swollen clear down his neck. The ship's doctor (who didn't inspire a lot of confidence) gave him a shot and some pills and told him to take it easy. The next morning he was not any better, and we were still at sea, so back to the ship's doctor for another shot. The next day we docked at Cozumel, Mexico. Keith was worse, and I knew the best thing to do was to get him home as quickly as possible. There were no flights to Texas from Cozumel that day and he would have to wait until the next day when the ship arrived at Cancun, Mexico.

Keith was now very ill. The ship personnel were no help in arranging any flights. As we had bussed to Galveston, we had no airline tickets at all. We took a taxi to the airport to purchase a ticket, only to discover that we had to buy the tickets at the downtown airline office. Back we went to town, bought a one-way ticket for $300 and returned to the airport. I went to check him in, and the agent would not accept the ticket because he did not have a stamped Mexican tourist card. As the ship was going round trip Galveston, a tourist card was not required. I asked to see the immigration supervisor. In his office were three officers in official uniforms. I explained our situation.

"You cannot leave without a stamped tourist card. Otherwise you are here illegally," the man at the desk stated.

"This is a port of entry, is it not"?

"Yes," he replied.

"Then you have tourist cards in your desk. How much is it going to cost for you to get one out and stamp it so I can get my sick husband on the plane? Or do you not have a bit of feeling to help someone in need?" I pleaded, and I was almost in tears at this point.

He looked around at the other men, and I knew he could not take a bribe in their presence. He reached in his desk drawer and handed me a tourist card. I immediately filled it out. He stamped it. I said, "Thank you very much" and quickly went over to the check-in counter. We had just a short time to get Keith a boarding pass and on the plane.

I returned to the ship and, for the first time in my travel history, I was alone on a cruise. I sat down and cried. I heard a knock at the door and there was our darling little steward with a cup of tea. He had been so solicitous while Keith had been sick, always straightening his bed and bringing food to the room.

The next day I called Keith from Cayman Island. He told me he had gone to a different dentist who took care of the infection that had resulted from the original dental work. He was feeling much better.

When we received a bill from the first dentist for $350, I wrote back:

"Due to your unsatisfactory dental work on my husband, we had the following expenses:

Ship's Doctor — 2 visits @ $50.....$100

Medication on the ship....................$60

Airline ticket home.......................$300

Cab fares for tickets and airport..........$40

Total spent................................$500

"This does not cover my husband's pain, the inconvenience, and the fact that he missed the cruise, so I think you really owe us money, but we will call it even."

I never heard from him again.

There are some stairs you don't want to fall down (Tikal, Guatemala)

While we stalked wild game in Africa, Keith herded luggage

Another reason you always come home with more stuff than you left with (Ecuador)

5

BAGGAGE BLUES

Twenty people were on a tour to Ecuador and the Galapagos. When we arrived at Quito, Ecuador, we had twenty bags. There were so many excellent bargains on native handicrafts and at the village markets that everyone just went wild. When we left, we had a total of forty-two bags. Needless to say, we certainly were good for the economy of the country.

Celebrating the hundredth birthday of the Statue of Liberty in 1986 was a great excuse to visit New York for three days. Add on a seven-day cruise of the New England islands and it became a once-in-a-lifetime experience. So it wasn't too surprising I had 126 people in our group and 156 pieces of luggage! We were staying at the Halloran House Hotel, right across Park Avenue from the Waldorf Astoria. The Halloran is a very nice hotel but, like many older hotels in the Big Apple, it has a very small lobby.

The day we were leaving for Newport, Rhode Island, for the cruise, the hotel bellmen had collected everyone's luggage from outside their rooms and piled it in stacks in the lobby. In such close quarters, with the bags stacked so high, it was impossible to get an accurate count. Finally, I said: "Just load 'em up, we have to get on our way to Newport."

We arrived at Newport and boarded the ship. Passengers dispersed to their cabins and we distributed the luggage. The Price family discovered they were missing all five of their bags!

Buckshot, the father, said, "Y'know, I was *afraid* the bellman wouldn't see our luggage. It was kinda tucked around the back in a corner." Now he tells me! A call back to the hotel revealed that the bags were located right where Buckshot said they were, kinda tucked around the back in a corner.

The manager of the hotel went beyond the call of duty. When he got off work at five, he delivered the Price's bags to Newport, about 150 miles away, in his own car. He arrived after midnight but well ahead of our morning sailing. Then he turned around and drove back to New York to be at work by eight. Because of his extra effort, the Prices were able to sail the next morning with all their clothes. Don't tell me there aren't caring people in the world. Even in New York City.

ð. ð. ð. ð.

In all our years of travel, Keith and I were responsible for hundreds of bags. On numerous occasions we would be missing a bag upon arrival at an airline destination, but it was always recovered eventually. We had only one piece totally lost or, to be more specific, stolen. It happened on a bus trip to Houston. When we arrived at the hotel, as was my custom, I had the bellmen come out and start unloading the luggage while I went inside and obtained the room keys. I always had the passengers remain on the bus during this process.

Kermit, a frequent passenger, had a hang-up bag containing an ultra-suede leather sports jacket that was popular at that time. You could see the collar of the coat at the top of the bag. As we were settling into our hotel room, Kermit called to tell me that the bellmen had delivered one of his bags, but he was missing his hang-up bag. We checked with all our people and no one had it in their room by mistake. The hotel was alerted and we had to leave that evening to attend a Broadway show. Of course, Kermit had to go without his fashionable suede jacket.

The next morning I met with the hotel manager regarding the lost bag. He said that the bellman who had unloaded and delivered our baggage did not show up for work that morning, and the evidence was rather clear to me. I knew the hotel had insurance to cover this type of incident, so I filed a claim. It took about a month of hounding the hotel, but Kermit finally received reimbursement for the contents of the bag which also included his dress pants, and his wife's dress and shawl.

ъ ъ ъ ъ

We were ready to transfer to the airport after a stay in Las Vegas. Our group's luggage had been collected by the hotel bellmen and placed on the sidewalk outside the Rivieria Hotel. Keith always took the responsibility of looking after the luggage, while I was responsible for the people. (He had the better deal because the luggage couldn't complain!) He had our tote bag with him and a couple from my group came up and asked him to watch their tote bag as they wanted to play the slot machines while waiting for the bus to arrive. When I appeared after taking care of all the departure formalities, Keith handed me our tote bag and the other one to watch. He went out to help load the bags when the bus arrived. I went back into the lobby, sat the bags down and stood nearby.

Shortly thereafter, the bus arrived and it was my duty to round everyone up from the casino to get on the coach. As I am not accustomed to having to think about luggage, that is exactly what I did — not think about it. I gathered the group together, herded them to the bus, noted all present and accounted for, and checked that Keith had the luggage loaded, so off we went to the airport.

On the way to the airport, Keith queried: "Where's our tote bag?"

To my horror realized I had left both bags in the lobby of the hotel. When we arrived at the airport luggage check-in area, I sent all the people in and told them I would meet them at the departure gate with their boarding passes after I had checked in all the luggage. This was back in the good old days before strict security regulations when I could check the all the passengers' luggage and obtain the boarding passes, too. The client never had to go up to the airline check-in counter.

Keith immediately summoned a cab to go back to the hotel and retrieve the tote bags. The small bag belonging to the couple was there, but ours was missing. It was a practically new large tweed tote bag. When Keith alerted the hotel security, they just said, "You never should have left them unguarded," as if we didn't know better. There was nothing for him to do but pick up the one remaining bag and get back to the airport as quickly as possible to catch the plane.

In the meantime, I had fifty bags to be checked to Austin. When the bus arrived at the group baggage area at the airport, there was no skycap on duty. The driver unloaded all the luggage and left. I went to a phone in the area and asked for a person to check my bags. Finally, one porter arrived and I showed him the tickets and said I needed all the bags tagged. As he slowly filled out the tags (again, before the days of computerized luggage tags), I attached them to each bag. The skycap never touched a suitcase. When all bags had been tagged and he handed me the receipts, I gave him $25, for I felt he did not deserve $1 per bag when I had done over half the work. I started for the terminal door.

"Wait up, missy," he hollered, "you're short on the tip."

"Since I did half the work, I paid you for just half."

"Do you want to see these bags arrive in Austin on time?" he warned.

So what could I do but accept the blackmail and hand him another $25. I sure was relieved when I saw all the bags arrive on the carousel at the Austin Airport.

To continue the saga of the Brooks' missing tote bag: I had purchased a new bag, plus all new supplies such as cosmetics, medical prescriptions, curling iron, and on and on. About a month after the trip, UPS delivered the bag to our home with everything intact. What is surprising is that it came from Bally's Hotel in Vegas, quite a distance on the strip from the Rivieria Hotel. When I called Bally's, they said that it was turned in to their lost and found department. They were able to send it to us because of our identification tag on the bag. Apparently whoever took it was disappointed that it did not contain any cameras, jewelry, or money and just decided to get rid of it. We will never know, but it certainly was nice to have it back.

ع& ع& ع& ع&

We had a group of eighty-eight people for the Nashville Country Christmas tour at the Opryland Hotel. It was time to leave and the bellmen had collected the luggage from each room and had stacked it on carts at a back loading entrance. Keith and I went down there and carefully counted the correct number of bags. Upon arrival at the Nashville airport, I checked the bags as a group. Then, on the plane, I counted the airline luggage stubs and found that I had only eighty-seven, when I should have had eighty-eight. I was hoping the porters at Delta had made a mistake. When we arrived in Austin, we discovered that June's bag was missing. I immediately phoned the Opryland Hotel. Sure enough, it was there. Somehow, it had fallen from the cart at the hotel as they wheeled the baggage out to load on the bus. How they could not notice when a bag fell off is beyond me, but they sent it on the next plane and Delta delivered it to her the next day.

ع& ع& ع& ع&

The culmination of our Cunard cruise around the British Isles was at Southampton, England. On most cruises you are requested to place your checked luggage outside your door the night prior to disembarkation. I always remind my passengers never to pack anything in the bag that they will need the next morning for travel home. Alene had her pants suit all ready to put on the morning we were leaving, only to discover she had not kept out a blouse. Fortunately, she was wearing pajamas, so she just used the pajama top as a blouse. The colors were even compatible.

While I was occupied with a passenger who needed wheelchair assistance, I told my group to go to dockside, identify their bags and have the porters put them on our bus for transfer to the airport in London. By the time I reached the bus with my patient, everyone was there and they said everything was OK. Again, when I got to the airport, I group checked the bags. When we arrived in Atlanta to go through customs and change planes, everyone had their bags except Alene and Bob. They stood waiting for theirs to arrive on the carousel. "Did you pick them up from the dock and see that they got on the bus?" I asked.

"No, we thought you were going to do that."

What could I say?

When I returned to my office, I contacted Cunard. They had found the two bags left on the dock in England, and the Cunard officials put them on the QE2 bound for New York, certainly an elegant way for two bags to travel. Then UPS brought them to me at the Austin bank and I finally returned the missing suitcases to the owners. This took about a month, but at least everything worked out all right.

We had just completed a seven-day cruise in the paradise of the Tahitian Islands. The ship docked at 8 a.m., and all the ship's passengers were taken to a hotel in Papeete and then transferred that evening to the airport for a 10 p.m. flight out. The ship would deliver the checked luggage directly to the airport.

Five busloads with a total of 180 passengers arrived at the same time at the airport. A huge mound of luggage greeted us. We had been told it would be unloaded and put in separate alphabetical areas. Either the workmen did not know the alphabet, or, I rather think, they didn't give a damn, and about three hundred bags were thrown in one big pile in the airport lobby. The airport at Papeete at that time was a large open-air facility. It was about ninety degrees with about ninety percent humidity and there was no air conditioning. It was like a sauna in there and everyone was hot and bothered.

As this was a charter flight, we could not obtain boarding passes in advance. We had to get them when we checked in. This could be a disaster if the plane was overbooked and, judging from the crowds, it looked as if it might be.

As I surveyed the situation — people digging around, throwing bags everywhere, trying to find theirs — I commanded: "Keith, you and Paul get in there and find our group's bags. The rest of you form a human chain to the front desk. As they hand you a bag, quickly pass it up to me. I'll have the ticket and get the bag checked and get the boarding pass."

Our bags had special bright yellow tags, so they were easy to spot. Much to the other passengers' distress, my system worked very well and we were the first ones to get our bags checked through and receive boarding passes, guaranteeing everyone in my group the best seats on the plane. When I had finally finished and started to leave the check-in desk, I heard someone say: "Now that the Bitch is through, maybe we can get ours checked."

I just turned around and left as quickly as possible. But, because the "bitch" had done her job, we had the front seats on the all-coach-class plane, which meant we were served first, had a little more leg room, and didn't have to contend with the roar of the engines on the ten-hour flight from Papeete to Los Angeles.

≈ ≈ ≈ ≈

We had sailed from Ft. Lauderdale, Florida on the Star Princess, through the Panama Canal, disembarking at Acapulco, Mexico. When we arrived at the non-air conditioned airport, the bags were once again dumped in one area, but this time at least all the luggage for Delta Airlines was in one pile. So we had to find ours. Thanks to those bright yellow tags, Keith quickly spotted our bags and brought them to me at the counter. I noticed that at the Delta desk there was a stack of luggage tags already marked for Austin.

"To expedite matters, could I go ahead and put the luggage tags on each bag and hand them to you?" I asked.

"No, it is a federal offense for anyone but airline personnel to attach the tags. If you do it, you could go to jail."

I certainly didn't want to end up in a Mexican jail, so I stepped back and watched as they slowly processed the bags. Keith came up with the last of our bags from the pile, but we only had twenty-four out of fifty-eight pieces. It was now just twenty minutes before departure. I ran up to a Princess representative and explained I was missing thrity-four bags. He just handed me a Lost Baggage Claim Form! That was all I needed at this point.

I had already sent the passengers up to the gate, and I had no idea what their individual bags looked like. Also, since I had group-checked, I didn't know which bags had already been sent to the plane. Five minutes before departure, I saw the Princess luggage truck approaching. I ran up the stairs to the departure gate to ask them to hold the plane until I could get everything checked. It was so hot and humid my clothing was stuck to my skin with perspiration. As I reached the gate desk, I saw a sign — "Plane delayed one hour due to weather." Back downstairs, I got the other baggage taken care of and made it in plenty of time.

This delay caused a late arrival at DFW. As we rushed out of customs, I was delighted to see that our gate for the Austin flight was right next door. We had come in at Gate 35 and were scheduled to go out of Gate 34. When I got everyone to Gate 34, they announced the Austin flight was departing out of Gate 29, in another terminal building, typical at DFW. I told everyone to hurry on and I ran at breakneck speed ahead of them to Gate 29. When I got there, I found out that this flight, too, had been delayed due to weather. I was about to collapse. When we finally got on the plane, the pilot announced that we were number fourteen in line for take off, (another great thing about DFW) and we were on the runway for another fifty minutes. We arrived in Austin over two hours late. The girl who was to pick Keith and me up had given up and gone home. We took a cab and, to make my day complete, the driver charged us an extra $2.80 for using the trunk! If I had known that little rule, I would have sat on the darn luggage inside the cab.

એ એ એ એ

One evening as I entered the dining room of a hotel in Honduras, I immediately was drawn to an unusual painting in a large basket hanging high above a door. It was a three dimensional picture of a village with a cathedral high on a hillside, very much like a charming village we had passed through that afternoon. The canvas had been molded inside the basket, the background painted, and then life-like miniatures of a bridge, the light poles, and rocks had been added for a 3-D effect.

"How much for the basket painting?" I asked the waiter.

"I will have to ask the manager. He isn't here, but we can call him," was the reply.

Later he returned and said "$100."

"Sold! Please take it down and see if you can wrap it for taking on a plane."

When the item was at my feet on the floor, I was amazed at how large it really was. The round basket frame was eight inches deep and over three feet across. The waiters found some cardboard and with tape formed a makeshift wrapping.

As we toted the thing back to our room, Keith pointed out that there was no way would we'd be able to get it on the plane in this condition. I had hoped to carry it on the plane, but now realized it would have to be checked. I hardly slept that night, wondering how I would manage it.

The next morning our guide said there was a cabinet shop in a nearby village that could make a wooden box in which to ship the painting safely. So off we went. The carpenter said he could do the job for $10 and I told him to get started. We went to eat breakfast, and when we returned, he had the picture totally encased in a very sturdy wooden box.

"Twenty dollars," he said. "It took more lumber than I originally planned."

What could I do? The picture was already nailed inside the box, so I paid him. That was just the beginning of my problems. When we arrived at the airport to check in at American Airlines, I found out why that hole under the counter that you put your luggage through is thirty-six inches high. If your luggage can't fit through, you pay an extra fee for oversize luggage. I was assessed $60. I paid American, got our boarding passes, and was on the way to the departure gate when over the loud speaker I heard: "Joyce Brooks, please report to American check-in immediately."

"You need to go back to security. That box is too large to go through the luggage x-ray," they told me.

I followed a clerk back to where three men were squatting down by my box, prying it open with a crowbar and hammer.

"We're going to have to open it to check for explosives and drugs," they explained.

I was afraid that if they tore into the box they might damage the painting and I would never get it back together again. But since this was Honduras, I knew American officials were extra cautious about drugs.

"Please wait," I pleaded. "I am going to be on the same plane, so I don't believe I'd plant a bomb and risk my own life. As for drugs, don't you have some drug dogs that can sniff instead of tearing into the box?"

Miraculously, they agreed. As they brought in the dogs, I suddenly had a fear that the artist might have hidden something there, but it passed the sniff test.

So off we flew to Miami, our port of entry for the United States. I had no idea what problems we would face with customs officials there. When we arrived, we had to go to an area where "oversize" items are held. We put the huge box on a cart with the rest of our luggage and proceeded to customs.

I was shaking as I wheeled the cart up to the lady official. I handed her the customs form where I had listed a painting under items purchased.

"What's that?" she asked pointing to the big box.

"A painting in a basket," I answered.

She just waved us through. That was it! I couldn't believe it. We promptly went over to the American baggage crew and handed it off with our other luggage.

It was a relief to pick the box up at the Austin airport, take it home and uncrate it to find everything in fine condition. Of course, the painting that started out costing just $100 ended up costing nearly double that, but we love to look at it and remember our times in Honduras.

No matter where you break down, you'll attract rubberneckers

The 'main terminal' (the tree) and shuttle van at Bololo, Papua New Guinea

*The leg sticking out from beneath our derailed 'Machu Picchu Express'
belongs to a worker, not a victim. Thank goodness it didn't go off the other
side of the track or we might have ended up in the Urubamba River,
hundreds of feet below!*

GETTING THERE IS HALF THE FUN

6

Our American Airlines plane was taxiing along the runway at the Austin airport when we suddenly came to an abrupt stop. If we had not had our seat belts fastened, we would all have been thrown from our seats. There was no explanation until later in flight when the pilot came on the p.a. system and drawled: "Sorry for that little incident on the runway. Just wanted you folks to know we brake for armadillos." What the real problem was, we will never know.

Considering all the traveling we have done, we have been very fortunate to escape any serious problems. Our worst scare came on an inspection tour to Jamaica before I brought a group. Our plane left Miami in a fierce rainstorm. As the plane gained altitude, we encountered a wind shear, a particularly violent type of turbulence associated with storms. This was an L-1011, the kind that seats 2-4-2 across, with luggage bins suspended overhead down the middle of the plane. When we hit the wind shear, the plane began to toss about wildly and the center luggage racks swayed back and forth. I was certain they would rip free from the ceiling. Everything was rattling and shaking, and I thought, "This is it." Thank God, the pilot was able to pull up and out of the rough weather, and we were quickly on our way to Jamaica.

Of course, statistically, flying is the safest way to travel. You have a greater risk of injury driving your own car around your own town! The worst part about flying is the overcrowding and the delays. I have noticed recently that, regardless of where you are going, the plane is always full. In the '70s and '80s, overseas flights were frequently half full, giving you room to stretch out and get some rest. Not anymore. They are usually overbooked and packed to the gills. Another problem that's getting worse by the year is planes not being on time. My advice is to book early morning flights, because the later in the day your flight, the more it seems to be delayed.

On the ground, tour companies make every effort to assure that the vehicles they use — planes, trains, boats, or buses — are safe and operated by professionals. Still, there were times in my group travels when things became a little sticky. Many incidents seemed terrible at the time, but afterwards, once the shock and discomfort had worn off, they provided excellent material for cocktail party chatter and even a few laughs, proving the old adage that getting there can be half the fun.

&a &a &a &a

My group was returning from a Las Vegas gambling trip when our luck ran out. We had been in the air just a few minutes when the pilot announced calmly, "We've lost number one engine. No problem. We have three others. But, we can't fly to Houston in this condition, so we're going to go out over the desert, dump some fuel, and return to Vegas."

As the plane turned around, I looked out the window. What an apprehensive feeling to see a stream of fuel being discharged from the wing tips! I had a horrible vision of the fuel being swept into the back of the plane and catching fire. One woman started screaming, "We are going to crash and die!"

The pilot landed safely, but they had the crash unit and foam trucks out to meet us just in case. We were told not to leave the gate area while they assessed the problem. Most of the passengers scrambled to other airlines to book other flights. There was no way I could find thirty-six seats on any single plane, so I told my group to sit tight.

This was in the '80s, on Pan American Airways when airline service meant something. The flight attendants were great. As the wait stretched from 10 a.m. through the lunch hour, the stewardesses served us the cold portion of the plane lunch. (This was also back when hot meals were available on all flights of one or more hours.) So we had an appetizer, salad and dessert. They also brought out the snacks and liquor cart from the first class compartment and started pouring drinks. As the afternoon wore on, everyone from the plane had departed except my group and two guys from Houston. The booze kept flowing, and everyone was having fun and feeling no pain. I knew I had to keep my senses to get this group home, so I didn't join the party. A replacement part arrived from San Francisco, but it didn't work.

At 7 p.m., they announced that a plane that had departed from Los Angeles was detouring to Vegas to pick us up. My group staggered and weaved onto the plane and after we took off, the following announcement was made: "Welcome to our passengers who just boarded in Las Vegas. Since we weren't expecting you, we're sorry that we do not have enough food on board to serve you dinner. However, we are pleased to offer you unlimited free cocktails."

A loud groan came from my group. Just what they didn't need — another drink! When we arrived in Houston, we had missed our connecting flight to Austin, so I had to find hotel rooms and PanAm picked up the bill. The next morning my group made it home — many with a hangover, but with a great story to tell about their trip to Las Vegas.

ε❧ ε❧ ε❧ ε❧

Keith and I were on a personal trip to Papua New Guinea. We are butterfly collectors, so when we discovered that one of the best spots for butterflies was at Bulolo, located in the jungles in the center of the country, about two hundred miles north of Port Moresby, we just had to go. Papua New Guinea itself is off the beaten tourist path, and Bulolo is not even a trail. The only way to get there is on a two-engine, twelve-seat Otter plane, usually piloted by Australians. The "airline" that flew this route was Southwest Air, which reminded me comfortingly of the airline of the same name in Texas.

After we had been in the air about forty-five minutes, flying over high mountains and dense jungles, I noticed the plane was descending. I looked all around, but saw no buildings, no runway, nothing to indicate an airport. Just then, we swooped down and landed in a grassy clearing I hadn't even noticed. A large tree served as the terminal.

Keith and I were unloaded from the plane along with a bundle of newspapers and two cardboard boxes. Then the pilot climbed back in the cockpit, waved a cheery goodbye, and took off. There we stood, all alone in the jungles of New Guinea with no one in sight. After about twenty minutes, up drove a pickup with a lady driver.

"We were to have someone from the Pine Lodge Resort meet us," I told her.

"Oh, they are just probably running late. Come along with me," she said in a friendly manner. So the papers, the two boxes, Keith and I were loaded into the pickup and off we went. About halfway into Bulolo, we met an old station wagon.

"There's your ride," she announced. She stopped, and we transferred to the other vehicle.

"I'm Easygo, the cook. Your guide had to go out of town, so I am filling in," we were informed by a pleasant little man of about sixty.

We were later to discover his great ability as a chef. That evening we dined on delicious grilled barrimundi fish accompanied by excellently prepared vegetables. What made the evening exceptional were our table companions, the only other three guests at the lodge. One was an Australian who was traveling around Papua New Guinea seeking qualified scholarship students for an Australian college. On the side, he was peddling metal detectors.

The other two were an Italian couple, both doctors. They had to come to Bulolo for the same reason we had — the butterflies and insects. He showed off a beetle that had cost $400! (He was definitely more into collecting than we were, and obviously more financially able to indulge his hobby.) With Easygo's delicious food and charming dinner companions we had a delightfully civilized dining experience in the depths of the jungle.

Our accommodations at the Pine Lodge were basic, complete with several geckos (little lizards) that ran in and out of the thatched roof, but were obliging enough not to join us in the bed. What was truly surprising was the television set in the room with telecasts via satellite from Australia and the United States.

The next day our guide, Ken, showed up and took all of us to the butterfly farm and processing plant where we were able to obtain some rare and unique specimens for our collection.

Gold was discovered here in the 1920s and '30s, but the gold began to peter out by the start of World War II, and the mines never returned to full production. Dredges can be seen along the creek-ways, rusting reminders of the days when prospectors flocked to the area. We saw many places where there had been mines, but only one was in operation when we were there and, according to Ken, not too profitably.

When we returned to the "airport" for our flight back to Port Moresby, a violent storm unleashed torrents of rain, accompanied by lightening and thunder. As we sat in the station wagon under the tree "terminal," I thought there was no way a small plane was coming during this storm. About thirty minutes after the scheduled arrival time, Ken said: "I hear it."

Darting down through the clouds came the plane, sliding in on the grass with water splashing up to the wingtips. As Ken held umbrellas, we boarded the plane, and with the rain still falling, off we went into the clouds. When we emerged from the low-lying fog, a monstrous black storm cloud loomed in front of us. Our pilot calmly banked the plane and we flew around it. The small craft bumped up and down something fierce before we found smooth flying, but I had faith in our Aussie pilot. I was confident he knew where the high mountains were, and would get us to Port Moresby safely, and he did.

᠈᠕ ᠈᠕ ᠈᠕ ᠈᠕

Hiram Bingham, a Yale professor, discovered Machu Picchu, the "lost city of the Incas," in 1911 when he hacked his way through centuries of dense vegetation high in the Peruvian Andes to find the largest Inca settlement never to have been discovered or plundered by the Spanish. I got there a little later with a Collette tour of senior citizens. We didn't have to hack our way to the top of the mountain on which Machu Picchu sits, but the journey was memorable anyway.

The only way to reach Machu Picchu, other than by foot on the old Inca Trail, is by train, a seventy-mile, three-hour journey from Cuzco. The incline from Cuzco to Machu Picchu is so steep that the train cars, each with its own engine, go forward for several miles, then backward, zigzagging their way up the mountainside. Nearer Machu Picchu, the track levels out and you have a panoramic ride full of natural splendors between high mountains covered with bromeliads offset by the raging Urubamba River. The train stops at villages along the way where the tourists bargain for Indian crafts and food items. We have several souvenirs we obtained through the train windows, including a large black spider, about eight inches across, safely mounted in a glass frame. Finally the train stopped at a small station where we transferred to a bus for the last 1,000-foot leg of the journey on a switchback road up the mountainside.

What a breathtaking sight at the summit. The Machu Picchu ruins have to be an all-time high for travelers, in more than one sense of the term. Lush green foliage covers the terraced gardens and the towering mountain peaks. Before your eyes lies an entire city of rock buildings perched on the sides of precipitous slopes. It is believed that this secluded village high in the mountains was a haven where sacred virgins of the sun escaped from the Spaniards during the 1500s.

At 8,202 feet, with the Urubamba churning below, we were amazed at the superb construction of stone buildings that have stood for centuries without the aid of mortar. With the exception of the original straw roofs, the city is pretty much intact, with a maze of plazas, chambers and palaces connected by solid stone stairways. I was also overwhelmed by the water system that flowed from terrace to terrace.

A special mystical feeling came over me as I stood in the presence of the spirits of the ancient Incas who so many years ago went about their daily lives in this mountaintop retreat. You could easily see how they could worship the sun up here where you somehow felt closer to it. After climbing in and around the ruins in for about two hours in absolutely fabulous sunny weather, we had lunch. All of sudden a heavy rain began to fall and it was announced that the train would leave at 2 p.m., an hour early. Everyone rushed to get on the buses for the trip down the mountain. It was push and shove to get aboard in the rain and I assumed all my chickens were there, so I did not take time to count. I had started to board when up ran Cindy.

"What's going on?" she yelled.

Unknown to me, Cindy had gone back up to the ruins area to take more photos. She had seen the commotion and ran back down. I shudder to think what would have happened if I had left one of my group on top of the mountain because I hadn't stopped to count.

As the bus departed, a young Indian boy hollered and waved at us. Each time the bus came around a bend, there he was, standing by the side of the road, waving and yelling. After about four hairpin turns, everyone in the bus was looking for him as we drove down the switch back road. He would always be there, standing in the rain and waving. We couldn't figure how he could continually beat the bus until we spotted the trail leading straight down the mountain. When we reached the bottom, he boarded the bus to a loud cheer and everyone donated money and food for his effort.

I saw a report that the Peruvian government is planning to install cable cars to take tourists up the mountainside. Not only would this destroy the natural beauty of the site but it would eliminate the little Indian boys' means of making money from their hillside runs. Let's hope it never happens.

It was still raining when we reached the train station and our local guide led us a long way down the track, only to discover that it was the wrong car. Back we trudged in the rain and got settled in the right car only to hear them announce that the train would leave at 3 p.m. after all. Delays like this are why I always advise my chickens to bring books along on a trip. At 3:05 p.m., the train slowly chugged out of the station.

It all happened so suddenly. A quarter of a mile out of the station there was a loud noise and our car started swinging from side to side and seemed about to topple over. I looked out and all I could see was the swift river so close to us I could almost touch it. I knew if we landed there, we would all perish. The side-to-side vibrating ended with a loud thud as the car dropped down off the track and stopped, still upright. We were shaken up pretty good, but no one was injured.

It turned out that the person who switches the tracks had not fastened the switch securely. It held for the first two cars, but then shook apart as our car hit it and we jumped off the track. For nearly two hours we sat by the side of the river while the train personnel tried to get the car back on the track by piling rocks under the wheels. Finally, using the individual engine on the car, supplemented by brute strength, they accomplished the feat. We arrived in Cuzco three hours late but safe, and with a good story to relate.

ða ða ða ða

On a Princess Cruise through Alaska's Inside Passage, we stopped at Juneau. Since we had been there many times before, Keith and I decided to take the raft trip at Mendenhall Glacier. Three of my "little ladies" joined us and 60 or so other people from the ship for this excursion. Buses transported us the fourteen miles out to where we were outfitted and boarded the rubber rafts. "Outfitted" meant being issued a poncho and rubber boots. My little ladies had such small feet that we had difficulty getting boots to fit them. By the time we had completed their ensembles, all the rafts were already loaded and starting down the icy river that flows from the glacier with chunks of ice floating all around. A girl was in charge of the only raft left, and she smiled gamely as the guys piloting the other rafts jeered that she was last.

The passenger list for this last rubber raft were our three little ladies, a huge man weighing easily over three hundred pounds, his medium-size wife, Keith and me. When the heavy man got on the raft, it just sank down where he was sitting, so it was decided he should get in the middle. This made the boat drag bottom, but in deep water we could at least float upright. The rest of us climbed in and sat around the edges of the boat and away we went. The other rafts were nowhere in sight.

Shortly after we pushed off, you guessed it, we hit high center. Our poor oarswoman could not budge us off with her paddles. So Keith and I volunteered to get out and push. Did I mention that this water was coming off a glacier? We thought it wouldn't be deep enough to get in our boots — but no — as we stepped into the stream the ice-cold water bubbled right into our boots. We were able to bounce the raft off high center and crawl back in, shivering and shaking as we poured ice water out of our boots.

The brochure for the excursion promised that halfway along we would stop and have a picnic and a drink of "Mendenhall Madness". By the time we reached the stopping place, the earlier rafters had devoured all the food and drained the "Mendenhall Madness" to the last drop. At this point, I was the one who was mad! I felt so sorry for our lady captain; she tried so hard in a very difficult situation. We made it back to the ship and it took several hours for my feet to warm up and to this day I have not had a taste of "Mendenhall Madness."

ॐ ॐ ॐ ॐ

One segment of a nine-day tour to Costa Rica was a night's stay at the Rio Colorado Lodge, located where the mouth of the Rio Colorado empties into the Caribbean Sea. The lodge, noted for its fine fishing, also offered many jungle wildlife adventures. The only way to reach the lodge is by small plane or by boat. You can arrive by water two ways. I had groups experience both. One option is to take a bus from San Jose south to the seaport of Limon where you board a motor launch and travel seventy-six miles north on inland rivers and narrow waterways. Along the way you see monkeys, tree sloths, and a wide range of jungle and water birds, plus numerous other boats of all sizes.

The other way to the lodge was to bus from San Jose for about seventy-five miles northeast to Puerto Viejo and catch a large motorized canoe. You travel on the Sarapiqui River north for about thirty miles to reach the Nicaraguan border. My group went in February 1990, shortly after the peace treaty between the Contras and the Sandinistas and this route had just been opened for tourism. Since we were crossing an international border, our local guide had obtained our names and passport numbers prior to departure. As our boat approached the Costa Rican guard post, we hardly realized that this was a checkpoint. One guardsman was swimming around the edge of the river in a bikini bathing suit. The other guard on duty was dressed in combat boots, shorts, and a brightly colored surfing shirt. He took the list from our guide and waved us on.

One minute later we reached the Nicaraguan border. Here were three guards, all in combat uniforms, armed with rifles. None of them could have been over fourteen. The one in charge took the passport list, smiled and waved us on. Meanwhile, the other two were willingly posing for the photographs being snapped by everyone in the boat. As we continued down the San Juan River, which forms the border between the two countries, we noticed uniformed guards with guns at intervals along the banks.

About thirty minutes later, the canoe's motor coughed and died. Here we were in no man's land between two countries, and one side was armed. Our boat driver and our guide started working on the engine and, thankfully, the current took us slowly downstream in the direction of the lodge. There were no villages in sight and not even a Sandinista. The one and a half hour boat ride to the Rio Colorado Lodge had stretched to three hours and it was getting dark. There was no radio to alert anyone of our problem, so the only thing to do was just float slowly along. Finally, around 8:30 p.m. we heard a boat approaching. The lodge had sent a rescue boat for its stranded guests. It tied onto our boat and pulled us in.

The lights of the lodge certainly were a welcome sight, since I was dying to go to the bathroom. This was yet another occasion on which I envied men their anatomical advantages. During our long journey I noticed several of them leaning way over the boat, and I don't think they were looking for fish.

ટ**ા** ટ**ા** ટ**ા** ટ**ા**

You would think that something as simple as a canoe ride would not create a problem, but this was an exception. We took a group of senior citizens for a weekend on a dude ranch near Bandera, Texas. Activities included horseback riding, a hayride, golf, and a canoe trip down the Medina River. Keith and I assisted the entire group, two by two, into their individual canoes, making sure to tell them all to be extra careful. I sent them all happily floating down the gently flowing river, hoping they'd make it through okay.

Then we climbed into our boat. I had never been in a canoe in my life, and had no idea how to maneuver the thing. I was in front with my paddle and Keith was in the back, giving instructions and trying to steer. The first thing we did was go right up a cypress tree trunk. After getting out of that situation, we tried to paddle downstream. Obviously, I was doing everything wrong and Keith was getting upset that I was not following his instructions.

We hadn't gone but a few feet when we hit a whirlpool and immediately capsized head first into the river. Conveniently, the water was just about four feet deep. I stood up laughing, and then realized I could not see Keith. He emerged out from under the boat, minus his glasses. We tried to feel around and find them, but no luck. So, I guess today there is a catfish in the Medina River with excellent eyesight.

Of course, he did not have an extra pair and had to do without until we could get back to Austin and an optometrist. But that inconvenience was nothing compared to the embarrassment we felt when we finally arrived downstream, bedraggled and soaking wet. All of the "old folks" that I had been so worried about stood there, perfectly dry, laughing at us.

ʠ ʠ ʠ ʠ

I had heard many wonderful things about Costa Rica, but after many unpleasant experiences in Mexico, I wanted to see for myself before recommending it to my groups. The local Costa Rica tour operator agreed to bring me (Keith had to pay) down for an inspection trip. I discovered that Costa Rica is the only country south of the Rio Grande where you can safely drink the tap water. They have no military and use the money they save for education, making Costa Rica one of the world's most literate nations. Violent crime is very low.

Costa Rica has over 850 species of birds, more than all of North America, and 10 percent of all the butterflies in the world — more than the entire continent of Africa. The country has allocated 8 percent of their land to national park systems that range from rainforests to volcanoes to beaches. Sounded like a place I would like to take my FF's (frequent followers).

One day on the Pacific coast, we were walking along the beach in Manuel Antonio National Park when a lady approached us.

"Pardon me, are you from Texas?"

The cap I was wearing, with the logo of the Austin bank for which I organized the tours, had given me away, so we fessed up. She excitedly told us she was from West Texas and we sat down and had a nice visit. She was the wife of the American Vice Consul in Costa Rica. We had dinner with the family that evening and I explained my mission — to look things over and then bring back tourists. When I mentioned this, she suggested that we bring the group to the embassy for a reception upon my return. I was flabbergasted — that would be something neat for me to promote the trip.

When I advertised the Costa Rica tour to our bank customers, I was overwhelmed with the response. Immediately I had eighty-eight people sign up and I had to cut it off there, for we could handle only two busloads. I wrote the embassy in Costa Rica of my success and they replied that the embassy could not accommodate that number, but offered to arrange for a reception at a local restaurant. They selected The Tiquicia, an open-air café high on a mountaintop overlooking the city of San Jose. From this vantage point, you could see the twinkling lights of the city below and the surrounding mountains.

The night of the party I questioned our transfer drivers when they arrived in school bus type vehicles, instead of the regular motor coaches we had been using.

"The roads are not suitable for that type of bus," they answered. That should have been a clue right there. Although the road along the fifteen-mile trip was rough, we arrived at the restaurant without any problem.

I had told everyone that we were to be the guests of honor of the American Embassy and to dress up for the occasion, so everyone was decked out in their finest. The evening consisted of an open bar, a delicious Costa Rican meal, culminating with entertainment by a group of colorfully-attired native children. A fabulous view of the city lights made the evening complete. Our special hosts were the Vice Consul and his wife, the Costa Rican Minister of Foreign Exports, and the Embassy Consul General and his wife. Each made a brief welcome speech and explained his position. At ten, aromatic Costa Rican coffee was served. I reveled in the glory of the evening and thought to myself: "Joyce Brooks, you pulled off a great one this time."

When I led the group out to board the buses to return to the hotel, I noticed that it had rained while we had been inside. The restaurant was located at the end of a dirt road about a third of a mile downhill from the main road at the top of the mountain. The dirt road had become exceedingly slick and the buses couldn't get any traction.

"Everyone out," said the driver.

I stepped out of the bus first and immediately slid about two feet in the mud in my open-toed sandals. We formed a human chain to unload everyone. The driver suggested that we walk up the mountain, and he would try to get the bus up there. It was pitch dark as everyone trudged up in the mud. About half way, Kermit, who had a history of heart trouble, started having difficulty breathing. Keith and Larry got on either side of him and helped him to the top where he was able to sit down on the side of the road and loosen his tie. Shortly he seemed to get better.

There on the mountaintop, stood ninety people, including the Vice Consul and his wife who had come with us on the bus. We were stranded and it was turning cold. The other hosts had already left in their private cars. Many of the ladies had no wraps, and the Southern gentlemen relinquished their coats. After one hour up there, and no sign of the buses, Keith walked down to see what was going on. When he got there, he discovered they were pouring water under the wheels — why they thought that would help I'll never know! All they were accomplishing was making the tires spin faster. Our local guide sent word that he had called the city and more buses were coming for us.

About halfway up the road, I had noticed a small house. The lady who lived there walked up and invited us to come down to her home to escape the cold. Can you imagine having ninety strangers show up at your place around midnight, and you have only a tiny living room? Her husband built a fire in their outdoor barbecue grill to warm those who could not fit in the house. One of my ladies was so eager to get to a warm spot that she stumbled on the porch step and sprained her ankle.

Our hostess apologized that she did not have any tea — who has enough tea on hand for ninety people? Most of the women were in her small living room, sitting on every available chair and mostly on the floor. She graciously offered us her one bathroom, which I thought would surely clog from overuse. The woman and her husband were from Canada and had two small children who were asleep; how they managed to stay that way I will never know. He was a writer struggling to make his mark in the literary world.

Finally, one bus showed up, and I packed in as many people as I could. They were standing in the aisle and sitting three to a seat. Then came several taxis. Kermit, Virginia, Keith, and I were the last ones to depart in a cab. When we reached the top of the mountain, the cab just went straight, instead of turning onto the correct road. Kermit noticed that we were going the wrong direction, so I tried to advise the driver as best I could in my poor Spanish. He got on the radio, and all I could understand was "Cinco!" When we were about halfway down the mountain toward the city, I noticed all *five* of the cabs were stopped in the middle of the road. (This was what the "Cinco" was about.) I jumped out.

"What in the world is going on now?" I screamed to my local provider.

"They want more money before they will continue to San Jose."

At this point I had about had it. "Take care of it," I responded, and to this day I don't know what he did, but the cabs started off, each going about 100 miles an hour and running every red light until we reached the hotel. Fortunately, at this time of the night the streets were nearly deserted.

I had to make out notes to slide under everyone's door advising them that we would not be leaving on the next morning's tour until 9 a.m., instead of the previously scheduled 8 a.m. I finally fell into bed around 3 a.m., thankful that we had escaped this tribulation without any serious injuries.

Everyone was so overwhelmed with the friendliness and generosity of the Canadian couple's hospitality during our terrible ordeal that we collected $300 for them. I had been advised not to send money through the mail, so before leaving Costa Rica, I delivered the money personally to the American Embassy with a note asking them to hand-deliver it. Some time later I received the following letter:

Dear Joyce,

The couple from the US Embassy here in San Jose stopped by to visit us this morning. They brought us two nice thank you notes, and the collection of money donated to us by the members of your tour group.

That was some night, when the buses from the Tiquicia Restaurant collapsed, and we found ourselves hosts to a few score of unexpected visitors. We still refer to it locally as "The Night of the 88 Texans." And we are still impressed, I should add, with the resilience, good humor and warm friendliness of your group.

Now, this unexpected sum of money has arrived and we felt we should write immediately to express our thanks in turn. Really, you didn't have to do that. But now that you have, thank you.

It's funny how a couple of broken buses led to an exchange of kindness between all of us. I suppose if we could all just find a few more reasons to act this way regularly, the newspapers would eventually run out of bad news.

In the meantime, thanks again. And if any of you come back to Costa Rica, do stop by and say hello. This time, though, take a 4-wheel drive taxi when you come up our mountain.

Yours faithfully,

John and Deanna

❧ ❧ ❧ ❧

In January, 1991, I escorted a group of thirty-six to Belize with a side trip to Tikal, in Guatemala. I had been advised that our local guide was an American, with degrees in marine biology and wildlife, who had come to Belize to conduct ecology research in 1982, met and married a local man and had been living there ever since. When we arrived at the Belize City airport, a smartly dressed woman approached me, extending her hand in welcome. "Ellen" I said in greeting, as I had been informed that was our guide's name.

"No, I am Judy, director of your local tour company. Here's your guide, Ellen."

Turning to face me was a woman dressed in cut off jeans, with a baseball cap over her long, stringy hair, and a faded T-shirt revealing her *extremely* pregnant condition. I could not see how this person could possibly be our tour guide. That evening, we had a welcome reception at the hotel and she appeared in a nice dress, her hair neatly combed. I was happy to find out that she was indeed very well informed on the flora and fauna of the area. I also learned that, at age forty, she was seven months pregnant with her first child. This would be a new experience, I thought, having to deliver the tour guide's baby!

Our first two nights were in the Cockscomb Basin, southwest of the capital, a tropical jungle with many species of colorful birds and many animals. But when thirty-seven people are tramping through a jungle at once, it is hard to see much wildlife. Ellen pointed high in a far away tree and said "Toucan!" We could barely see it, it was so small, and someone remarked it had to be a "One-can." We were advised that most of the animals were nocturnal. We certainly did not need to be tramping through the jungle in the dark looking for a jaguar, one of the wild animals the park was known for.

On the third day, we began a bus trip of about two hundred miles to San Ignacio near the Guatemala border. As this was to be a long trip, we prepared box lunches and drinks to take with us. We traveled along the "Hummingbird Highway" and that is the only thing that could travel it in comfort. The semi-paved road was incredibly rough, filled with large potholes and washboard-like asphalt.

About two hours into the ride, I smelled something burning. Ellen spoke to the driver who said that the motor was heating up due to the mountainous terrain, but not to worry. It was the old standard reply, "No problem!" Twenty minutes later there was indeed a problem as the bus came to a complete stop. A bearing had gone out on one of the front wheels and we were about three hours from Belize City and a replacement vehicle. Another problem. Before anyone could send help, they had to know we were in trouble. There was no radio and this was before the wonderful days of cell phones. We were many miles from a phone.

We were stranded next to a running stream of water, and we did have our food and drinks. So I told everyone to find a shade tree and get as comfortable as possible. That proved difficult thanks to the "no-see-ums," mosquito-like insects so tiny you can't see them (thus the name). They were everywhere and would attack any skin that was not covered. They even found the little area at my wrist where my long sleeved shirt was buttoned! We sprayed repellent all over us and, by wearing long sleeved shirts and long pants, were able to keep most of the pesky critters away.

Finally, a pickup truck came by. When I saw the letters UN (as in United Nations), I thought we were rescued. I could see an antenna and figured they should have a CB or some type of radio communication. Two local men were inside. We flagged them down and I asked if they could make a call for help for us on their CB radio. "No," they replied. Then Ellen asked them in Spanish if they would take her to locate a telephone. They just said, "No!" and drove off. So much for the UN. This was the first time in all my travels that I met local people who would not help others in need. Ellen then walked about an hour until she found a farmhouse and made a call to send another bus. The nice farmer brought her back, so we should not judge all Belizeans by the two in the UN truck.

We rejoiced when we saw the rescue bus approaching. We had been on the side of the road for five hours. It was dark when we reached our hotel in San Ignacio in northern Belize and since dinner was scheduled at 7p.m. and it was now 6:45, I rushed to tell the kitchen staff to hold everything until 8.

In this remote hotel, the only television set was in the bar area. As I passed through there, I heard: "This is CNN reporting live, January 16, 1991. I am standing on the streets of Baghdad witnessing the bombing of the city."

The first thought that ran through my head was, "Here I am responsible for a group of people in a remote area in Belize and we are at war with Iraq." I suddenly realized that we were probably in the safest place an American could be at that moment. When I told everyone the news, they all had to go watch our "prime-time war."

The next day, we crossed the border into Guatemala for the approximately thirty-mile journey to Tikal. I had been warned that the road was rough and unpaved, but it had rained recently and the road was now an unbroken series of three- to four-foot ruts. Half the time the driver had to leave the road entirely to get around the deep holes. It took us four hours to make this very uncomfortable trip, and I kept thinking as I was bouncing up and down, what if this shaking brings on the baby?

The ancient city of Tikal is overpowering. Inhabited from as early as 2,000 BC, it was at its peak in population and culture from 250 to 900 AD. Its ruins cover some 222 square miles of jungle, but only six square miles have been explored closely. Complex multilevel palaces are built like mazes around courtyards. Smaller temples, baths and shrines surround ball courts and large plaster plazas. Colorful macaws and other birds are visible everywhere.

All this made the rough ride to get there worthwhile, but I did not want to think of returning the same way. So I had Ellen check on the possibility of chartering a plane back to Belize City. I was advised we could charter a nineteen-seat plane for $70 per person. I presented the plan, and quickly had seventeen takers. Keith and I would go with the group on the plane, and Ellen would return with the others on the bus. Some did not want to fly in a small plane and others didn't want to spend the money, so it worked out fine.

The next morning, my flying group was to go to the airport at 7, then the bus would return for the others and they would depart at 8. At 6:45 I was making sure all the flyers were ready to go and started looking for Ellen to say good-by until Belize City. I found her in her room, cradling the commode. She said she had gotten very sick to her stomach during the night.

"Here comes the baby," I thought in panic. She assured me that everything was OK in that regard, adding that she was feeling a bit better and I should go ahead. The bus riders told me later she lay down the entire trip back to Belize City, but seemed fine when she reached there.

We boarded the plane and took off. One of my passengers started throwing up, and on a plane that size, there are no "barf bags" or flight attendants. I rushed to my purse for the plastic Baggies I always carry, and the Wet Ones to minister to him as best I could. By now we had probably been in the air ten or fifteen minutes and Bill, sitting at the front hollered, "Joyce, the pilot wants to see you."

I went to the cockpit and he asked, "Where are we going?"

"I hope we are going to Belize City," I said.

"No problem," and with that he turned the plane in the direction of Belize City.

"You really didn't know where we were going?" I asked in disbelief.

"I was instructed to pick up nineteen people at Tikal who had chartered a plane. No one mentioned where to."

Twenty minutes later we landed in Belize City and there was a transfer bus to take us to a hotel where we had day rooms. But everyone wanted to stay in the lounge and watch the Gulf War on TV, since there were no television sets in the rooms. As the conflict was in its fourth day, the sortie reports were coming in fast and furious.

As we waited for the overland group, I noticed various members leaving the lounge and not returning. A check of their rooms revealed that they were sick to their stomach, just like Ellen, but without being pregnant. Apparently, we had gotten more out of Tikal than a walk back in time.

The bus people showed up around two that afternoon, and we transferred to a boat to cruise over to Cay Chapel on the Belize Barrier Reef, which is second in size only to the Great Barrier Reef in Australia. We were there two nights, and here I discovered that our Ellen, portly in her maternity bathing suit, could swim like a fish, and call each of them by name. That evening, after a shrimp dinner, she had a very interesting slide show of her extensive work in the marine biology of the area. Apparently, the shrimp were not as fresh as they should have been, because the next day, several more were sick, including me.

But the tour must go on, and off we flew to northeastern interior Belize and landed at Gallon Jug. The airport consisted of a short runway and a thatch-covered open stand with benches around it. From there we went in vans to Chan Chich, a remote paradise located on a

Mayan site in the heart of a 130,000-acre private reserve. The acreage belonged to the man who had the Coca-Cola and beer distributorship for Belize. The individual cabanas were constructed entirely of local materials harvested from the surrounding jungle. The resort operators were a man and wife from the United States. The only means of communication was radio.

Here you could take guided trail walks to Mayan ruins and watch numerous species of birds, including oscillated turkeys, parrots, and toucans. We were told that there were jaguar and howler monkeys, which we didn't see. But that night, I had just dozed off to sleep, when a loud noise pierced the quiet of the jungle air. I nearly jumped out of the bed. It sounded like a child screaming. That was the howler monkey, heard but never seen.

We toured the resort's coffee and banana plantations, which were under the direction of a man from Louisiana. He was experimenting with Hereford cattle and other range animals to see if they could grow well in the tropics. It was obvious how busy this man was and I began to feel sorry for his wife who had been brought here from Louisiana and deposited in the middle of the jungle. We went to their lovely home, with all the modern conveniences. I immediately saw she was a lady of resources. She had developed raised gardens, in which she, with the aid of a native gardener, planted vegetables in rotation. With the continuous growing season, she provided fresh vegetables for their table year-round. She collected leaves and decomposed vegetation from the jungle floor, bagged it, and sold it as fertilizer. She also dried some leaves, added spices or flavoring, and marketed it as potpourri.

She had noticed that the shark bones at the local fish market were being thrown away, so she asked for some of the bones, took them home, and buried them in the ground to let the ants clean them. Afterwards, she washed them, and had all sizes of perfectly formed round beads, with a hole in the middle, which she dyed different colors and fashioned into necklaces, bracelets, and earrings. Her business flourished and she had hired four native women to assist in assembling the jewelry. Here was a lady who could have sat around moaning about being alone in the jungle who turned out to be a very busy and very successful businesswoman. She certainly had my admiration.

(A couple of years later Keith and I were with a group tour of the Pacific Coast. We were at a trout farm in Oregon. As we were returning to the bus, we encountered the managers of Chan Chich, their two sons and her brother, who was the bartender at the lodge. We had a pleasant short visit, amazed to meet each other again in Oregon!)

We flew back to Belize City to connect with our TACA flight to Houston. Everyone was taking this war thing very seriously. Airport security officials went through all our bags and had everyone remove any batteries from cameras, clocks, flashlights, etc. As I started out to board the plane, an airport representative came running up to me and handed me a box full of batteries. "These belong to your group."

When we reached Houston to change planes, things were also in turmoil. Over at one side sat a man with a parachute strapped on his back. He said he was not going to get on the plane unless they let him wear it. The Continental agent said firmly, "No parachute inside the plane."

When we got on our flight, I noticed he was sitting there in the boarding area, parachute still intact. I have no idea how he thought he would have time to parachute from a plane if there were an explosion, not to mention how he would survive at the altitudes at which the plane flies.

Back in Austin, I was so glad that we were home safely and everyone had their luggage that I forgot about the box of batteries I had in my tote bag. I later sent everyone a memo saying they could stop by the bank and pick up their batteries, but no one seemed to want to be bothered, so I finally threw them in the trash.

≥ ≥ ≥ ≥

Sometimes a breakdown can be a blessing. In 1984 I led a group on a week's safari in Kenya. My group was in a caravan in three Land Rovers and I was in the lead vehicle with the lead guide, Godfrey, who spoke Swahili and fairly good English. He was an expert on Kenyan birds and frequently would come to an abrupt stop, throwing all the passengers around in the van, to point out a particular bird.

This was a time of terrible drought in Africa so the first part of our trip was over extremely dusty roads. The dust was so thick that we had to cover our noses and mouths with scarves to breathe, and the dirt formed in rivulets on the windowpanes of the van. We spent four days bumping along in an almost constant cloud of dust.

Then we crossed the mountains to the Serengeti National Park and, surprise, the landscape turned a lush green. The roads that had been so dry and dusty were now muddy and slippery. You guessed it, we got stuck. All during the safari, Godfrey had cautioned us sternly to never step out of the Land Rover while we were in the wild. "$300 fine," he continuously reminded us. Of course, I never saw any official around who might enforce this rule, but we complied. Now that we were stuck, Godfrey bellowed, "Everyone out!"

While the men tried to extricate the vehicle from the mud hole, the ladies strolled over to a nearby stream that had, as best count, twenty-seven hippos lazing around like gigantic black blobs in the water. What a sight! I looked back to see how they were progressing with the van, and there was a giraffe who had wandered up and was leaning its long neck down to investigate the operation. I guess we would still be stuck there if a group of German campers had not come by in an over-sized Mercedes safari truck. A quick tie of a rope to the Land Rover, and the huge truck pulled the stuck van right out and we were on our way.

After seven days of bumping along on the dusty and muddy roads, we could not think of enduring the long ride back. So I chartered a plane to fly us to Nairobi. Funny how the specter of a four- to five-hour journey over those same roads convinced everyone to pay $90 for a forty-five-minute plane ride.

That experience came in handy a few years later on a safari to Tanzania. I thought the roads in Kenya were bad, but Tanzania wins the prize. The roads were a never-ending series of potholes and it took hours to travel a short distance, even without breakdowns. Many times we would hit a hole so hard that our heads would hit the roof of the Land Rover. We had two Land Rovers for our group on this tour, and it seemed that one or the other was always breaking down. At least there was good radio contact between drivers, and one could usually go back and assist the other, but this was very time consuming. We had overheating problems (even without air conditioning), flat tires, and even lost the spare tire fastened underneath the car when we went over one particularly nasty bump in the road.

After six days on the these roads, I was informed, that to reach our next destination, we had to go back over the same route — in a single day! Eight or nine hours of misery. That is, if the Land Rovers could even make it. I checked with the local operator to see if chartering a plane was possible. "No problem at all," was the much-welcome reply.

In my capacity as tour guide, I called Collette Tours and filled them in on our situation. The company graciously agreed to pay for the forty-five-minute charter flight. It was exciting to fly over game preserves, seeing from the air the areas we had traversed by land. As the plane approached the Tarangire National Park airport runway, zebras and wildebeests covered the entire area. The plane buzzed the herd on a low fly-by. The animals scattered and we were able to land on the next try. We reached our destination hotel in time for a swim, some much-needed relaxation, and a game drive.

That evening our entire group was in the bar area laughing and having a wonderful time when a bedraggled member of another tour group came up to us.

"Have you folks been here long?"

"No," we replied, "we just flew in this morning."

"So that's why you're so happy! We're exhausted. We drove all day on those horrible roads to get here, and wish we felt like having a good time with you."

Several members of my group shot appreciative glances my way and a few raised their glasses in a toast. I beamed with pleasure because, in the eyes of my little group of happy hunters, I was the hero of the day. All group leaders try to make everyone's experience as happy and hassle-free as possible. Sometimes the fates conspire against us, but most of the time we succeed. And, every once in a while, we get to enjoy a special moment like the one I savored in that Tarangire hotel bar, basking in the glow of a job well done.

Another day, another long walk out on the tarmac (Central America)

Up a rainy river, looking for monkeys, in Borneo

7

MOTHER NATURE
CAN BE UNKIND

When you consider the number of trips I have taken, we have been very lucky where the weather is concerned. Bill, one of my most frequent travelers, always said that we had good weather when he was along, and maybe that was the reason. Of course I was careful not to schedule tours to places that predictably would have bad weather during our visit. Still, no matter how carefully you plan, Mother Nature does not always cooperate. We have had our encounters with downpours and droughts and, on occasion, worse.

Each year the charming town of Fredericksburg, in the Texas Hill Country, holds a "Candlelight Tour of Homes" and a "Kris Kringle Market" prior to Christmas. I had planned a bank trip including a private tour of the homes, concluding with dinner at a local tearoom. In making my arrangements with the local historical society, I was told that the tearoom did not serve wine, but that I could bring my own and serve it to the group.

The response to this event was so overwhelming that I immediately filled the bus with forty-six and, so as not to disappoint anyone, had Keith take an additional eight people in our personal van. As so often happens in Texas, this December day started out warm and sunny, but around three in the afternoon, just as we arrived in

Fredericksburg, a "norther" hit with extremely cold gale force winds. Naturally, the outside vendors at the Kris Kringle Market closed up early, so the little Christmas shopping spree I had planned for the passengers did not work out. Improvising, I had them browse the town's various shops until our historical guide appeared. Right at six, a young man, no older than thirteen, approached me. "Are you Mrs. Brooks?" he inquired.

I nodded my head.

"Welcome. I'm Tommy, your guide," he said with an outstretched hand.

This was quite a shock, as I was expecting a gray-haired historian of the area to tell the group all about the city's colorful German heritage and the houses we were to visit.

"Well, Tommy," I said, "how nice. Are you a native of Fredericksburg?"

"Oh, yes, ma'am. I've lived here two years."

When we arrived at the bus, I introduced him and handed over the microphone. Poor child, he was so scared his hand was shaking and he could hardly hold the mike. So whatever information he may have known about the properties vanished through fright. It was obvious that no one had prepared him to speak to a bus load of senior citizens.

We began the home tour and Tommy, who was still years away from his first driver's license, couldn't give the bus driver directions to the homes. When we did stumble on the first home, he took us in the back way up some dark stairs where I was afraid that someone would fall. Since it was so cold and our guide did not seem to know exactly where to go, we decided to cut the tour short and go to the tearoom where we would at least be warm.

When we dropped Tommy off, I told him I felt so sorry for him because he was a very nice young man who had just been put in an uncomfortable situation. I gave him a nice tip that I hoped would make him feel a little better. My real beef was with the historical society for sending a youngster clearly unprepared to handle such a large group.

According to our schedule, we were supposed to arrive at the tearoom at eight. We got there at 7:50 and there was only one person working there and the dining area was set up for just forty-four people. This meant I had ten people standing around with no place to sit, and from the look of things, nothing to eat. When you have a problem, I have always found the best strategy is to put food or drink in people's mouths — fast. That way at least they won't complain as much. We rushed out to the bus and brought in the ice chests with the wine and cold drinks. I went in the kitchen to get wine glasses. But, of course, the tearoom didn't serve wine so there were no wine glasses. So I said, "Just give us some glasses, anything will do." Well, the tearoom apparently didn't do a booming business, because after the first fifteen glasses were handed to us, we noticed they rest were covered with dust. Stanley, one of my passengers and a member of the bank's board of directors said, "Hand them to me. I can give 'em a quick wash." So Stanley washed, Keith dried, and I poured wine and delivered it to the customers.

About this time, the owner of the tearoom appeared, none too pleased that we had, one, arrived early, two, taken over her kitchen and, three, brought ten more people than she was expecting. I explained that I had paid the historical society for fifty-four. She was very nice and said that she had cooked extra in case someone wanted seconds, and with Keith and me taking very small portions, everything seemed to work out. After everyone had eaten the traditional Fredericksburg meal of sausages, German potato salad, cooked red cabbage, local baked bread, apple bread pudding for dessert, and been plied with two or more glasses of wine, all was calm in the tearoom as the storm raged outside.

❧ ❧ ❧ ❧

On a bus trip to the remote Big Bend National Park in West Texas, we ran into another Texas weather demon.

I had arranged for a private tour of the University of Texas McDonald Observatory, the third largest in the nation, in the nearby Davis Mountains. They admit the public only one night a month, so it took more than a little creativity, and a request by a local friend of ours, to have the rules bent to allow my group to come at an unscheduled time. I was very pleased with myself for pulling off this coup and made sure to tell everyone how privileged we were to receive this special treatment.

We arrived at the impressive round building perched on the mountaintop just as it was getting dark. An observatory employee showed us around, explained how the telescope worked, and filled us in on what the scientists were studying at that time. We went to the telescope room where we would get to first hand view the stars. A push of a button and the ceiling of the room began to open. At that moment, a driving gust of wind hit, causing the top of the room to start rotating around. Quickly, the technicians began closing the roof, and consequently, our chance to look at the constellations and Milky Way was, quite literally, gone with the wind.

We were asked to depart immediately because, with the change in the weather, they wanted to close up the station. When we stepped outside, the wind was blowing so hard we had to form a human chain of forty-four people to keep from being blown off the mountain. We proceeded in this fashion until we reached our bus at the bottom of the hill.

It had taken me several weeks of wheedling and cajoling to get that special tour permit and in one minute it was rescinded by Mother Nature.

❧ ❧ ❧ ❧

I had an exciting weekend planned for my group. First we bussed from Austin to the King Ranch, one of the largest ranches in the world, located in South Texas. The management of the ranch graciously offers tour groups a ride through a small portion of the spread, topping it off with a BBQ lunch served at one of the "line shacks" where cowboys camp while working on the range.

After lunch, we stopped at the King Ranch Western Store in Kingsville to stock up on items such as a King Ranch Cookbook and western apparel. A short drive brought us to Rockport, the winter home of the almost extinct whooping crane, one of the largest and rarest birds in the world. The adult birds stand up to five feet tall. In the late 1980s, only thirty-seven "whoopers" were in the flock that came back to the Aransas National Wildlife Refuge in Texas each winter. Through a protection program sponsored by Canada and the United States, the whooping cranes had increased their numbers to over one hundred by the year 2000, but are still on the endangered species list. I had booked a breakfast cruise for the next morning for an up-close look at the whoopers and other water fowl.

We were staying at a condominium complex managed by the tour boat owner. When we arrived about three that afternoon, the weather was sunny and beautiful. The manager was concerned, though, because the weather forecast called for bad weather in the morning. "But they are usually wrong," he said cheerfully, "so we'll just have to see."

About 3 a.m. I was awaked by the roar of wind and when I opened the door, I noticed the temperature had dropped considerably. What to do? I had two bus loads, eighty-eight people, whom I had told to be ready to board the boat at seven for the cruise. At 5 a.m. I got up, dressed in my cotton slacks and a windbreaker, the warmest clothes I had with me, and noticed the light was on in the manager's office. I went over to discuss the disaster.

"The wind is too high to go out in the boat this morning," he concluded. "I suggest you have the people come over to the boat at eight and we can serve them breakfast as planned. But we won't be able to sail."

There were no phones in the condos, so at 6:30 a.m. I had to knock with cold hands on forty-five doors and tell them that we were not sailing at seven, but to be at the boat at eight for breakfast. As it is normally warm this time of the year in South Texas, nearly everyone was as unprepared for the cold weather as I was. Most people had nothing more substantial than a windbreaker or a light jacket.

After eating a hearty and delicious breakfast, I had to find something for the bunch to do. I checked with the Wildlife Refuge a few miles from town and they said to come on over and they'd show us a film on the whooping cranes. They had a small museum and there was an observation platform from which we might spot the birds. By this time, the cold wind had turned into driving rain.

At the museum, we were ushered into the viewing room. I thought that at least my people could enjoy a film and learn about the whooping cranes if they could not see them personally. No sooner had the projector started than the film broke! We drove around to the observation platform, but it was raining so hard that no one wanted to venture out. So no seeing the big birds, on film or in feather.

When I was lamenting to the lady at the museum about how my entire morning's activities had been ruined, she suggested we visit the Fulton Mansion. Cattle baron George Fulton built this thirty-room mansion in the mid-1870s. The house was definitely ahead of its time. It had central heat and ventilation, hot and cold running water, flush toilets, and gas lights. I called and explained the situation. The house manager said that they were closed because of the bad weather, but that she would open for me and my group. Bless her.

I loaded the bunch back on the buses, and off we drove to Fulton, three miles north of Rockport. A group as large as ours could not be admitted to the house at once, so some people had to stand out in the cold and rain to wait their turn. This did not make for happy sightseers! When we finally got inside, it was still cold, as the heat had not been turned on, because they had not planned on having guests that day. So people rushed through as quickly as possible and did not take time to enjoy the unique beauty of the place.

Finally, it was time to start home. In one of the buses, the toilet reeked terribly. We had been gone three days and there had been no dumping station available to empty the lavatories. At the first stop, I bought two cans of Lysol spray and tried my best to correct it, but this did not completely take care of the problem. Was I ever glad to get back to Austin after this weekend of agony!

🐦 🐦 🐦 🐦

One of the most beautiful man-made sights in the world is the Nashville Opryland Hotel decorated for Christmas. Approximately two million clear Christmas lights sparkle in the night outside the impressive hotel building. Inside, the holiday decorations are unbelievable. Mechanical figures of skaters and elves move constantly and giant snowflakes are suspended from the high glass ceiling. Thousands of poinsettias are colorfully placed among the permanent foliage and waterfalls of the atriums. When I was taking groups there, the hotel had two areas, the Magnolia and the Cascade, each with glass-roofed gardens with over ten thousand tropical plants and numerous water-falls. In 1996 they opened the Delta area, four and a half more acres of plants and waterways making a total of nine acres of spectacular tropi-cal gardens. Today the hotel boasts 2,883 rooms, making it the largest hotel in the nation outside Las Vegas.

I took four groups to the Opryland Hotel during four different Decembers. The trips were always popular with my core group, but Nashville's winter weather can be unpredictable, which made for some annoying moments.

On one trip, I had offered my group the choice of a regular room or, for an extra $150, a balcony room that faced one of the atriums. This was a special feature of the hotel; from your private vantage point, you could look down on all the gorgeous decorations and watch the activities of the people as they strolled below you. About half of the group opted to have the balcony rooms. When we arrived at the Opryland Hotel, I was advised that there were no balcony rooms avail-able for my people. Apparently, there had been a mix-up when Collette Tours requested our rooms. Great! Now I had over forty people expecting to spend their four days enjoying their balcony, and no balcony. Not only that, but they had paid $150 extra! After going round and round with the hotel personnel who insisted that there were no balcony rooms available, I saw that I was getting nowhere. So, I had to break the news to my clients, never a fun thing to do. Most of them took the news remarkably well, but there were some critical comments. I called Collette and asked them to send me the refund checks by overnight courier and order an "amenity package for each room," which they did. It was a smart move. My customers felt consid-erably better when I handed them checks for $150 each while we were still on the trip.

It can be difficult to find your way around the Opryland Hotel with so many trails through the atriums, shops, and restaurants. Mrs. F could never find her way to her room. She was traveling alone, and I had to either have a bellman take her to her room or escort her there myself. One evening we attended the television taping of "Nashville Now."We were instructed to be there by six, even though the program did not start until eight.

The studio was inside the Opryland Park, about four blocks from where the shuttle buses drop you at the entrance. Just as we stepped off the bus, a heavy rain shower unleashed itself on us. No one had an umbrella or any protection other than the coats on their backs; one gentleman had on a beautiful suede jacket that was ruined. When we arrived dripping wet at the studio, we discovered that the only restrooms were about one hundred yards away and to get there you had to run through the rain again!

As we had to get there at six, I told everyone to eat early or plan to have a late dinner after the show. When we returned to the hotel around ten, Keith and I stopped at one of the numerous restaurants inside the hotel for a light snack. At 11:30, Keith was already in bed sound asleep and I was in the bathroom doing my nightly bedtime ritual when the phone rang.When this happens at a late hour like this, I know someone is sick or dying. It was Mrs. F, the little lady who couldn't find her room. But I knew she had made it, because I had delivered her there myself.

"Joyce, I'm hungry," came the voice at the other end of the line.

"Call room service and order something to eat," I replied.

"That costs too much."

"Then, go down to one of the restaurants inside the hotel. Rachel's Kitchen in the Magnolia Lobby is near your room and stays open all night," I advised.

"I'm afraid to go out by myself. Can't you bring me a sandwich?"

"I am already undressed and in my nightgown. You will be perfectly safe within the hotel, and you can always get a bellman to escort you. Just give them a call." I was getting a little irritated with her at this point.

"Have Keith go get me a sandwich."

"He is already asleep!" I said.

"Then I'll just starve!" She slammed down the phone.

The next morning, I approached her and said: "Mrs. F, my job as group leader covers many things, but not going out in the middle of the night to get you something to eat when room service is available and the restaurants are in a secured area. I am sorry you felt differently."

"Never mind," she retorted. "I managed to live, no thanks to you."

One event included in the Opryland Country Christmas Package is the "Christmas Musical Revue and Feast," an intimate dinner for two thousand held in the grand ballroom. This particular year, the routine was that you found your assigned table, went through one of two buffet lines for your salad, returned to your table and had your entree served by waiters. When one of my gentlemen passengers arrived and saw the line of hundreds at the salad areas, he became very upset.

"I did not pay for a dinner to stand in a damn long line. That just chaps my ass!" he proclaimed loudly.

"Just sit your chapped ass down at the table and our waiter will get your salad. What kind of dressing do you prefer?" I asked calmly.

Our table waiter, whom I had already met, had heard the conversation and could hardly keep from laughing.

"Yes sir, you will have your salad shortly," he said as he rushed off.

Later the man confessed to Keith that a woman had never talked him to like that and he admired me for it. To this day we are the best of friends and he has been on several other trips with me.

On one trip for the Country Christmas, we awoke to a snow-covered fairyland. About four inches of glistening snow adorned the trees outside the Opryland Hotel and the twinkling lights created the most perfect Christmas card you have ever seen. Everyone was so excited about the wondrous addition to our trip.

All this was lovely to look at and by evening the weather had cleared. I was thankful, for we were scheduled to go about fifteen miles out of Nashville to "Twitty City," Conway Twitty's showplace and family compound which was all decorated for Christmas. The snow was no longer falling, but the temperature was below freezing. When we unloaded the two bus loads at the park entrance (yes another full house of eighty-eight people!) I told them to meet the buses back at the same place in one hour because we had tickets to the Grand Ole Opry back in town. The empty buses proceeded to the bus parking lot about a half a mile away. As I entered the "city," a security guard said that we were not supposed to unload guests there in front, but in the parking lot and from there they would be picked up by shuttle vans. I explained I was sorry, but was not aware of this rule, and what about picking them up in the same place (the entrance) when we got ready to leave.

"No, they must go back to the parking lot by the shuttle vans. We cannot allow buses to block the entrance area," he said with authority.

At this point, I noticed the size of the shuttle vans. They carried twelve people and there were only two of them. At that rate, I figured it would take an hour just to haul them back to the parking lot, and we had to get to the Opry.

"I need to talk with the chief of security," I said urgently.

Finding the man in charge, I explained my quandary. He agreed to let the buses return to the entrance to pick up the passengers, but said that I needed to do it quickly before most of their customers starting arriving around seven. Now I had to find Keith and Wanda, a passenger who was helping me on the other bus. They had to round up the group and tell them we needed to leave right away.

The security chief and I then climbed into a golf cart headed for the parking lot to get the buses. They had not used the cart since it had snowed, and the floor and seat were still covered with ice. Off we raced in the freezing night to the bus parking area. There were our two buses, but alas, they were locked and the drivers were not there. Thinking they had a free hour, they had gone for coffee. The security chief called the main office to have them paged to return to their buses immediately.

We located the drivers, and they drove back to the entrance. I had no idea how Keith and Wanda would be able to round up all the people, but there they all stood ready to board the buses. I was flabbergasted.

"It's a miracle," I whispered to Keith when we were settled in the bus. "How did you ever manage it?"

"No miracle," he smiled. "It was so darn cold no one wanted to go see the decorations. They all huddled together in the gift shop and the restaurant."

Thanks to the biting cold, we made it to the Grand Ole Opry on time. If you have not been to the Opryland Hotel during December, I heartily recommend that you not miss this holiday treat. I can assure you that it will put you in the Christmas spirit.

ə& ə& ə& ə&

It was January and we had just returned from a pleasurable cruise along the Mexican Riviera from Acapulco to San Diego. As we were waiting in the departure lounge in San Diego, someone announced she had just called home to Austin and it was snowing. Hard to believe when we were sitting there in our lightweight cruise clothes and the weather outside was a sunny 75 degrees.

As the plane began its descent into the Dallas-Fort Worth airport, I noticed everything was white. I was advised that our connecting flight to Austin had been canceled. As this was an "Act of God," the airline made no effort to assist in finding a place to stay. I ran to the phone and to my surprise found twenty-two rooms available at the airport Holiday Inn. They said they would send shuttles to pick us up.

I approached the group clustered in the waiting room.

"This is the situation. The flight to Austin has been canceled. We hope to get out in the morning. I have rooms reserved for you at the Holiday Inn. However, you will have to cover the cost of the room as the airline is not taking care of it and it is not included in the tour cost. We have to leave our checked luggage with American, so just take your carry on and follow me out to get the shuttles."

Everyone accepted the arrangement without comment except for one lady.

"What am I going to do? My nightgown is in my checked luggage," a fiftyish woman cried. Her husband seemed embarrassed that she was making such a fuss. I couldn't imagine what to say when inspiration struck.

"Try sleeping without your nightie," I replied with a wink. "You might like it."

The next morning, as we flew back to Austin, I was pleased to see that the lady with no nightgown seemed to be in an exceptionally good mood.

❧ ❧ ❧ ❧

On a January excursion to Houston, my group of forty-four en-joyed a day of upscale shopping at the city's famed Galleria shopping mecca and two Broadway shows — *Me and My Gal* Saturday night and the Sunday matinee of *Showboat*. On the way home, we stopped in LaGrange at The Bon Ton, known in this area of Texas as a great place for "good ole home style cookin'." As our bus pulled out from the res-taurant at around 9 p.m., snow mixed with sleet was falling. The farther we went toward Austin, the worse it became, but I had faith in Ben, our excellent bus driver. Not far from LaGrange, as we approached a small hill, red lights were flashing. We were stopped by the Highway Patrol who informed us that an eighteen-wheeler had jack-knifed, causing two on-coming cars to slide into each other at the top of the hill. There was no way for the bus to get through. He advised that we go back to a nearby motel and spend the night.

"There's no way they'll have twenty-eight rooms available," I thought, as I had several single women on the trip. To my amazement, the motel said they could accommodate us if the single women doubled up. I came on the bus and announced:

"We have enough rooms, but we have to make some adjustments. Single ladies, please pair up and come with me, as we have to assign the rooms with two beds first. Just take what you have with you on the bus because it would take forever to unload and sort out the luggage in this cold weather."

The passengers were wonderful. Not one complaint about not having any gown to sleep in. I guess they were just glad that we were safe at the motel.

By midnight I had everyone settled. The next morning, Ben and I called Austin to check road conditions. South Texas has so little experi-ence with ice and snow that people are not prepared for it when it comes. They have no snow moving equipment. Another problem was that the snow hit on a Sunday. The highway patrol told us to wait until mid-morning, saying that, if we were careful, it should be okay to travel.

Ben had been driving for me for years and I had total confidence in his ability to maneuver the bus in all kinds of weather. We set a departure time of 10:30 a.m. I had two people who refused to go with us, saying it was too dangerous and that they were going to stay right there. So they did. They had their family come get them the next day.

We made it safe and sound, but this encouraged me to be more cautious in planning any bus trip during the winter months. I had thought going south to Houston would be fine, but you can never be sure about Mother Nature.

🐫 🐫 🐫 🐫

I was leading a group through the rich history and splendid scenery of North Texas and Oklahoma. We toured Palo Duro Canyon State Park, where a series of canyons cut jaggedly down through the escarpment of the Texas panhandle to form colorful shapes that, according to the brochures, resemble a "señorita's skirt." Depending on the light, which is at its best early in the morning or late in the evening, the colors of red, coral, and yellow create striking vistas. After drinking in the scenery, we went to the grounds of the musical drama, *Texas!*, to enjoy a pre-show BBQ dinner. Everyone had gone through the serving line and was just sitting down at the outdoor tables to relish this Texas feast when a sudden, strong wind hit. Rosa had just sat down at the table when the wind blew her plate and its contents right into her lap. What a mess! BBQ, beans, and potato salad all over her. Not only did we have the wind to contend with, but it also started raining mud balls, a good old West Texas weather trick. Everyone was rushing to the buses and, as I tried to herd my group to our coach, I noticed some little lady was blown completely under a bus. Thank goodness she was not one of mine. Some men pulled her out and she seemed to be okay.

Just as we all got to the bus, the skies really opened up, but in about twenty minutes the deluge passed on through, which is also typical of Texas rain storms. The play officials announced that as soon as they could dry the outdoor theater seats, the musical would start. This show is a recreation of pioneer life in the Texas Panhandle performed by eighty singers and dancers. We were ushered to our assigned seats, the show began, and the rains came again. The show was cancelled, but at least they set off the fireworks that end the show, so we did get to see something.

Next morning, with that catastrophe behind us, we continued north to Oklahoma City where we visited the National Cowboy Hall of Fame and Western Heritage Center. This is the world's largest exhibition of western lore including art by Russell, Remington, and other famous western artists. John Wayne's Kachina doll collection fascinated me, as we have a few of these Indian carvings ourselves.

That evening was the second outdoor show of the tour, Rogers' and Hammerstein's *Oklahoma*. Ten minutes into the show we heard thunder and saw flashes of lightning. At first I thought it was part of the production. Then, when the raindrops began falling on my head, I knew it was the real thing. We all scampered to the covered pavilion and waited, which proved to be a boon for the concession stand business. After about thirty minutes, the rain stopped, the seats were dried off, and the play continued. This time we got to see the production to its conclusion, because the constant light mist that fell was not considered bad enough to cancel the show. We all looked like drowned rats when it was over, but we at least saw it.

The third show of the tour was *Trail of Tears*, a musical drama that tells of how the Cherokee tribe was uprooted from its ancestral home in the Carolinas and forced to march to Oklahoma. And, yes, it too was outdoors. It was staged at Tahlequah, not far from Muskogee where we stopped at the Five Civilized Tribes Museum. Here we marveled at the art and culture of the Cherokee, Chickasaw, Choctaw, Creek, and Seminole Indians. Movies have brainwashed us to think of all Indians as "savages." In fact, as the "Trail of Tears" so poignantly relates, the Cherokee Indians of the Carolinas had assimilated quite well. They were farmers, knew how to read and write, and dressed in western clothes. They lived a very civilized lifestyle until forced from their land by the U.S. government and marched to Oklahoma.

As we again took our seats, I could see lightning in the sky. "No, not again," I thought. But this time, the rain waited until the performance was complete. Like they say, two out of three ain't bad.

≈ ≈ ≈ ≈

It sounded like a fabulous cruise — fifteen days up the Mississippi from New Orleans to Chicago aboard an intimate vessel of the American Canadian Caribbean Line that accommodates just eighty passengers in a very relaxed and comfortable environment. The vessel has a six-foot draft that allows it to enter areas other ships cannot navigate and a retractable pilothouse that lets it slip beneath low bridges. One night the entertainment for the evening was watching the crew take the pilothouse apart and reposition the steering wheel at a lower level.

This cruise poked into a number of rivers besides the Mississippi, including the Mobile, Tombigbee, Tennessee, Ohio, Illinois, DesPlaines and Chicago Rivers. The ports of call were Mobile, Demopolis, and Waverly Plantation in Mississippi; the Tenn-Tom Canal and Shiloh National Park in Tennessee; Paducah, Kentucky; St. Genevieve and St. Louis, Missouri; and Havana, New Salem, and Chicago, in Illinois. We cruised during May and it happened to be a very rainy May. It rained every day, sometimes downpours. We would get drenched at nearly each stop. As we continued northward, the captain became increasingly concerned about the flood debris we were seeing in the river. You could sit on the covered verandah in the stern and see large trees floating by.

When we reached St. Louis, we sailed right up under the famous arch and dropped anchor, for the flood had covered our assigned docking area. Ship dinghies shuttled us to shore where we had to climb out in knee-deep water that covered the sidewalks and wade to dry land. Fortunately, it was not raining at this time, but we made quite a sight arriving in St. Louis carrying our shoes and socks and a towel.

Our view that night was glorious. Out on deck you could look up right overhead and see the lighted arch that towers above the river — an incredible feeling! I can now say that I spent the night *under* the St. Louis Gateway Arch. Sometimes, weather disasters can ruin a trip. In this case, a "natural disaster" created an unforgettable experience for some very happy, if slightly soggy, vacationers.

This village church in Honduras inspired the purchase of a large basket painting

Rio: Soft breezes and 'soft crime'

8

TRAVELER
BEWARE

People are always saying to me: "Aren't you afraid to travel in all those foreign countries?" To that I reply, "The United States has the highest crime rate in the world."

In this day and age, crime is everywhere and, of course, more in some places than others. You hear horror stories of things that happen to travelers all the time. So even though the risks are very slight, I tell my passengers: (1) Leave all your valuables at home. (2) Bring a minimum of jewelry and only pieces of little value. (3) Do not go out in dangerous areas or at night alone. Always travel in groups. (4) Assume a low profile. (5) Keep your passport, large sums of money, and credit cards in a money belt or similar hidden pouches. Carry only a few dollars in the local currency in your pocket or purse. (6) Ladies should carry their purses with the shoulder strap across the front so they can easily protect it. Never put your purse on the floor in a public place.

Americans stick out like a sore thumb abroad, even when they follow these guidelines, but by being alert and carefully guarding purses and possessions, we have been very lucky. We have had very few problems.

After three days in Paris, our group was scheduled to take the train to Zurich, Switzerland, where we were to board a ship for a cruise down the Rhine to Amsterdam. We were waiting for the bus transfer in the hotel lobby. Our guide, Willie, requested that we bring our carry-on bags and wait outside so we could load quickly when the coach arrived. While we were standing there, two men came up to two of my ladies and one started talking to them in some foreign language; they couldn't recognize it, but it wasn't French. The ladies were taken aback by this approach, and started explaining to the man that they could not understand him. At this point, the other man picked up the two bags that were on the sidewalk by the ladies' feet, and both men ran around the corner down the alley.

"Willie!" they screamed. "Two men just stole our bags."

Willie, our Dutch guide who speaks six languages and is 6'6" tall, ran after them as fast as his long legs could take him. In no time at all he returned with a big smile and the three bags.

"What happened?" I asked.

"They thought they had escaped and were just sauntering down the alley. I ran behind them, batted their heads together, and picked up the bags. There is one extra here that they must have stolen from another hotel. Go inside the hotel and give the extra one to the desk clerk and have him call the police. We have to catch a train."

At that point, the coach arrived. We loaded up and went away with all our luggage and a very good story.

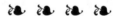

A stop on the city tour in Quito, Ecuador, was at La Cathedral, the city's ageless classic beauty of a building where the national hero, Mariscal Sucre, is entombed. Cecelia, our guide, informed us that this was a very dangerous part of the city, and told us to leave our purses and wallets on the bus. She said our trusted driver would circle the area while we visited the cathedral.

The entrance to the church was two heavy wooden doors, of which only one was open for passage. Keith was bringing up the rear and carrying my camera case, which I had asked him to hold when I had to assist a lady passenger who had fallen in the square earlier. The next-to-last person from our group to enter was George. Keith noticed that as George started to cross the threshold, several people suddenly were gathering in the passageway pushing and shoving and he was having difficulty getting through the entrance. I was waiting inside to see when everyone was present to start the tour. George emerged from the doorway and first thing I noticed was that his right front pants pocket was cut. It was a very professional job. They had cut through the pant material and front part of the pocket, extracted a calculator (which I am sure they thought was a wad of folding money) and left the back portion of the pocket intact. All this happened and George never knew anything except that he was having a difficult time getting through the door.

While this was taking place, Keith was still outside waiting his turn when he felt someone pulling on the camera case that was over his shoulder. A little lady, about four and half feet tall, had unzipped the case and was trying to pull the camera out. I had the zoom lens attached to the camera, and it fit snugly in the case. Keith just elbowed her out of the way and, with the doorway now clear, came on in.

Inside, we gave thanks that we had all made it into the cathedral without any great loss — just a calculator and a ruined pair of trousers.

ॐ ॐ ॐ ॐ

Gypsies are infamous in Italy for using a variety of distractions while they cleverly pick your pocket. I had warned my group about this and told them to stay away from deserted areas.

Some did not heed my warnings. While out on a shopping expedition in Milan, four of my ladies decided to cut through the park on the way back to the hotel. There they were approached by a group of gypsy women, one of whom was holding a baby wrapped in a blanket. She started talking in Italian about the baby, which naturally caught the attention of the American ladies. While the hubbub about the baby was in progress, one woman unzipped Barbara's purse and stole a calculator. Barbara had her money in an underarm pouch, and before she knew it, the gypsy was trying to get to it. Barbara started screaming and the women ran off.

The same day, Lois and Julian were standing on a street corner, consulting their city map to see where they were. A gypsy came up and unzipped Lois' fanny pack, but Lois was too quick for her and the thief failed to accomplish her mission.

ஐ ஐ ஐ ஐ

About eighty-eight miles north of Lisbon, Portugal, is Fatima, a world famous pilgrimage site. Devout Catholics believe that on May 13, 1917, the Virgin Mary appeared over a small oak tree and spoke to three shepherd children. That oak has long since disappeared, thanks to souvenir collectors. So a nearby oak was pressed into service as a substitute and it still stands near the chapel. Today a cold, white basilica in the neoclassic style stands at the end of the wide square.

Conrad and Kathleen visited one of the prayer nooks scattered around the grounds to light a candle and say a prayer. As they were getting their candles, Kathleen noticed a well-dressed man and woman in their mid-forties next to them who seemed to be having all kinds of trouble lighting their candle. They dropped it once and could not seem to get the match to burn. Conrad paid no attention, as he was taking this opportunity to commune with God. He lit his candle, closed his eyes, and said his prayer. Just then he thought he felt a slight nudge, but didn't think anything of it until he reached into his front pants pocket to make a contribution to the collection box. Where his money clip and bills had been he felt nothing. At this point the well-dressed couple was nowhere in sight. In the money clip he had his Visa card, $800 in American Express Travelers Cheques, $300 in U.S. cash and about $100 in Portuguese currency. This was just the third day of a fifteen-day trip, and all their finances were gone.

Our Collette guide, Jose, quickly took care of everything. He notified the area police who only said that things like that happen every day. The only advice they gave was to check the trashcans in the area and we might find the money clip. No such luck. Conrad called and canceled the credit card and informed American Express about the travelers checks. New checks were ready for them at our next scheduled city. I loaned them "walking around money" until the funds arrived. I guess the lesson to be learned here is, when in public, pray with your eyes open.

&a. &a. &a. &a.

"We only have soft crime here, we do not kill people like you do in the United States," our local guide in Rio de Janeiro told us. But immediately after making that statement, he warned us not to wear any jewelry or carry handbags out in public, especially in the Copacabana Beach area.

Brazil is known for its precious and semi-precious stones and there are jewelry stores everywhere.

"With all this beautiful jewelry available, do local people buy and wear it?" I inquired.

"Oh, yes," he stated. "But they carry it in a small pouch inside their clothes until they get to the office or party and then put it on."

Having been forewarned, most of us were very careful. However, June and Ellen went strolling along the black and white mosaic promenade of Copacabana Beach. June had a very tiny gold chain without any ornamentation around her neck. A young boy came up behind her and with his index and third fingers grabbed the necklace. The chain broke, but became tangled in the loose weave sweater she was wearing. Loud screams from both ladies sent the thief away emptyhanded. June suffered two deep scratch marks on the back of her neck and a great scare.

Later that night, we were in our beachfront hotel when we heard gunshots ring out. We were told that rival gangs were fighting over territorial rights to the beach. So much for "soft crime"!

Despite the "soft crime," Rio is an exciting and wonderful city to visit. Even if you have never been there, I am sure you have seen the photos of the natural harbor bordered by the striking and sweeping design of the mosaic walkway along the beach where hundreds of skimpily clad people swim, dance to samba music, and relax in the brilliant sunshine. The backdrop for this picturesque scene is a seemingly endless procession of deep green mountain peaks. Some of the hills seem to rise up from the sea. The most famous is the 2,330-foot Corcovado Mountain that supports Rio's centerpiece, the world-renowned statue of Christ the Redeemer, His arms spread out over the city below. The concrete figure stands 125 feet high and the outstretched hands span 92 feet. By all means, come to this special vantage point for an unforgettable view of Rio. But remember: Watch your purse and wallet!

❧ ❧ ❧ ❧

Not all problems are in foreign countries. Our group was in Las Vegas at the Riviera Hotel when one of my ladies at the dollar slots fell victim to a fairly common scam. She had just won $300 and, as she was taking the coins out of the tray where they had landed with a wonderful and exhilarating clatter, two young men came and sat down on either side of her. Both started playing their respective slot machines. As Eva was placing her winnings in the coin racks and setting them on the space between the machines on her left side, the man on the right started talking to her about how lucky she had been to win, and telling her that he never won. He wanted to know her secret.

"There's no secret," she laughed. "Just be at the right machine at the right time."

"Well, I had better go find me another machine. This one sure isn't doing me any good." And with that, he got up and left.

When she turned to pick up her winnings from her left side where she had stacked them they were gone, and so was the guy sitting on the left. She reported it to the casino security, but they said there was nothing they could do since she couldn't even prove she had won the $300! So if you ever win big, keep your winnings in your sight at all times.

❧ ❧ ❧ ❧

When you consider all the places we have been, I feel fortunate to have had only two things stolen and never recovered. One was a new bathing suit that I had hung up in the bathroom at the Intercontinental Hotel in Miami. Reporting the loss accomplished nothing.

The other was in Fiji. We had been told by our guide that in order to save time, we needed to send our checked baggage the night before to the airport for international inspection. Because the local airport had no x-ray equipment, all baggage had to be searched by hand. We were asked to leave our suitcases unlocked for the inspection, and then we could lock them when we retrieved them before check-in the next day.

I had decided to wear a new cotton knit sundress and sweater that evening for our farewell dinner. I had already packed everything that afternoon, and all I had to do when we came in that night was put the clothes we had worn to the dinner in the bag and send it on to the airport. I placed the dress and the sweater right on top and closed the bag. When I got home to the United States and started unpacking, the first thing I noticed was that the dress was there, but no new cotton sweater. I guess the dress didn't fit the thief's wife or girl friend, but the sweater was just the right weight for Fiji temperatures and they couldn't resist. I hope some lady is enjoying it right now on those cool Fiji nights.

ê ê ê ê

Not all rip-offs are by theft. Sometimes you can lose a bundle through simple ignorance. We were on a cruise of the Canary Islands and Morocco. One stop was the famous city of Casablanca where I kept looking in vain for Bogart and Bergman. During the morning tour of the city, the guide pointed out the Royal Mansour Hotel, telling us that this was where the current king had a private suite and that they served tea in the lobby each afternoon at four.

Since we had the afternoon free, Keith and I decided to check out the Sultan's hideaway. Just as we were leaving the ship, two of my passengers, Jim and Ann, stopped us and asked where we were heading. We explained, and asked them to join us. We enjoyed the walk down to the hotel.

A magnificently dressed doorman in a white robe with a purple velvet cape welcomed us. The architecture of the building was Moorish, with an ornate entryway that made it seem like a palace right out of the "Arabian Nights." The lobby was dominated by a sumptuous hand-painted dome from which hung a large chandelier. As it was just four, we asked about "afternoon tea" and were ushered into the Winter Garden, an oasis-like area filled with palm trees and white wicker furniture with sink-into-cushions. A gentleman played soothing tunes at a grand piano in the corner.

When the waiter appeared, we asked for the "afternoon tea." We were served a sweet hot tea in small clear glasses, which the hot liquid made difficult to handle. Accompanying the tea was a three-tiered gold serving dish laden with all kinds of little sweets of stuffed fruits and cookies. We were the only ones in the lounge and felt very regal as we sipped our tea and ate one or two little goodies.

The waiter asked if we wanted anything else, and we said no. Jim immediately insisted on taking care of the bill. When it arrived, to everyone's surprise, especially to Jim's, the charge was $60 — as in U.S. $60! This was in 1990 and to us Texans $60 seemed a shade high for four little bitty glasses of hot tea and a few sweets. Jim did not have $60 cash with him, and Keith wanted to help him, but he would not hear of it. The hotel accepted his credit card. At this point, I regretted not having eaten more of the sweets.

After all that, I thought we should get something extra, so I asked if we could see the Sultan's suite. Opportunely, he was not in town, and the hotel staff graciously took us up to his private quarters, which consisted of four rooms, a living room, meeting area, bedroom and bath. It was luxurious, but not nearly as impressive as the $60 bill for afternoon tea.

ða ða ða ða

You don't have to leave the country to get ripped off at a fancy joint. Keith and I were going to a conference in New Orleans and when Buckshot, a close friend of ours, found out, he said that we *must* have brunch at Brennan's and, not to worry, he would make the reservation through the manager who was a personal friend of his. When we arrived at Brennan's that Sunday morning, we were directed to a lovely table overlooking the courtyard. I commented that Buckshot had done well in getting us such a nice table in such a crowded restaurant. Before we could place our order, a waiter rushed up to our table.

"Mr. and Mrs. Brooks! I am so sorry. You do not belong here. We have your table in our private dining room."

Speechless, we followed him to the small dining room with two tables. No view, though. In fact, there were no windows; for privacy I guess. As we were seated with great ceremony, I noticed there were three ladies at the other table. After introductions, we found out they were from Toronto and one was the mayor of that city.

Sanders, our waiter, appeared with a bottle of wine. "Compliments of the manager." At this point, we were feeling pretty superior to be receiving so much personal attention.

Sanders said, "I will bring you Brennan's Traditional Breakfast. Is that agreeable with you?" At this point, we would have agreed to anything.

The first course was fruit and crepes, followed by eggs Benedict and a small steak, accompanied with all types of rolls. As we were relishing the first course, Sanders, very proper with a white cloth over his left arm, was attending to our Canadian partners. As he served each plate, he did it with a grand flourish and a bow. Just as he started to deliver the Lord Mayor's plate, somehow in all the pomp and circumstance, the plate slid out of his hand and the contents splattered all over Lord Mayor and onto the floor.

Without any change of expression, Sanders stood up straight and, with the white cloth still in place over his arm, said: "Madam, I seemed to have spilled your breakfast on the floor. Please remain still, and I will have it cleaned up promptly and bring you a fresh plate, compliments of the establishment."

I thought I was going to die laughing, but managed to stifle myself. Sanders went about wiping the eggs off the mayor and the floor, and quickly returned with a fresh plate for her. The mayor took it all in good spirits and soon everyone was chatting and enjoying the meal.

Sanders served the rest of the meal without incident. When we asked for the check, we nearly had a heart attack. The cost of our breakfast was $75 (and the wine was free). This was in 1975, mind you, when $75 meant something. At this point, I wished he had spilled our breakfast on the floor so we wouldn't have had to pay for it.

In the fullness of time, as we look back at how many laughs we've had over the incident, it makes it worth the price. We will certainly never forget Sanders.

೭ఽ ೭ఽ ೭ఽ ೭ఽ

The only time during our travels that I have been truly frightened for my life and possessions was in the remote Baliem Valley of Irian Jaya, the western half of the island of New Guinea, governed by Indonesia.

Our group was traveling in two vans. In the first van were our Travcoa guide, David, our local guide, Freddie, and some of our group. In the second van, where we and the other members of the tour were riding, we had just the driver and a young man whose duties, as far as I could tell, were to open the van doors and assist the passengers in an out. He was riding in the very back of the vehicle.

We were driving through the countryside en route to a native Dani village when we came to a bridge over a river. Standing in the middle of the bridge were three hoodlums. The first van was quite a distance ahead of us and had already crossed the bridge and gone on. We were stopped by the bridge's self-appointed toll takers who requested money. Our driver explained that Freddie in the first van had paid for us. They insisted that he had not and demanded the money, in loud and, even though I could not understand them, not very nice words.

At this point, our little man (and he was little, barely over five feet tall) jumped out the back of the van. He started screaming at the three, and right away, one hit him squarely in the eye. Our little man started hitting back and the larger one continued to pound him with blows to his face and ribs. I thought that, when they got through with him, we were going to be robbed and who knows what else. Our driver then pulled out the amount of money they were requesting and handed it to one of the guys not involved in the fight. If I had realized it was that simple, I would have shelled out the money immediately.

We opened the back door, our man crawled in and we went on our way. About a mile or so down the road, the first van was waiting for us. I was upset that they had gone off without checking first to see if we had cleared the bridge. Our little man suffered a black eye, bruised ribs, and several other abrasions. Freddie did not seem very concerned about his assistant's condition. He came over to our van and began assuring us that he had paid for us. I felt that he should have been aware of the danger and not left one of his vehicles at the mercy of thugs.

On the return trip, David rode in our van, and when we reached the bridge, the collectors were gone. Guess they had taken in all the money they wanted for the day. From that day on, we had a responsible guide in each van for the rest of the tour in Irian Jaya.

⁊⁊ ⁊⁊ ⁊⁊ ⁊⁊

We were in Acapulco in 1974, and my brother Delbert and Keith wanted to go deep-sea fishing. They found a captain who agreed to take them out for a half day for $50; if they didn't catch anything, the captain would charge them $100 for the whole day. When they told me of this deal, I said, "I won't see you until late this afternoon, because no way is he going to let you catch a fish in the morning!"

I had gone shopping and had just settled comfortably beside the hotel swimming pool with a book when, about 11 a.m, there stood Keith.

"Come see my catch!" he said with glee.

We rushed down to the dock and hanging there was his sailfish. It was seven feet long and weighed 168 pounds. Delbert had caught one too, but he had released his. Smart move.

It was November and I had told Keith that if he caught a big fish, I would have it mounted for him for Christmas. Now I had to make good my promise.

We agreed to pay a $100 deposit. The Mexican officials would skin the fish and give the meat to the poor. They would have a taxidermist mount the fish and it would be shipped to the nearest port of entry, in

143

our case, Laredo, Texas. We would then pay an additional $100 and pick up the fish.

This sounded fine, as we always enjoy going down to Laredo for a weekend to shop and stay at the Camino Real Hotel right next to the border.

Christmas came, and no fish, so I found a little plastic sailfish for Keith's stocking. Finally, in February, we were notified by mail that the fish was ready and we should send the remaining $100. We took the gamble and sent the money.

I was getting very uneasy when a month had passed and we had heard nothing about going to Laredo. Then one day the phone rang.

"Mrs. Brooks, this is Braniff Air Freight at the Austin airport. We have a package for you C.O.D. in the amount of $240."

Needless to say, this was not what we had anticipated. Back in 1974 you could fly round trip to Acapulco for that amount; probably you still can. But what are you going to do?

So now we have swimming on our wall one very expensive sail-fish, and a terrible taxidermy job it is, too. But each time we look at it, we think about what suckers we were and get a kick out of it.

It cost more to bring the fish home than to send Keith on the trip

No matter where you're cruising, Baked Alaska is sure to be on the menu

9

WHAT TIME IS THE MIDNIGHT BUFFET?

What is it about cruises that makes seemingly intelligent people take leave of their common sense? Maybe it's the sea air. Here are some questions I've been asked, in all seriousness, by folks I've escorted on cruises:

"Does the crew go home at night?"

"I'm sitting on the sofa, but where is the bed?"

"Do these stairs go to the upper decks?"

"Do I have to eat at all the dining times?"

And my all-time favorite...

"What time is the midnight buffet?"

I entered the group travel game just as cruising became the rage. The television series, "The Love Boat," had ignited interest in this form of leisure travel, and everyone was ready to go on their first cruise so I had no problem enlisting my clientele to join me aboard ship.

We took forty cruises during our tour group leader term, seventeen of them with Princess Cruises. I chose Princess because they represented the "Love Boat" in most people's minds and was an easy sell. I also had a Princess representative whom I liked very much. I usually filled my quota on every sailing that I presented. In fact, I was so successful that at one point the Princess reservation department said that I was booking too many passengers. Still, Keith and I managed to set a record (at that time) for having sailed the most days with Princess, a feat which the cruise line recognized with the magnanimous gift of . . . a clock!

Because of the volume of business I produced, Keith and I were guests of Princess Cruises for the inauguration of the Star Princess ship in San Francisco in 1989 and the christening of the Crown Princess in New York City in 1990. At the Star Princess introduction, we were among hundreds of travel agents and press people who were invited to the city by the bay to preview the newest ship of the Princess fleet. We were wined and dined and stayed overnight on the ship, which was moored in the harbor.

It was an honor to attend both events, but the one in New York City was the most exciting. Here we witnessed Sophia Loren as she smashed a gigantic bottle of champagne over the helm of the Crown Princess. Then, after a lavish cocktail party and dinner, as the ship sailed around in New York Harbor, Tony Bennett (one of my favorite singers) entertained all the guests. This was climaxed by a fireworks display from the deck of the ship with the glittering lights of New York City as backdrop. Then, to make this fairy tale evening complete, I was waiting for the elevator when out stepped Sophia herself. I gaped in admiration at this gorgeous woman as she graciously gave me her autograph.

Cruises appeal to many people for many reasons. For starters, you do not have to throw your bag outside the door each day as you do on a bus tour. You just unpack, hang your clothes in the closet, and settle in for a week or so.

If you like to eat, a cruise is the vacation for you. A typical cruise, offers the option of a breakfast buffet on deck, ordering from the menu in the dining room, or a Continental breakfast served in your room. Around ten in the morning you can have coffee or tea with rolls. Lunch is also available on deck or in the dining room. Afternoon tea is served at four with all kinds of goodies. Dinner is a multi-course event in the dining room and of course you need to save room for the midnight buffet! (Be sure to bring skirts and pants with elastic waistbands.) The newer and larger ships have even more dining possibilities, such as snack bars, pizza parlors, two dining rooms, and so forth. Most ships also have 24-hour room service.

On most large ships, you are assigned a dining time and table. You had better hope you have compatible dining partners, for they can make or break your cruise experience. Nothing is worse than someone who monopolizes the conversation with senseless chatter or gripes about everything. Nearly every table has or one more Mr. Know-it-all, Mrs. I've-been-everywhere, Miss This-is-the-worst-cruise-I've-ever-been-on, or Mrs. What-are-you-eating-can-I-have-a-taste?

One morning at breakfast a couple we had not met before joined us. I noticed she had a ring on every finger, plus earrings and several necklaces.

"Your jewelry is lovely. You must like jewelry very much," I said to make conversation.

"Oh, dear, I'm scaled down for this cruise. You should see what I wear at home."

I prefer the smaller ships with open seating and dining times. This way you can choose when you go to eat and select your dining partners. It is a great way to meet new people, and if you don't care for them, you can avoid them at the next meal.

Usually the entertainment on the large ships is first class and Princess rated number one with its splashy Las Vegas extravaganzas. The only downside was that we went on so many Princess cruises that we saw the same performances several times. There are other activities, too, such as bridge, crafts, trap shooting, dancing, exercise and gym equipment, a library, lectures on ports of call — just about anything you could want to keep you occupied. And don't forget the bingo; very popular on the ship. You can always leave a little money at the shipboard casino, or you may prefer to just lie out on the deck and read a book or take a nap.

A Cunard cruise of the British Isles presented a magician one evening. The seas were rather rough and the ship was rocking back and forth as he launched into his act. He called for a volunteer from the audience to assist him and, when no one volunteered, he selected me. Reluctantly, I went on the stage where the ship's movement was much more evident than it had been in the audience. The magician took out a piece of rope.

"Now, ladies and gentlemen," he announced, "I have here one long piece of rope. I am going to fold it in half and have my assistant (what did you say your name was? Oh yes, Joyce), take these scissors and cut the rope in half."

I took the scissors, and just as I started to cut, a big wave rocked the entire ship. The scissors slipped and I cut the rope in the wrong place (much to the magician's grief). As we stood there and he tried unsuccessfully to get the rope back together, another wave hit. This time the little table with all his apparatus fell down and two rabbits started hopping out on the stage. He quickly grabbed the hoppers, his equipment, table and all and, without further ado, exited the stage, leaving me standing there with the whole audience laughing loudly. My brilliant stage career was at an end.

My major complaint about cruises is that you usually have only a few hours to enjoy most ports of call. The large ships have to unload about two thousand people to go on excursions or shop. Before you know it, it's time to get back on the ship and eat.

Another problem is seasickness. When it strikes, it is terrible. Most people are not prepared for the feeling you have when the ship is rolling side to side. The best thing to do if this occurs is to take a Dramamine (or some other motion sickness medicine) and go to bed. Usually things will be better when you awaken or, heaven forbid, you might have to miss a meal. Some people get the "ear patch," a sort of medicated Band-Aid that is supposed to prevent motion sickness. Most people I know who have tried this method complain of dry mouth and some dizziness. I had one lady pass out because her first patch came off in the shower and she slapped on another one and practically OD'd from over-medication.

Another thing that bothers me on a ship is that there is always something creaking. I am a very light sleeper, and I used to lie awake during the night with the ship sounding like someone was closing a door on "Inner Sanctum." Then I discovered earplugs. They have been a lifesaver for me, not only on ships, but in noisy hotels and jungle camps alive with the din of insects. So if noise bothers you when you try to sleep, get those little spongy type earplugs and shut out the rest of the world.

Another of my cruise pet peeves is the picture taking. On the larger ships there is a photographer snapping away at every moment — when you embark, in the dining room, on shore excursions, when you disembark — I even expect to see them when I step out of the shower. The worst time is boarding the ship. You've been up for sixteen hours or more, been hassled by the airline with delays and ghastly food, stood in long lines to go through immigration and customs, wrestled with the luggage, looked for the transfer bus, crammed into it with other irritable passengers, and been taken on a bumpy ride to the ship in un-air-conditioned misery in a tropical, humid climate. At last you arrive at the ship, dig out all your documents, go through the registration process, put your luggage through the security x-ray, and finally drag yourself up the gangplank and — FLASH — right in your face. Your hair is a mess, you haven't repaired your make-up since early that morning, and you are generally exhausted. Now you can purchase a "Welcome Aboard" picture for just $6! Of course, you don't have to buy the snapshot, but you do have to endure the embarrassment of seeing your horrible picture displayed for all to see on the sale boards.

🐦 🐦 🐦 🐦

There are some places that can only be fully appreciated on a cruise. The Panama Canal is one of them. To really see this man-made wonder, you must sail through it. I heartily recommend that you spend the extra bucks and book a verandah room. Book even the cheapest room with a balcony, and you will be rewarded during the entire cruise. While all the other passengers are pushing and jostling for position out on the open decks to see the canal operation, you can watch everything in comfort and privacy. You'll also have a better view because you're lower down, closer to the action. We have been through the canal twice, once with a verandah and once without, and the two experiences cannot be compared.

The Panama Canal opened in 1914 and provided a vital route for ships traveling between the Atlantic and the Pacific Oceans. In 1903, the U.S. signed a treaty with Panama to construct a ship canal across the Isthmus of Panama, an engineering feat that required digging through the Continental Divide and building the most massive canal locks ever envisioned.

It takes about nine hours to traverse the fifty-mile canal. On both trips our ship had a reservation for 8 a.m. to provide daylight viewing. At the entrance we were in line with numerous other craft, from large ships to small sailing boats. It is exhilarating to see the largest canal gates ever created swing open. The ship maneuvers into position and is tied into place as little locomotives move alongside pulling the ship into place. Then the gates close and the water starts to rise. Coming from the Atlantic side, the ship is raised in a continuous flight of locks to reach Gatun Lake, a man-made lake covering 163 square miles. While on the lake, you travel a nine-mile channel that was carved through rock and shale. Originally known as Culebra Cut, it was re-named Gaillard Cut to honor the engineer in charge of this section of canal work. You pass Gold Hill, at 662 feet above sea level the highest place along the channel. On the opposite side stands Contractor's Hill. It originally had an altitude of 410 feet but this was reduced to 370 feet to stabilize it in 1954. The Gaillard Cut, too, has been modified. Origi-nally 300 feet wide, it was later widened to 500 feet to better accom-modate large ships.

The locks on the Pacific side of Gatun Lake start at Pedro Miguel where the vessel is lowered thirty-one feet to Miraflores Lake, a small artificial body of water a mile wide. Then there are two more locks be-fore reaching the Pacific Ocean at Balboa, Panama. The Pacific lock gates are the highest in the system due to the extreme tidal variation of the Pacific. The maximum allowable dimensions for regular transit of the canal are 106 feet wide and 950 feet long with a maximum draft of 39.5 feet. The Royal Princess, at 105 feet, 7 inches wide 805 feet, 9 inches long and with a 25-foot draft, was carefully designed to be "Panama Canal-friendly." Seemed like a tight fit to me.

ða ða ða ða

Panama Canal sailings usually embark at either San Juan, Puerto Rico on the Atlantic side or Acapulco, Mexico on the Pacific. Typically various Caribbean islands and Mexican coastal cities are included in a trans-canal cruise.

One of our ports of call on a Star Princess cruise through the canal was Costa Rica. I had been there before and knew an excellent guide, so I told my group not to take the ship's excursion. We would do our own. All forty of my group seemed pleased with this arrangement. Well before sailing, I contacted my Costa Rican tour operator, Tibor, told him exactly what I wanted for the day and requested Bobby as our guide. Bobby had been our guide on two previous tours and spoke very clear English, which is not always the case in some countries. He had an advantage because his mother was from Philadelphia and had met and married his father when he was in the U.S. playing baseball.

During the cruise itself, I wanted to reconfirm with Tibor that everything was in place for our private tour. This was before the days of e-mail and the ship charged $15 to send a one-page fax. Surely, I thought, I can do better than that. So when we docked at Cozumel, Mexico, I inquired about where we could send a fax and was directed to the Presidential Hotel. A $3 cab ride took us out to the hotel, where we discovered that the fax machine was broken. But the hotel's beach looked like a good place to snorkel, so for a couple of hours we swam among the many colorful fishes not far from the shore. I was informed that we could send a fax at the Carib Hotel, a half mile farther out. Since there was no taxi available, we walked to the Carib in the hot Mexican sun only to be told they did not even have a fax. "Go to the airline office downtown," they said. The cab ride there cost $6. This office actually had a working fax machine, so I sent my fax for a cost of $6, making the grand total for my little venture $15, same as it would have been on the ship but minus the aggravation. In the fax, I told Tibor that I would call him the next day between one and three from Grand Cayman.

When we docked, I went to the nearby harbor phone booths to call Costa Rica. The phone took only Cayman coins and I had none. A nice local man came to my rescue. I put in my coins and tried to place my call, only to learn that these phones were for calls to the United States only, so I promptly lost my Cayman coins. Someone suggested that I go to the phone company a few blocks away. There they placed my call and the person who answered in Costa Rica said that Tibor was in Peru and no one there knew anything about my tour. I said I would call "mañana."

The next day brought us to Jamaica. I was starting to wise up, so as soon as we disembarked, I looked for the phone company. We found it, along with a sign indicating that the office would open at 10:15. Of course, Jamaica runs on island time, which means about two hours late. At eleven, the girl who ran the office made her appearance and this time I did get to talk to someone who assured me everything was in place. We would have Bobby as guide and she had ordered the flowers. (We were to be there on Mother's Day and I wanted each lady to have a flower corsage.) Even though I had finally reconfirmed everything, I still felt uneasy. If anything got messed up, my people would miss seeing Costa Rica since I had told them not to book the ship's tour.

We sailed through the Panama Canal and the next stop was Puntarenas on the west coast of Costa Rica. That morning I rushed out on deck and saw buses everywhere, but no sign of Bobby. After breakfast, I donned my bank's red hat with the NCNB logo and went out on deck, and to my joy, I spotted another red NCNB hat on the dock. What a welcoming sight! I had given Bobby the cap on our last trip. As my group came down the gangplank, he greeted each one and pinned flowers on the ladies.

We had an extraordinary day tour of Costa Rica because Bobby knew exactly where to go and when to go there to miss the mob of fourteen hundred tourists from the ship. We saw the sights and went shopping without any delays and, to my great relief, returned to the ship right on time. I had this horror of not getting back to the ship by sailing time. Since we were not on a Princess tour, they would not know where we were and would leave without us. But it all worked out fine and it was a perfect day. We had a relaxing two days at sea before arriving at Acapulco where we caught our flight home.

ﻬ ﻬ ﻬ ﻬ

The Cunard Princess offered a one-week cruise departing from Galveston, Texas, and sailing to Cozumel, Cancun, and Grand Cayman. The sailing was in early May, and even though I knew that Mexico would be a little too hot at that time of year, I decided to give it a try. Since Galveston is just two hundred miles from Austin, we could go down by bus, and save the airfare. With my group discount, the savings made the cruise an exceptional bargain and I had 118 people sign up!

With that many people, you certainly cannot expect everything to run smoothly. And it didn't. This was the time that Keith had his tooth problem and had to fly home and that was just one problem on a cruise that had more than its share of minor annoyances.

First, just getting that many passengers settled in their rooms was a feat in itself. Very few of the group had cruised before, so even though I had warned them that their staterooms would not look like the huge cabins on television's "Love Boat," the tiny rooms were a shock to some. Several couples from one community had requested rooms in the same area. When one couple in this group discovered their cabin was not near those of their friends, the man threw a fit.

"I am a Texan and not used to being pushed around!" he yelled at me.

"I am a Texan, too," I fired right back. "And I was not aware of that birthright, and certainly no one is trying to push you. I have talked to the ship's personnel and the ship is full, so we cannot move you near your friends. My cabin isn't near them, but if you wish to change with me, I will gladly do so."

When I made that offer, he cooled down and said they would make do with things the way they were.

Then one lady rushed up to me. "One of our beds is folded up in the wall. How are we going to take a nap?"

Now that was a BIG problem! I informed her that all she had to do was to call the room steward any time she wanted the bed pulled down and she could nap whenever she wished. Or, if she was in a big hurry, she could reach up and pull it down herself. That crisis was no sooner settled than another one raised its head.

The ship announced that passengers could not book excursions to both Chichen Itza and Tulum, the Mayan ruins that had been promoted in the cruise brochure. I had many history buffs in my group who told me they had booked the cruise specifically to see these famous Mayan archeological sites. What a mess! Everyone was complaining to me about something over which I had no control. I advised them to take the half-day tour to Tulum, since the Chichen Itza tour was a full day and would be very tiring and hot at this time of the year. As it turned out, I advised correctly. The ship had mechanical problems, our arrival was delayed, and the Chichen Itza tour was cancelled. So much ado about nothing.

The entertainment one evening was "Big Band Night" featuring the Ronnie Renfro Band from Houston. Apparently he was well known in the Houston area, although I was not familiar with him. His band was on stage, and Ronnie was waiting in the back to make his appearance. Edith, one of my regular travelers, was sitting on the aisle, and she could not see around him.

"Could you please move, young man," she requested. "You're blocking my view."

"I'll just be here a moment," he said, taking a sip from a Dr. Pepper can.

"There's a seat over there," she hissed, pointing to a vacant place nearby. "Sit there."

"Just a minute," he said.

"Do you think you have special privileges just because you're dressed in a white tux?" she said, really irritated by this time.

At that moment, the cruise director announced: "Ladies and gentlemen, give a big welcome to the esteemed leader of our Big Band, Ronnie Renfro!" and the young man ran down the aisle to the stage.

Poor Edith wanted to crawl under the seat.

I had made arrangements for a group party the last day of the sailing in the Top Sail Lounge at 11 a.m. The night before I read in the ship's daily bulletin that there would be bridge classes in the Top Sail Lounge at 11 a.m., so the next morning at eight sharp I was waiting at the purser's desk to clear up this schedule conflict.

"Are you here for the crossword puzzle?" the young man behind the desk inquired.

"No."

"Then you're here to guess how far the ship's sailed since yesterday?"

"No. I am a group leader and have a problem I wish to discuss with the purser."

When the purser opened his window, I explained what I had read in the bulletin and I thought I had the room reserved at the same time.

"I know how bridge players are and I don't want to have to run them out with a stick," I said lightheartedly.

At that moment, I noticed a man standing behind me.

"I'm the bridge instructor and we terrible bridge players will gladly move somewhere to avoid getting attacked with a stick," he said.

I wanted to die: eight hundred people on board and I had to say that with him right behind me. I apologized to him, saying that I was just using a figure of speech. He cheerfully agreed to move his group, and we had the Top Sail Lounge for our party.

I had had RepublicBank blue T-shirts made for everyone with the route and date of the cruise printed on the front and I asked everyone to wear the shirts the day of the party. It was quite a sight to see over a hundred people walking around the decks in the same T-shirt. I had numerous other passengers stop me and ask where they could get one of the shirts.

"Put your money in RepublicBank and go with us on our next cruise," I replied happily. Since nearly everyone on that ship was from Texas, I signed up a lot of new accounts and gained quite a few travelers from those T-shirts.

While we were disembarking in Galveston, Wes and Dorothy came rushing up to me.

"Our bags aren't here! We've looked everywhere."

I had the ship's personnel make a check, but the bags were not on board. At this point, all the passengers had collected their luggage, and two suitcases were left sitting on the dock.

"Those look like ours, but they aren't," said Wes. "See the name tags?"

Sure enough, someone had grabbed their luggage by mistake. A few days later Wesley and Dorothy had their bags.

All's well that ends well, I suppose, but this was one trip I was especially glad to see end so I could rush home and look after Keith.

ટ• ટ• ટ• ટ•

In 1990, I presented to my bank customers a Cunard Princess cruise that visited Spain, Agadir, Casablanca, and Tangier in Morocco, Madeira, four of the Canary Islands, and the Rock of Gibraltar. The fourteen-day cruise cost just $2,198 for an outside cabin, including roundtrip airfare. The response was tremendous. I immediately filled my forty spaces with a waiting list. That's the good part.

Now for the bad. Two months prior to sailing, a couple cancelled. I sold their space to the first two on the waiting list, but Cunard said I could not change names as the cruise was overbooked. When I went over my list of passengers with the cruise company, two names were missing from their list, and the company said that it could not get them on the cruise. These people had made reservations as soon as I had an-nounced the cruise, so I called my Cunard rep, Betty, and she was able to get them re-instated. Two weeks later, they cancelled! I still had people on my waiting list, and I went as far as the Cunard Vice Presi-dent to try to put them in the cancelled spots. No luck. I worried around with this for days, and finally had to inform some of the people I had told could go that I was unable to get them on the cruise. I sent them flowers.

Next, Cunard sent out notices that we would have to overnight in London on the way back, which was not included in the original price. It was going to cost $100 per person extra. I notified all my people and was in the process of collecting the additional fees when Cunard called to tell me they had re-arranged the air schedule and we would not have to overnight in London after all. Now I had to refund the money to those who had paid and tell the others not to send pay-ments.

Later, Cunard called and said that, because of the overbooking, if my people would downgrade, the company would refund $530 per cabin. So I had to phone everyone again, and eighteen agreed. When I reported back to Cunard, they said they only needed six people to downgrade, so I had to call back the other twelve to advise them of this change. When we departed for the cruise on January 17, I still had not received the $530 for those who had agreed to a downgrade! That would be a battle to fight when we returned.

A week before departure, the Williams cancelled, so I had to contact Cunard and the insurance company and hassle around for their refund. Then four days before departure, Don called to say he had been diagnosed with an aneurysm and was to be operated on in two days. He did not take out the cancellation insurance because this was their fiftieth anniversary and his wife's birthday, and they had every intention of making the cruise. Given the circumstances, he insisted that Cunard give him credit for a later sailing. The company said no. So I had to call Betty again, and she was finally able to get the company to go along with a credit, since this was a special case and I was such a good customer. She asked me to write a letter to her explaining everything, and she would see about getting the credit. As I sat down to write the letter, I realized that I did not know how to spell "aneurysm" and I couldn't even find it in the dictionary. I called the library and they looked it up for me. I had almost finished typing the letter when the phone rang.

"Joyce, this is Don. The doctor just re-examined me and says his diagnosis was incorrect. I'm OK and we can go on the cruise!"

Back on the phone with Cunard. We were able to reclaim the cabin, but now we couldn't get seats on the plane. Finally, the day before departure, the plane reservations cleared.

Then Irene called. She had to cancel because her sister was dying. So back to Cunard and the insurance company. Since I had ordered a bottle of champagne for everyone's room, I called the ship's Amenities Department to cancel Irene's champagne. To my amazement, Cunard said they hadn't received any wine order from me, so I had to fax it to them. This unnerving experience taught me to re-confirm *everything!*

Totally exhausted from the many pre-cruise problems, I finally departed with thirty-five passengers. But my troubles were just beginning. Two gals coming from Lubbock got delayed and missed the flight from New York to Spain and I had no idea where they were. When our plane landed at Malaga, the Cunard representatives grabbed all the bags and had them on several carts ready for immigration when Camille realized she had locked her passport in her luggage. We had to go through the stack of suitcases to find her bag and remove the precious document. When we were on the transfer bus, Edith said she did not see her bags (now she tells me!), but when we arrived at the hotel in Torremolinos, her bags were there.

The next morning the group toured Mijas, a quaint village of white-washed Andalusian-style houses perched 1,476 feet above the Mediterranean Sea. This village has the only square bullring in all of Spain. We strolled through the cobblestone streets along the mountainside, stopping at the many souvenir shops and sampling the delicious caramelized almonds that vendors were cooking right out on the sidewalks.

When we returned in the afternoon from the tour, I had a message from my two missing ladies. They had not only missed their plane in New York, but the connection in Madrid as well. Still, they were on their way, arrival time unknown. I left word with the hotel receptionist to contact me when they arrived. Tired from the flight and hassles of the day before, I lay down for a nap. I had just dozed off when there was a knock at my door. There stood a lady. "I'm here, now what do I do?"

"Are you Mrs. Bennett or Mrs. Seale?" I inquired, as I had never met my Lubbock passengers.

"No, they told me you were the Cunard leader and I am on the cruise."

I explained that I was the leader for the Texas group and referred her to the cruise personnel. I returned to bed again and was just about to fall asleep when the phone rang. This time it was the Lubbock ladies. They had finally made it and said they were so tired they wanted to rest, so I told them I would see them later.

I lay back down and ten minutes later the phone rang yet again. "We got here late and missed the morning tour. What are you going to do about a refund?"

"Who is this?" I asked groggily. They weren't in my group either, but the ever-helpful receptionist had given them my name.

The next morning, as I was leaving the hotel, a desk clerk stopped me and wanted me to pay for two people who had left without taking care of their bill. I had to show them my passenger list to prove to them that I was not responsible for those charges. It was hard to explain to them that I was just the leader for the Texas group, and was not responsible for every passenger on the cruise.

We reached the Cunard Princess at six, after a tour to Granada and its magnificent Alhambra palace. I instructed my people to have their cruise documents and passports in hand to expedite the check-in process. As I walked down to where they were lined up, I noticed that one of my ladies had a different looking envelope in her hand. It was her airline ticket. I called this to her attention and she discovered that she had left her cruise documents in her suitcase, which was now aboard the ship. I went with her to the cruise officials and explained the situation. I showed them my passenger manifest with her name on it, and they let her go aboard with the promise to deliver the documents to the purser when she received her luggage on ship.

The next task was to get everyone settled in their cabins, with all of their luggage and the gift champagne. Miracles do happen — everything was in place, but no one, least of all me, was pleased with the condition of the ship. It was shabby looking. Even the coat hangers in the closet were broken. And on our deck, there were some plumbing problems and the odor was horrible.

Our first stop was Casablanca, Morocco. In the evening, after dinner on the ship, we were entertained by a local Moroccan troupe, six big, ugly, fat women dancing to music provided by three skinny men who played a drum, some kind of round iron cylinder and a stringed instrument. Every now and then the men would jump up and down and make loud noises. It was the worst cruise show I had ever seen. Toward the end of the act, the women came around asking passengers to dance. One approached Keith who jumped up and ran from the room. I followed him, laughing all the way.

After a day at sea we arrived at Madeira. The port city of Funchal was a picture postcard sight — blue water, colorful flowers everywhere, and little white houses with red roofs dotting the mountainside. The island was discovered in 1419 by the Portuguese explorer Joao Gonçalves Zarco who called it Madeira, meaning wood, for the island was covered with forests at that time. Today it is almost treeless, due to the clearing of the land for cultivation of sugar cane, bananas, and grapes. Madeira is probably best known for its fortified wine, the result of an accidental discovery in the eighteenth century. At that time, merchants added brandy to their wine to preserve it during long sea voyages. During several months at sea, the wine was subjected to heat and much sloshing around in the casks. At the end of the journey, the wine tasted much different from the way it had at the beginning of the trip and everyone liked the results. Today the vintners reproduce those same effects by fortifying the wine with spirits and baking and shaking it for three months. You might call it "shake and bake wine." They then age it for at least three years, creating one of the world's longest-lasting wines. The island is also known for its exquisite embroidery. Our guide said that over seventy thousand local women were employed in this industry and it was one of the island's main exports.

Our tour took us around the charming city and up a mountain for a fantastic view of the ocean and surrounding countryside. An exciting feature of this tour was the wicker basket sledge ride one and a half miles down a winding cobblestone run. Two people sit in what looks like a sleigh with a rope on each side while two men run alongside controlling the turns and the speed with the ropes. It was a wind-filled and jostling ride, and loads of fun.

The first Canary Island was Las Palmas, or Gran Canaria, which was a gran letdown. After the great tour on Madeira, this one was the pits! Six loaded buses drove up the mountain to see the extinct Bandama Crater. If you have seen the Hawaiian volcanoes, this was nothing. Then all six buses stopped for souvenirs and drinks at a little place that had *one* unisex toilet for over two hundred people. Fortunately, that evening a group of local youths in colorful native costumes presented a song and dance show that was the best shipboard entertainment of the entire trip.

La Palma Island, which is not to be confused with Las Palmas, is located in the northwest section of the archipelago. It's just twenty-nine miles long and eighteen miles at the widest point. The island is dominated by a mountain range, with the highest peak at 7,977 feet. The observatory here is one of the most important in the world because of the island's unpolluted air. The ride up was breathtaking. We went through a two-mile tunnel to the other side of the mountain and the weather changed completely. One side was foggy and overcast while the other side was sunny and bright. There were tall pine trees, almond trees in bloom, large ferns, cacti, and brilliant red poinsettias up to six feet high. We did not get to go inside the observatory, but the ride up there was reward enough.

The capital city of Santa Cruz was like a breath of fresh air, very quaint and not at all touristy. No one tried to sell us anything and there were very few souvenir shops. This cozy little village sits on a horseshoe-shaped bay that serves as an excellent harbor for one of the world's most gorgeous island paradises.

The explorers of the Canary Islands must have been partial to the name "Santa Cruz" because the capital of Tenerife is also called Santa Cruz. On this largest of the Canaries, you can, in the course of one day, pick bananas, throw snowballs, swim in the Atlantic, climb mountains, visit a botanical garden, and go to the opera. The city is a beautiful seaside resort, a favorite retreat for Europeans, and a retirement home for just about everyone, it seems. A ride through the mountains brought us to the Orotava Valley where two hundred years ago the German botanist Alexander von Humboldt, the fellow they named the current after, planted all types of tropical trees and plants. Today the lush valley is known for its baby bananas, avocado, mango, potatoes, and lots and lots of flowers and cacti.

As we returned to the ship, Keith and I were not feeling well. Several people on the ship had come down with the flu and we hoped we were not getting it too. That's another bad thing about ships — if there's a bug going around, many of the passengers get it because of the close quarters and restricted ventilation system.

We rested and took the antibiotics that I always travel with and we felt better when we arrived at our final Canary Island, Lanzarote where our guide was a personable young lady whose grandmother lived in San Antonio, Texas. She had spent six months there learning English in order to qualify as a guide and we enjoyed exchanging tales of Texas with her.

Lanzarote had recently experienced one if its infrequent rains and everything was green. The island has more than three hundred volcanoes and "fire mountain cinders," too hot to handle, can be scooped up from a few inches beneath the surface in some areas. Our guide told us that Caesar Manrique, an architect and artist who died in 1992, established the policy that buildings be no more than three floors high, and all painted white with green or blue trim. The result is charming.

We visited a grotto, open at both ends, where shimmering effects from natural light transform the still water of the transparent pool into a dazzling light show. Here thrives a species of small white spider crab found nowhere else in the world. It looks like a little lobster about half an inch long. Green ferns and plants add to the beauty of this magical spot.

After two days on rough seas, we arrived at Tangier, Morocco, the gateway to North Africa, lying at the crossroads of the Mediterranean and the Atlantic. Keith and I were still not feeling up to par and I had eight of my group ill with the flu or seasick. Still, it felt great to stand on solid ground in the wonderful sunshine after the tossing of the ship on the rough seas. The city is devoted to tourism. We walked through souks filled with snake charmers and peddlers offering all kinds of merchandise. The women were dressed in traditional and modern fashions, but all the children wore clothing just like the kids in the States. My favorite place was the Malcolm Forbes Toy Soldier Museum. Here, displayed in numerous glass cases, were millions of miniature soldiers arranged in true-to-life battle scenes. Unbelievable!

That afternoon, we sailed across the Straits of Gibraltar to the mighty rock. This landmark rises 1,396 feet out of the sea and covers just two square miles. A bus ride up the rock provided fabulous views. There were many tunnels that the army used for storage during World War II and, of course, everywhere were the Barbary apes who live there as pampered guests of the British Army. Legend is that when the apes go, so goes British power. We were told there were about seventy apes in residence on Gibraltar at that time.

When we sailed back to Torremolinos to return home, practically everyone in my group was sick. Two of my passengers, Edith and Mr. Connors, were so weak from the flu they were in wheelchairs. When we reached the airport, we discovered that passengers were to be taken out to the plane by bus, and that there was no accommodation for wheelchairs on the bus. So we had to take the elevator down to ground level and then hoof it across the runway to board the plane. After I made sure everyone else was on the bus, Mrs. Connors wheeled Mr. Connors and I pushed Edith for what seemed like a mile out to the plane. When we got there, Mr. Connors was so pale that I was afraid he was going to die right there. The flight attendants helped us get him and Edith on board. When we arrived at JFK in New York, I had a porter take them in wheelchairs through customs and immigration and to the connecting flight. When we returned to Austin that night, I said my prayers that this trip with all its problems was finally over. I wrote in my diary: "Thank God, one more trip without a death."

ka ka ka ka

If you want a relaxing tour of Hawaii, take the American Hawaiian Cruise around the four main islands. The ships are intimate, not at all like the new mega floating hotels. The staff and crew are American, so don't expect the high level of service you might receive on European ships. The food is also standard American fare; it's not gourmet, but many Americans prefer it that way. Those are just my personal opinions, of course. I took groups on two of these cruises and everyone seemed to have a marvelous time on both.

The cruise in 1982 was the very first cruise of my life, so it is very special to me. Because Keith and I had been to Hawaii two times before, the sights were not new to us, but Hawaii is always appealing. The only mishap on that tour occurred when Edith was preparing for bed. She was in her gown when she heard a noise outside her cabin door. She opened the door and, not seeing anyone, stepped out in the hall to look further. Then her door slammed shut, locking her out. Fortunately, I was in my room and could provide her sanctuary while I went down to the main desk and obtained a key to open her door. My robe protected her modesty on the return trip to her room.

In 1990 I brought another group on the same Hawaii cruise. The first full day of the cruise the ship sailed around the small island of

Molokai, known for the leper colony that was established by Father Joseph Damien in 1873 on the north coast. The entire island is covered with pineapple fields.

Our first port of call was Maui, dominated by the towering peak of Halaekala which rises 10,032 feet into the clouds. On our honeymoon, Keith and I had driven down to the unspoiled village of Hana, and we wanted to repeat this scenic experience. Ada and Wesley, two of our passengers, rented a car with us. Off we went on the fifty-eight-mile snake-like road that has 667 curves and fifty-six one-way bridges. Referred to as "Hell for the driver, but Heaven for passengers," this is one road where you need to take time to "smell the flowers" not only for the enjoyment, but for the safety. On one side of the road there were tulip trees in bloom (it was July), waterfalls, monstrous fern plants, outsized ivy winding up the trees, fuchsia and pink impatiens, and all growing wild and free. Most of the time on the left-hand side it was "Watch That Step – it's a LULU," as the road hugged cliffs that dropped sharply into the raging waves of the Pacific Ocean. God had certainly worked overtime in preparing this piece of ecstasy.

Hana is a quiet residential community at the end of that difficult, but gratifying road. We had lunch out on the terrace of the Hana Hotel and stopped at Hasegawa's General Store, which has been in business for over seventy years.

Just another fourteen miles takes you to the Seven Pools, where numerous basins (there are a lot more than seven) stair-step down the slopes. We returned to the ship via the same route. On our previous trip, Keith and I continued back on the island circle road, but from the Seven Pools it is unpaved, and definitely not recommended for your comfort, or that of your car's suspension.

On the 1990 cruise, the ship was sailing to Hilo on the big island of Hawaii. During the night we went out on deck to see the Mauna Loa Volcano, which was erupting at the time. It was a bizarre feeling to watch the glowing red stream of lava as it made its stately way from the top of the mountain to the water's edge, where it entered the sea in a roar of steam. When we docked at Hilo, we immediately rented a car to take a closer look. As we approached the volcano, guards stopped us from getting too close to the lava flow. Some trees were still burning and the ground was smoking; it was like an antechamber to hell. We chatted with the guards and they pointed out that their tables and equipment were on rollers so they could get out of the way quickly if the burning lava came their direction. One table was filled with pieces of lava rock. I picked up one piece with sparkling silver specks in it; it was about the size of a coconut and still warm.

"You may have that, if you wish," the guard offered.

I was thrilled to have such an unusual souvenir. The guard also told us about Black Sand Beach, explaining that when the hot lava hits the cool ocean water, it explodes and makes the sand black. So down to the beach we drove and I picked up a small jar of black sand. On the way back, we discussed how we would display our piece of lava on a bed of black sand as a special highlight in our extensive collection of curios.

As I walked up the gangplank carrying my prize piece of lava, a ship's officer at the entrance grabbed it right out of my hand.

"You can't take that on the ship! It's bad luck," he screamed.

"Who says we can't?" I retorted.

"The captain," he said, as he threw my treasure into the water.

I was so upset by the loss of my wonderful keepsake and the crewman's hysterical reaction. But before I could take the matter up with higher authorities, one of my ladies had to go to the doctor, so for the moment, my lava problem was forgotten.

The next day we arrived at Kona, where Keith and I took the snorkeling excursion offered by the ship. The ship's launch delivered us to a cove set aside as a Marine Life Conservation District, just perfect for snorkeling. Here we floated on top of crystal clear waters and observed hundreds of brilliantly colored fish of all sizes while the crew went fishing. This was one of the best snorkeling spots we had ever seen.

When the cruise launch came to pick up us for the return to the dive shop, Keith took out a banana from our tote bag and started to eat it.

"No wonder we didn't catch any fish. We had a banana on board," a crewman complained.

"What do you mean?" I asked.

Hawaiian legend holds that you will have bad luck if you have bananas on board your boat. When Keith finally finished eating the banana (he is a very slow eater), the sailor grabbed the peel and quickly threw it overboard. Since the sailor seemed knowledgeable in Hawaiian lore, I asked him about the lava. He said that the lava represents the wrath of Pele, the goddess of fire. Anyone who removes the lava from the island will incur Pele's revenge and have bad luck. He went on to say that there were many letters in the Volcano Museum from people who had taken lava rock home with them and had suffered terrible misfortunes. When they returned the lava to Hawaii, their luck turned.

Maybe it was for the best that I had my lava souvenir snatched away. When we got back from our snorkeling trip, there was a drawing for a T-shirt prize and I had the winning number! Now I have a lucky Hawaiian T-shirt instead of a cursed piece of lava. Thanks, Pele!

ê● ê● ê● ê●

Despite my personal reservations about cruising as a mode of travel, I must admit that there are some experiences you can get only by signing up for a cruise. The Amazon is a perfect example. The world's largest river, the Amazon in South America, is one of the most exotic regions on the planet. The Amazon Basin covers an area roughly the size of the United States, which may explain why even today it is still largely unexplored. The river begins as snow high up in the Andes Mountains and the run-off joins over a thousand tributaries to travel some four thousand miles to the Atlantic Ocean. Half of all known animal species are found in the Amazon Basin and over fifteen hundred varieties of fish swim in its waters. At the city of Belem, where the river empties out into the sea, the river is two hundred miles wide. The river and jungle around it occupy one-fourth of Brazil's total landmass, yet only four percent of the nation's population lives there. These natives' way of life has not changed much through the years and only in recent times have cruise ships intruded into this wilderness.

Our first Amazon cruise was aboard the Pacific Princess in 1990 and our first stop on the river was at Santarem, Brazil, 560 miles from the sea. A city tour revealed a dingy looking village with a population of approximately twenty thousand, the third largest city in the Amazon Basin. As we drove around the town we noticed big, black buzzards sitting on the home rooftops, hundreds of them. We then noticed they were eating the garbage thrown from the house windows and sampling leftovers from the fish factory. There is something hair-raising about having buzzards sitting on your roof, but it didn't seem to bother the locals. I guess they can do without a garbage collection fee and noisy garbage trucks.

Santarem, it turned out, had a number of connections with the United States. After the Civil War, more than one hundred Confederate soldiers and their families settled here and carried on their Southern way of life, complete with plantations and slavery, which continued to be legal in Brazil for twenty-three years after their arrival. In 1924 Henry Ford established large rubber tree plantations just south of the city.

Rubber trees are native to Brazil and local Indian tribes made rubber latex balls and figurines long before the Europeans arrived in the 1700s. In 1908, Brazil produced nearly 95 percent of the world's rubber. In 1876, rubber seeds were smuggled out of Brazil to Ceylon in the Orient. There, conditions were favorable for the cultivation of rubber and by 1913 Brazil was exporting less than 50 percent. Now the country has to import rubber for its own consumption.

We stopped at a hammock factory where our guide told us that they produce fifteen hammocks a day by hand weaving. A worker makes about $60 a month. I realized that our guide would probably make more than that today just in tips from the ship's passengers. It just goes to show the value of English as a second language in the developing world.

We also visited a home where they were processing manioc. Manioc leaves resemble marijuana and the roots look like sweet potatoes. To make manioc flour, they peel the root, grind it up, and put the mixture in a woven straw strainer (more advanced processors use cheesecloth) to extract the liquid, which contains cyanide poison.

"You have to be careful," our guide pointed out, "not to let the pigs or dogs get to the liquid." I guess it was considered okay for the kids.

After the mixture is dried, it is exported to be made into tapioca, that funny white gooey stuff that your mother tried to tell you was a good dessert. The rest of the mixture is used to make bread and added to other foods in cooking. The Amazon diet consists primarily of manioc, fish, fruit, and guess what – Brazil nuts! We saw a Brazil nut tree. The nuts grow in a large round pod like a coconut with fifteen or so nuts inside.

Leaving the buzzards contentedly perched on the rooftops, we continued up the river to Alter Do Chao, a small village of around two thousand people. Talk about the event of the century! We were the first ship to stop here and they had built a landing dock for the ship's tenders the night before. Fresh flowers and palm leaves were entwined on a handrail that was still wet with new paint. Everyone in the village was there to welcome us with dollar signs dancing in their eyes. Each passenger was ceremoniously given a rubber seed lei before being led to the souvenir market. Someone from Santarem must have paddled upriver to tell them about the "sucker Americans" who were coming. Everything was twice the price we had seen the day before in the buzzard village.

As Keith and I strolled around the village, it began to rain and I took out my umbrella. I was walking along when suddenly my right leg went down a hole right up to my knee. I fell down with the open umbrella on top of me, looking as though I had disappeared completely. Keith came to my rescue and pulled me out as the villagers nearby laughed and laughed. It was clear a new form of entertainment had reached Alter Do Chao. The only damage was very muddy white pants and a slightly bruised ego.

Two hundred and sixty-nine miles farther upstream we dropped anchor off Boca Da Valeria, a riverside village of twenty-two families. Their only means of transportation was by boat and the nearest town was about twenty miles upstream. These people had not heard about us, and we were the first ship to call on them. They were shy, but appeared happy to see us. As I stepped from the launch, I noticed a boy around four years of age holding a beautiful Tun sea shell. It was dark in color from the muddy river water. I asked him how much and he just shrugged his shoulders. I took out a $1 bill and he took it and handed me the shell. I had brought candy in my camera case and gave him several pieces. That did it. The camera case became a center of attraction for the other children and I gladly distributed the sweets to them.

The village crafts were primitive and a refreshing change from the tourist junk that is usually offered. We bought a hand carved alligator about a foot long. There were numerous exotic pets — monkeys, birds, and something that looked like a raccoon. One home had "Open House." It consisted of two rooms — the front one was open to the elements and the back one was closed in, serving as the bedroom. Hammocks were hung over a dirt floor. A large stone cooking area was outside in front.

As we started up a trail, a boy about ten years of age joined us. He knew but a few words of English. In his hands he held a boa constrictor snakeskin about five feet long.

"How much?" Keith asked.

"Three," he said and held up three fingers. Keith promptly produced the $3 and took possession of the snakeskin.

The boy then held up four fingers and indicated he wanted to know the English word. As we walked along the trail he pointed out a cocoa tree, various other fruits, a lovely blue butterfly, and some birds. I took the opportunity to teach him to count to ten in English. So now, the next cruise ship passenger will have to pay ten bucks for his snakeskins.

In my tote bag, the natives could see a small hand mirror I always carry to handle any problems I might incur with my contact lens. They kept pointing to it. I let them see their reflection, and then everyone wanted the mirror. As this was the only mirror of this type I had on this trip, I couldn't part with it, but I made a mental note to bring several if I ever returned.

We spent a wonderful morning with these friendly and uncomplicated people, but I am afraid the visit from our cruise ship, and the many that will surely follow, will bring many changes to their simple way of life.

Manaus, the capital of the state of Amazonas, is one thousand miles inland and flourished during the rubber boom of the late 1800s when wealthy rubber barons built the world-famous Teatro Amazonas, one of the finest opera houses in the world. When the rubber boom died, so did Manaus. Today you can see fine old mansions next door to shacks. In 1967, the Brazilian government declared Manaus a free port, and once again the city flourishes as a shopper's paradise for duty-free goods and as a focal point for the river tourist trade. It is also an industrial center with many Japanese, American, and German factories.

We explored the wilderness around Manaus on a sixteen-hour tour that took us deep into the Amazon jungle. Here we saw the "Wedding of the Waters," where the clear waters of the Rio Solimoes meet the dark black waters of the Rio Negro and they flow together for nearly four miles without mixing before becoming the one brown color of the Amazon. It looked like Chocolate Swirl Ice Cream.

We continued up the Rio Negro until the water became too shallow for our boat. There we transferred to a motorized canoe and pushed on to a lodge deep in the wilderness, where we were greeted by a jaguar. This was rather a jolt until we discovered he had a dislocated hip and the staff of the lodge had adopted him as a pet. He just loved to have his belly scratched.

After a break for refreshments, we trekked through forest so thick the guides had to hack through it with machetes. Small monkeys jumped around in the trees and we spotted macaws with their long technicolor feathers. All along the way we saw manioc fields, rubber, and rosewood trees. Then it began to rain, and we were soaked to the skin by the time we returned to the lodge.

After dinner came the big event of the day, the "Night Alligator Hunt." Now this was spooky. We zipped through the backwaters of the Amazon River in a small boat in the dark in search of an unsuspecting alligator. The only light was a flashlight. No spotlights or headlights for this hunt. The night jungle was filled with all kinds of noises from who knows what nocturnal creatures. As our shallow-bottomed boat glided close to overhanging tree branches in this flooded environment, big water drops from the afternoon rain would fall on my head and I imagined they were snakes or something worse. I am sure the guides knew exactly where to go, because after forty-five minutes of roaming up and down the inlets in the dark, we stopped. One guide jumped in the water and returned with two baby alligators, each about twelve inches long. Everyone in the boat got to hold the poor little creatures and then they were returned to their watery nest. The other boat caught a three-footer, about three years old. We finally returned to the ship around midnight, totally exhausted but delighted with our day in the captivating and exciting Amazon jungles.

In 1993, we returned to the Amazon with a group aboard the Stella Solaris for a cruise that began in Manaus and sailed down the river. What made this cruise outstanding was the presence of Captain Loren McIntyre, the man who discovered the source of the Amazon in 1971 and is listed in the *Guinness Book of World Records*. He lived three months with an Amazon tribe, explored the area by foot, dugout canoe, ship, and aircraft and has written numerous articles for *National Geographic*, complete with his personal photos of the people and scenery. I could sit for hours and listen to his stories of the people, and his photography was unbelievable. One picture of a jaguar resting on a tree branch with its tongue hanging out was particularly striking.

"How on earth did you get close enough for this photo?" I asked.

"By sitting a long time at the San Diego Zoo," he said with a laugh.

Each day he would lead us on a jungle walk or to a river village. He knew the village leaders by name and, through his expertise, we learned much more about the river way of life than on our previous cruises. Unfortunately, as we started in Manaus and were going down stream in a flood situation, the river current was very strong. We had only three days before we reached the buzzard town of Santarem. So the highlight of this cruise was the wealth of information, spiced with unbelievable photos, that Captain McIntyre provided. If you want to read an exciting and intense story of the Amazon, pick up *Amazon Beaming* by Petru Popescu. It is the story of Loren McIntyre's astonishing experience with the "cat people" of the Amazon basin. Captain McIntyre collects clothes and medical supplies for the people of the river and when we returned home, I sent him a large box of clothes.

We marveled at the Amazon Water Lily, the largest of which is called Victoria Amazonica. The pad of this plant can be as large as three to four feet in diameter and is strong enough to support a twenty-pound child on its surface. In fact, Captain McIntyre had a photo of a year-old child lying in the middle of a lily pad. Large white blossoms lift upward to make this look like a lily pond for the Jolly Green Giant. We also glimpsed the rare pink dolphin, which has adapted to the fresh waters of the Amazon basin and is the topic of many folk tales in Amazonia.

As I mentioned, we took this trip during the flood time. As our ship left the mouth of the large river, all of a sudden there was a BUMP. Items fell from cabin shelves and passengers were shaken about. We were later told that the ship had hit a massive silt patch that had collected on the ocean floor from the river's flood.

Our last Amazon journey was in 1994 aboard the Columbus Caravelle, a small luxury ship operated by MarQuest. The crew was from Germany, North America, and the Ukraine, and both German and English were spoken on board. Since there were only one hundred twenty passengers on a ship that could accommodate two hundred fifty, my group of twenty-six received special attention and service.

The most outstanding of the four naturalists on board was Jorge Sanches, a Brazilian with fourteen years' experience as a jungle guide, who led all the village walks. He had spent most of his time research-ing the daily lives and cultures of the Yanomami and Wapixana Indians of Brazil. His extensive knowledge of the rainforest as well as his flu-ency in Portuguese provided great insight into the region.

We boarded the ship in Iquitos, a shabby Peruvian town in the middle of South America, almost exactly three thousand miles from the Atlantic and the Pacific. It once thrived on the rubber industry, but today it serves as a center for small ship river trips such as ours. We ar-rived there in the dead of night and, after a short sleep in a modest (brochure lingo for rather bad) hotel, I was awakened by a roaring noise in the street below. The street was packed with motor scooters, many with a small cab at the back, that served as taxis. Where they were all going this time of the day I have no idea, but it certainly was early morning rush hour. There was not a car, truck, or bus in sight, just all these funny motorcycles.

The first order of business on board the ship, after finding your room, was to select knee-high rubber boots to wear on all shore excursions. One of the recurring pleasures of the cruise was hearing the cruise director announce in her commanding German accent, "Time for everyvon to put on your rubbers."

At each destination, the ship would drop anchor in the middle of the river and we would pile into twelve-passenger Zodiac rubber boats to go ashore or travel along the river tributaries. The only thing wrong with this procedure was that ten little boats would go single file along the river route and if there was any wildlife, only the lead boat would get to see it. Whatever had been there would be long gone by the time nine more fully loaded boats with motors roaring came passing by.

When we were on jungle treks, Jorge would take off with about seventy-five people trailing behind. We had been cautioned to be quiet, but of course there is no way seventy-five people can tromp quietly through the jungle. One day the herd was following Jorge single file when he waded right through a small stream. Like blind sheep, we all followed, and the water was so deep it filled our rubber boots. While I was pouring the water out of my boots, I felt annoyed that Jorge had taken us through this deep water. Then I was reminded that Jorge, native that he was, was barefooted and didn't have to worry about overflowing boots.

It was the stops at remote Indian villages that made this cruise special. Large cruise ships don't come this far up the Amazon, so these villages had not been corrupted by previous waves of tourists. Most communities consisted of several wooden huts with straw roofs and about forty or fifty inhabitants. In some places, there would be a school, with almost no supplies. Max and Cassandra organized a collection from the ship's passengers and gave the money to several schoolteachers to purchase materials for the youngsters. The villagers live off the river and jungle and have small gardens. Most wear old and tattered clothing. The men wear shorts and T-shirts; the women wear a skirt and blouse or, in many cases, just a grass skirt and bare top. Most of the children are naked or wear shorts.

In one village a young man wanted to sell us a jaguar skin. We did not want to encourage the killing of these beautiful cats and no one would buy it. I know they need to provide for themselves, but hope they can find a way to do so without killing their endangered animals.

I saw a man wearing a headpiece with long blue and red feathers. I traded a mirror for it and his wife was so excited. Our guide said the native woman had never seen a mirror before.

Each evening the naturalists on board presented in-depth lectures on the area visited that day. The scenery was spectacular, but the wild-life sightings were disappointing due to the large numbers of people on the excursions. Even so, this cruise was one of my favorites because it offered a rare personal glimpse of the people of the Amazon Basin and their lifestyle, an experience that was possible only by taking a cruise.

🐢 🐢 🐢 🐢

While the "Love Boat" type of cruise has its attractions, it gets bor-ing after a while and I was constantly looking for new and different cruising experiences for my loyal cruisers. One ship that especially caught my eye was the Sea Cloud, a magnificent sailing vessel origi-nally built in 1931 for heiress Marjorie Merriweather Post and finan-cier E. F. Hutton. A German company acquired this glorious vessel and in 1986 began offering high-end cruises. I contacted them about a fa-miliarization cruise, or "fam trip" as it's known in the trade. Cruise lines and tour operators will offer free trips to travel agents and tour leaders like myself in the hope that they will return home and eagerly sell the cruise or tour to their customers. To my pleasant surprise, the Sea Cloud offered a complimentary cabin to Keith and me on a cruise departing from Cozumel, Mexico.

Just to be on board this elegant ship was worth the trip. Hutton and Post spared no expense when they created what was then the larg-est private sailing vessel ever built. Some of their guests during the '30s and '40s included the Duke and Duchess of Windsor, Franklin D. Roosevelt and Sweden's King Gustavus V. And now Keith and Joyce Brooks!

The four-masted ship is 316 feet long and 50 feet wide at the beam. You can nearly break your neck looking up at the 191-foot main mast, as high as a twenty-story building. There are twenty-nine sails with a total sail area of 34,000 square feet. And, to add to the atmosphere, there are handsome young men and women in nifty shorts and "Sea Cloud" shirts scampering up and down, setting and adjusting the sails. You do not need a destination to make this a great trip. The ship itself is a fantastic voyage.

There are just thirty-four cabins that accommodate a maximum of sixty passengers. To serve these sixty passengers (if the ship is filled to capacity) is a crew of sixty. So in reality, you have one crew member to each passenger, a very novel approach to cruising since some of the large ships have two thousand passengers and about two hundred fifty crew.

The showplace of the ship was the Owner's Suite Nos. 1 and 2. No. 1 was designed for Marjorie. It featured French décor with Louis Philippe chairs and an opulent French Bed with overhead canopy. There was even a fireplace, although why you would want one on a cruise is beyond me. The bathroom was eye-popping with its Carrara marble, finely etched wall-sized dressing mirror, and golden swan faucets with water spouting from their beaks! The cost for Suite No. 1 in 1986 for the seven-day cruise was $30,000 a couple, a little over my budget. The couple that had these classy quarters certainly did not seem to be enjoying them. He stayed intoxicated most of the time, and his wife looked like she had never smiled in her life. Maybe she was the reason he drank or maybe he was the reason she didn't smile; we never found out which. I guess it just goes to prove that money can't buy happiness, just swanky cabins on the Sea Cloud to be miserable in. They were, however, gracious enough to host a cocktail party in their suite one evening so we were able to see how the other half lived.

We made do on the top deck with a small outside twin-bedded stateroom, which was good enough for us and, after all, we were there gratis.

You could sit where you wished at meals with the exception of the Captain's Table, which was reserved by invitation only for six passengers each evening. Everyone on board was included in this elite group at least once during the cruise. Complimentary fine wines, beer, and soft drinks were available for lunch and dinner, which were gourmet delights.

After leaving Cozumel, the ship stopped at several small islands for snorkeling and bird watching on the way to Honduras. We especially enjoyed snorkeling in the Blue Hole near Lighthouse Reef off the coast of Belize. Jacques Cousteau dove into it in 1970 and since then divers from around the world have braved the deep, dark pit. The Blue Hole is an isolated area in the ocean that was formed by a collapsed cave in the coral. Its depth has not been determined and from a distance it looks like a dark blue hole, thus its name. As we were snorkelers, we floated on top while watching the brave scuba divers explore the cavern with Gothic-style stalactites adorning the walls. The divers had food, and we could watch from above as they fed the many fishes and a few blacktip reef sharks. (Another reason I snorkel instead of scuba.)

We became close friends with the ship's doctor and his wife from New York City. Like us, they were guests of the ship, bartering his medical skills for free passage. She was a stockbroker. They were a young couple just getting started and, like us, were not extremely wealthy like the other passengers. We later had dinner with them at their apartment when we were in New York City on a tour.

This cruise ended all too soon, but we had lived for a brief time in old-fashioned elegance on this unparalleled sailing ship. Sadly, the Sea Cloud rates were too high to entice my clientele, so back to the Love Boat we had to go.

ε& ε& ε& ε&

Still, I hoped to expand my, and my customers' cruising horizons, so when an opportunity to join a Special Expeditions fam trip in the Sea of Cortez came up, I jumped at it. This was our kind of cruise: no fifteen meals a day, no lavish entertainment, no dressing up for dinner, no extra charge for shore excursions, and the main focus on natural history.

Keith and I flew to Los Angeles where we met the other members of the tour for the flight to Loreto, on the eastern side of Mexico's Baja California peninsula. I was sick with a cold, but thought when I reached the warm climate I would feel better. No such luck. After we had bumped over a rough road for forty-five minutes through the cold desert night, I felt even worse and, to make matters worse, was running a temperature.

Our ship, the Pacific Northwest Explorer, was docked at the tiny port town of Puerto Escondido. I could hardly hold up my head when being introduced to our captain, the expedition leader, and three members of the natural history staff. Even the cocktails and hors d'oeuvres didn't help, so you know I was sick! I was taking medication prescribed by my doctor and hoped I would see some improvement soon.

The Pacific Northwest Explorer is a comfortable ship with thirty-nine bare bones cabins accommodating a maximum of sixty-six passengers. Life aboard the ship was strictly casual and the forty-five people on this cruise were very compatible. They all had a common interest and were there to see and study the wonders of nature in this part of the world. They came from England, Canada, and all over the United States. Nutritious and wholesome meals were served family style at one sitting. Each evening before dinner the group gathered in the ship's lounge for cocktails and the naturalists would recap the day's stimulating activities, answer any questions, and brief us on the next day's activities.

When we woke the next morning the ship was cruising along the smooth Sea of Cortez waters. During the pre-dawn hours, a tiny dark least petrel bird crash-landed on the ship's deck. Sue, one of the naturalists, rescued the poor fowl, showed him to the passengers, and then carefully sent him on his way.

I was feeling a little better this morning, but was not up to joining the snorkelers as they left the ship. Keith reported that the event was exhilarating — the water was perfectly clear and a very cold 65 degrees. He described the sightings of the day: a large male Mexican hogfish, a jewelfish, schools of sergeant majors, and a colorful crown-of-thorns starfish. He was most excited about swimming with the sea lions. The sea lions looked like they would run right into your body but then slid right by. It made me even more eager to get better.

The third day, I felt like I could join the living. That afternoon we took the inflatable boats, called Humbers, into the small port town of Bahia de Los Angeles. This village was owned and run by the colorful

Papa Diaz. He operated the only motel, the only restaurant, all the tourist activities, and any other business that might be around. He was a character right out of the movies, around sixty years of age, heavy-set, with a large handlebar mustache, all decked out in long boots and a big sombrero.

Papa had a motley collection of vehicles awaiting our arrival at the beach. There were beat-up old vans, not-so-late-model sedans, and pickups in various stages of repair and disrepair. Our group piled into the closest conveyance and off we drove into the bleak desert. Surprisingly, we had only one flat on the ten-mile ride to the Boojum Forest. The odd-looking Boojum plants are found in only two places in the world, on the Baja Peninsula and in one small section of the Sonora Desert, near Libertad, on mainland Mexico. This cactus is related to the familiar desert ocotillos, but has an outlandish appearance uniquely its own. Boojums grow to seventy-six feet in height and live up to eight hundred years. During the rainy season the leaves on the tapering, columnar trunk grow within seventy-two hours after a rain. These massive plants with their long swooping appendages reminded me of a giant green octopus ready to wrap its tentacles around you.

While walking among the Boojums, we caught glimpses of mule deer, coyote, a side-blotched lizard, and black-tailed jackrabbit. In the underbrush, colorful California quail darted back and forth. Zooming around us were hummingbirds feeding on the red tubular flowers of the ocotillo that had bloomed after a recent rain.

Papa Diaz also had a sea turtle nursery for the three species of sea turtles found in the Sea of Cortez, the hawksbill, from which tortoise shell is obtained which has nearly led to the turtle's extinction, loggerheads, and greens, both exploited for their meat and leather. In the nursery, they hatch the eggs and then release the little ones out to sea when they have grown large enough to be safe from predators.

That evening at Papa's restaurant, we feasted on Mexican specialties including tasty hand-made tortillas, and were entertained with Mexican folk songs sung by Papa himself and a "compadre." The songs, slightly out of tune, added to the atmosphere of the setting in this tiny village in remote Mexico. We returned to the ship and continued our sail on the Sea of Cortez.

The next morning we awoke to an over-powering odor. We had dropped anchor on the lee side of San Pedro Martir Island. As I came out on deck, the air was filled with flying boobies, gulls, and pelicans. The incessant barking of sea lions pierced the air. But most overwhelming was the aroma of countless tons of seafowl guano. That's bird shit to us common folk. This tiny landmass, totally white from the droppings, is home to over 13,000 brown boobies and 16,500 blue-footed boobies. (I don't know who the booby counters were, but that is what the naturalists told us.) The fowl are drawn to this area for the nutrient rich waters that make fish plentiful.

After breakfast, which was none too appetizing with the odor, we went ashore. It was not what I call a "fun hike." First, it was impossible not to step in the guano, but what made it even worse was that it was slick! The trail was up a steep incline. Slipping and sliding, I was in total fear of falling down in the mess. I could hardly breathe from the stench. Then the naturalist cautioned us to be careful not to frighten the nesting boobies for, when alarmed, they will flee their nests and the eagerly watching yellow-footed gulls will quickly dive in and devour the boobies' unguarded eggs or chicks. So not only were we knee-deep in shit, we had to be careful not to be accessories to murder as well.

The naturalists pointed out that it was easy to tell the male and female blue-footed boobies apart. The larger female honks and has a ring of dark pigment around her iris that makes her pupil look large. The male, smaller in overall body size, makes a whistling call and has an apparently small pupil because he lacks the pigment ring. That's just fine. I was not going to crawl around in the guano to look the boobies in the eye and check their sex. We were also told that the blue-foots (and they really do have bright blue feet), lay one to three eggs at five-day intervals. Therefore, the chicks hatch on different days and, depending on the availability of food, one or more chicks survive. Usually the first chick to hatch gets the lion's share of the food and the younger siblings starve.

Leaving the birds and their stinky habitat behind, we sailed on into the Sea of Cortez searching for whales. We spotted several spouts and with the aid of binoculars were able to see six orcas, or killer whales, cavorting in the waves.

As the rosy dawn of the following day crept upon us, we were called out on deck to see a huge pod of several hundred tightly bunched common dolphins feeding on fish. It was a feeding frenzy as the dolphins churned the water from below and the brown boobies plunge-dived from above and double-crested cormorants joined in the banquet. The ship and the dolphins glided together for over an hour with the dolphins forming a horseshoe effect about fifty yards in front of the boat. We watched in amazement as they stayed in perfect formation. Suddenly, the entire pod leapt far out of the water, stood up on their tails and then, just as if the leader had given a signal, they dashed dramatically out of sight.

Another interesting mooring was in the peaceful bay of Enseñada Grande off the Isla Partida. Here we hiked up a red rocky canyon that periodically echoed with the melodious song of the small brown canyon wren. Six species of cacti made their home in the canyon floor. We were told that one of them, the pitaya dulce, or organ cactus, had a sweet red globular fruit the size of a tennis ball that, when ripe, tasted like watermelon. It was reported to be one of the main sources of food for the indigenous Indians of Baja.

We came across mounds of discarded oyster shells from which fishermen had extracted the exquisite black pearls that once flourished in this area. After seeing the large refuse pile, I can understand why they are rare now.

Later the ship's Humbers took us to the rocky islet of Los Islotes where hundreds of sea lions were lounging on the shoreline rocks and frolicking in the water. This must have been birthing season, for little sea lion pups were everywhere, crawling all over the beach or swimming around in the shallow water. Sea lion babies nurse for up to a year, even though they begin to fish at five or six months. It's not hard to pick out the dominant males. With their thick necks and large size, they stake their territory and defy other males to enter. If one is brave enough to cross the line, a battle is engaged with furious vengeance until there is a winner. We spotted some smaller males recuperating from bloody wounds.

This time I got to snorkel with the sea lions and what a thrill! They will swim all around you, but never touch you. They are so swift and graceful that they made me feel inept as I paddled around the in water and watched them swooshing past me.

Up in the sky elegant black frigate birds would gracefully dive into the sea for lunch. In contrast, brown pelicans would crash into the water, clumsy and splashing, and scoop up a pouch full of water and fish. They then would return to the rocks to enjoy their meal.

We docked at La Paz, our first city stop of the cruise. Taxis took us to a charming seaside restaurant for a Mexican meal that included everything on the menu. A mariachi band played while the waiters generously filled our glasses with beer or margaritas. To this day, when Keith and I hear a mariachi band or sip a margarita, we always remember this glorious day at La Paz. All was right with the world, good friends were enjoying wonderful food, drink, and music in an exotic place, and any thoughts of work and responsibilities were put on hold. It can't get any better than that!

Next on the itinerary was the seamount known as Gordo Banks where upwellings occur and the marine life is very rich. We had been advised that this would be an excellent place for whale viewing and, sure enough, at around 6 a.m., the captain announced on the loudspeaker: "Whale ahead!"

I jumped up, quickly slipped into my shorts, grabbed my camera, and rushed up on deck. There, just a few feet off the starboard bow were "whale tracks," slick round spots on the surface of the water. I climbed up on the bench next to the ship railing. All at once a blue whale surfaced, spraying me and the other photographers with a salty morning shower from his blowhole. I was so close I could see his eyeball. As I looked down at my dripping wet clothes, I realized that I had put on my shorts, but had not taken off my knee-length nightgown. Oh, well, no one was looking at me with a blue whale close by. The whale played around the boat for over an hour, diving below the bow, rolling on his side with his large white flippers waving to us as he went under, rocking the boat with his wakes. The naturalists estimated he was around fifty feet long.

During the day we were lucky to sight more blue and humpback whales. They lead an idyllic life, summer in Alaska and winter in Hawaii or Mexico. Later we caught a fleeting glimpse of a gray whale and two Bryde's whales. Several bottlenose dolphins were riding the whales' bow-wave and led us to their location.

That afternoon the Pacific Explorer rounded the cape of Cabo San Lucas and we realized that we had left the calm waters of the Sea of Cortez and entered the not-so-friendly Pacific Ocean. We had to leave the cruise at Cabo, as I had to return to work. The ship continued on around the Baja up to San Diego, California, encountering many whales along the way. If you love sea life and bird watching with a Mexican flavor, a cruise on the Sea of Cortez is for you. This is a trip I would gladly repeat.

Unfortunately, my regular customers preferred the Love Boat, so it was back to leading groups on big ships to gaudy ports. Like they say, it's a tough job but someone has to do it.

The old and the new in Dubrovnik, Yugoslavia

Heading aloft aboard the Sea Cloud

A parade of tall ships salutes Lady Liberty's 100th

A ringside seat for a passage through the Panama Canal

10

WE WERE
THERE WHEN

I have been to Costa Rica several times, but one of my fondest memories is of being there during their elections. Costa Rica has held free and open two-party elections since 1889, a feat that many Latin American nations have achieved only recently, and even then there is some doubt as to just how free some of those elections are. Politics are very important in Costa Rica and, as we drove through the cities and countryside, we saw colorful party flags flying from every rooftop as the owners emphatically showed the world their party preference. On election day, at the polling places, young girls dressed in cheerleader costumes, waving pompoms in their party's colors, cheered loudly for their candidate.

Ticos, as the Costa Ricans call themselves, are very proud of their right to vote — they have nearly 100 percent turnout — and when they cast their ballots, everyone's right thumb is marked with ink to indicate they've done their patriotic duty. All day we saw people proudly giving a "thumbs up" salute to show you they had voted. It was a thrilling sight and we Americans could certainly learn a lesson from the Ticos about exercising our precious right to vote.

Many times I have designed my tour offerings specifically to take advantage of such special occasions. Other times I just got lucky.

When I heard about the big celebration that was planned for the Statue of Liberty's hundredth birthday party, I contacted my tour company in New York City to see what we could do. Since the celebration would just be for the weekend, I wanted to include something else to justify the air fare, so I chartered the M.V. Savannah for a cruise around the New England islands. This small ship accommodates 126 people, and I hoped that I would have enough interest to fulfill my commitment. I kept my fingers crossed as I mailed my newsletter advertising the tour. Almost immediately I had 126 people registered and a waiting list.

I did not realize what a tremendous task I was undertaking. A group this large required three buses to get people from place to place, so I was on bus #1 and Keith was on bus #2. Since my bank president and his wife were on the tour, I put them in charge of bus #3.

The next problem was reserving the required space on one plane. I worked with the airlines about a year in advance to accomplish this feat. I also reserved space on the Circle Line Cruises' Number One ship to get my group a prime viewing location for the Parade of Tall Ships.

But we had another problem to worry about. There was some speculation that Libya's dictator, Colonel Muammar Gaddafi, might launch a terrorist attack during the event. And I was responsible for 126 people if anything happened!

We left Texas on July third. Everyone arrived at the airport on time, which was a miracle itself considering the number of people on the tour. Eight passengers needed wheelchairs. I knew from experience that it is almost impossible to find eight wheelchair attendants when you need them, so I had pre-ordered the chairs and enlisted the aid of some of my younger male travelers to serve as pushers. This worked out fine.

To help guide a contingent this large through airports and elsewhere I brought along a medium-size Texas flag, which I would hold aloft when we were on the move. It seemed like a great idea, but it proved unsatisfactory. Not only was it something extra to keep track of but I always seemed to be poking someone. I later discovered that a red cap perched on top of my head (at 5'8" I am fairly tall) and held high in crowded situations worked best. From that time on I have always worn a red baseball cap when leading tours. Bill, one of my "frequent followers," said that the group would follow that red cap anywhere, so I had better not walk off a cliff.

We were staying in New York City at the old Halloran House Hotel across from the Waldorf Astoria Hotel on Park Avenue. That evening the hotel served us a buffet supper on their rooftop terrace. They had several large-screen televisions placed around to let us watch the "Unveiling and Lighting" of the restored Statue of Liberty by President Reagan. As the President pressed the button to flash the laser beam that lighted the Lady, he said, "We are the keepers of the flame of liberty; we hold it high tonight for the world to see." From our vantage point on the hotel rooftop, we could watch the fireworks over the harbor.

The Statue of Liberty dominates the approach to New York Harbor and has been a symbol of freedom to countless immigrants seeking a new life. I had seen the Statue of Liberty before, of course, and had always found it impressive, but before attending this event, I had never realized its full significance.

In 1865, a group of French noblemen led by the Marquis de Lafayette, a passionate admirer of American ideals, conceived the idea of a statue of freedom as a gift from France to the United States. French sculptor Frederic Auguste Bartholdi began designing an immense female figure with a torch. It would be the biggest statue in the world at that time. He came to America and selected little Bedloe's Island in the middle of the New York harbor as the perfect site for his masterwork.

"I feel the spirit here, and it is certainly here that my statue must rise," he wrote. "Here where people get their first view of the New World and where liberty casts her rays on both worlds."

It was agreed that the statue should be in place for the centennial of the American Revolution in 1876. Unfortunately, the sculptor had difficulty obtaining funding and only the hand and torch were ready by that date. This portion of the sculpture was sent to America, but it arrived too late to be part of the celebration. So the hand and torch gathered dust in a corner of Madison Square Garden for four years before they were returned to France.

In 1879, Bartholdi turned to Gustave Eiffel, of Eiffel Tower fame, to assist in the construction. Funds were raised through a French National Lottery and, in 1884, the statue was finally completed.

Meanwhile, back in America, the money to build the pedestal still hadn't been raised. Newspaper publisher Joseph Pulitzer waged a campaign to raise the cash from the "little people" and in two months collected enough to complete the pedestal. Mark Twain, Bret Harte, and Walt Whitman auctioned off manuscripts to help raise money. A young New York poet, Emma Lazarus, was asked to write a sonnet whose final lines, inscribed on the pedestal, express the real promise of the New World.

"Give me your tired, your poor, your huddled masses yearning to breathe free, the wretched refuse of your teeming shore. Send these, the homeless, tempest-tossed to me. I lift my lamp beside the golden door."

The 151-foot copper statue was unveiled July 12, 1886, on Liberty Island, and one hundred years later, a refurbished, shining, and gleaming Lady Liberty was presented to the masses.

July 4, 1986 — the big day! So far, so good. The three transfer buses were at the hotel on time. There was just a minor delay when one lady was locked *in* her room. I had to send hotel security with a master key to solve that one.

We boarded the Number One Circle Line Ship. There were other passengers on board, but it was not crowded and we had the run of the ship, so we could view the parade of ships from any deck or angle. A bountiful Continental breakfast was served, and each person was presented with a souvenir red, white, and blue tote bag with a surprisingly tasty lunch. We sailed out into the harbor and, when the ship took up its position, I realized we were in the front row, right between the luxury liner Queen Elizabeth II, packed with celebrities and dignitaries, and the aircraft carrier John F. Kennedy with President and Mrs. Reagan. The guest of honor, Lady Liberty, was visible just down the harbor.

From ten to four, we had a front row seat for the parade of ships. It was reported that some twenty thousand vessels of every conceivable shape and size were there that day. The parade included twenty-two elegant sailing ships from eighteen countries, massive Navy destroyers, frigates and battleships, interspersed with all kinds of small boats from canoes and Chinese junks, to posh French yachts.

A special thrill ran through the group when the battleship Iowa stopped right in front of our ship to give President Reagan a twenty-one-gun salute. It is hard to explain the pride and patriotism of that moment. I felt I was witnessing a piece of history, which, of course, I was. It will always be a special memory for me.

Still, I couldn't help but feel uneasy. I had this fear that Gaddafi would blow the statue right out of the water, or something similar, and I'd have to deal with 126 panicky people, eight of whom could hardly walk. But God blessed America that day and everything went according to plan.

That evening my New York operators had planned the ultimate climax to a perfect day. They had rented an area on the New Jersey side at the Alice Austen House overlooking the Statue of Liberty and the bay. From this excellent vantage point, we were able to see the spectacular fireworks display around the Lady with the city of New York as a backdrop. We sipped a drink from the open bar and we dined on mussel steamers, clam chowder, barbecue chicken, steamed lobster, corn on the cob, fresh fruit, and a salad bar. It was the fireworks show to outdo all fireworks shows. Splashes of vibrant color, accompanied by loud booms, filled the skies around the statue with the twinkling lights of the city's buildings in the background. It was a beautiful clear night, and the colors reflected in the water were indescribable.

I was so proud to be an American that night and thrilled to be part of this Liberty Weekend. I think the country needs a celebration like this every ten or twenty years, to remind us of the greatness of this country and the privileges of citizenship.

ใ๊. ใ๊. ใ๊. ใ๊.

My New York Statue of Liberty Tour had been such a success that I decided to offer the Golden Gate Bridge's fiftieth birthday celebration in San Francisco the following year. It wasn't as a big a draw as the New York trip, but I did have a busload of forty-two sign up. And after the trauma of dealing with three buses in New York City, I was just as glad.

We flew to Los Angeles where we took in the usual LA sights — Beverly Hills, Rodeo Drive, Mann's Chinese Theatre, and Universal Studios. Then we drove south to see the J. Paul Getty Museum, an artistic extravaganza featuring gardens and thirty-eight galleries filled with paintings, period furniture, and sculpture.

The next day we drove north to the delightful little town of Solvang, known as "Little Denmark," where the architecture and food have a Scandinavian flavor. We continued up the coast highway to San Simeon, the palatial estate of William Randolph Hearst, where we toured the mansion and grounds to see how the rich and famous unwound in the heyday of Hollywood. On the way north, we drove through the striking landscape of the Big Sur and the Monterey Peninsula with its Pebble Beach Golf Course. We spent the night in Carmel, and many of us went to Clint Eastwood's café, "The Boar's Breath," for a cappuccino. Before arriving in San Francisco, we stopped at the Almaden Vineyards for a private tour and wine tasting. The final three nights were at the Holiday Inn at Fisherman's Wharf in San Francisco, my favorite city in the United States. San Francisco — never call it "Frisco" — has so much to offer, spectacular views of the bay, great food, and an exotic atmosphere.

On Saturday, we drove across the Golden Gate Bridge to the houseboat community of Sausalito where we had brunch at the famed Alta Mira, overlooking the bay. That evening we were on a chartered boat out in San Francisco Bay to observe the "lighting of the bridge." After the twenty thousand boats in New York harbor and all that pomp and dazzle, this seemed very calm and uneventful. It was estimated that about 350 boats were on hand to view the affair. There was a bountiful buffet supper provided on board and at 9 p.m., we all gathered out on deck where we had a direct view of the Golden Gate Bridge for the big moment.

To our dismay, when the lights came on, only the pillars of the bridge were illuminated, and you could hardly tell that anything had happened. It looked pathetic, especially since you could look across the harbor and see the Oakland Bridge lit up like a Christmas tree with gleaming lights strung all over the structure. Fireworks followed the "lighting," but after the New York extravaganza, this looked like a neighborhood Fourth of July festival, and not a very big one at that!

The next morning, television showed the mob of people that marched on the Golden Gate Bridge, and according to news reports, the structure sagged with the excessive weight. I was glad none of my group had decided to join that spectacle.

Even though I was disappointed in the celebration, everyone told me they enjoyed the tour of Los Angeles up to San Francisco, which taught me a valuable lesson: always try to over-deliver on a tour. That way, if one element falls short, the others will more than make up for it.

᷃ᷱ ᷃ᷱ ᷃ᷱ ᷃ᷱ

Being of Irish ancestry on my father's side, I thought how great it would be to celebrate St. Patrick's Day in Dublin, Ireland. So in 1989, I put together a tour and had a nice size group sign up. After seeing St. Paddy's Day in San Antonio, Texas, where they dye the river green, and in Savannah, Georgia, where the newspaper headlines read "Green Condoms Available for Celebration," I thought we were in for a wild party in Dublin, Ireland.

Was I ever wrong! We were more than a little surprised to find out that, in Ireland, St. Patrick's Day is a religious holiday. All the pubs were closed. People all over the world were having a big party but Dublin was quiet as could be! Of course, it wasn't a complete ghost town. After all there were plenty of other misinformed Americans like us who had come expecting to whoop it up. We had tickets to the Lord Mayor's Ball, but he was smart, he was in New York City living it up. We had to settle for the Vice Lord Mayor, a charming lady who was most gracious to us. It seemed like all the participants at the ball were American tourists who were gullible enough to have come to Ireland for a St. Patrick's Day celebration.

The morning of March 17 found us huddled in our coats for protection against the brisk temperatures. From our reserved front row seats we viewed the Grand Parade in downtown Dublin. It was a long and impressive parade, as parades go, but 80 percent of the bands and marching groups were from the United States.

I found out *after* the tour that the first St. Patrick's Day celebration, as we know it today, was hosted by the Charitable Irish Society of Boston. In Ireland, St. Patrick's Day was a time to atone for your sins and have a "dull day," but the Boston Irish chose to toast their patron saint in celebration of their arrival in the United States and their escape from Ireland's many troubles. When I spoke to an Irish gentleman at the Dublin parade about our coming over for the holiday, he replied: "Ireland is the worst place in the world to spend St. Patrick's Day."

So don't go to Ireland for the St. Patrick's Day festivities; stay in the States where the Irish really throw a big party. But by all means go to Ireland. It is truly the Emerald Isle with impressive and startling scenery. The people are exceptionally friendly and the pubs are entertaining. The country is only about the size of the state of Maine, but each bend of the road brings a new vista of quaint towns, medieval castles, coastal cliffs crashing down into frothy waves, barren rock piles, peat bogs, emerald green meadows and, in the late summer, a violet haze of heather.

One thing every visitor to Ireland must do is kiss the Blarney Stone. Legend has it that when you kiss the stone, you will receive the "gift of gab." I already had that, but I wanted to try the stone anyway.

The village of Blarney is five miles northwest of Cork. Here lies Blarney Castle with its massive square tower, eighty-three feet in height. The stone is set underneath the battlements that crown the tower.

First you have to climb 127 steps to reach the stone area. I was not prepared for the contortions required to complete the "kissing" feat. You lay down on your back and a guard holds your ankles. I was glad I had chosen to wear slacks that morning! You then lower yourself *backwards* between the battlements and press your lips to a well-burnished rock. As I was in this impossible position that only a gymnast could easily manage, I suddenly did not want to kiss a spot that had been kissed by countless people throughout the ages. Maybe germs can't live in the cool Irish weather, but I did not want to take a chance. So I puckered up and kissed the air about one inch from the rock. I figured blowing a kiss was just about as good as the real thing.

Doris, one of my travelers, went through the awkward process and as she surfaced she screamed, "Shit, I did it!" It seemed like this refined, retired schoolteacher got something a little extra with her gift of gab.

So, take a trip to Ireland. Just don't go on St. Patrick's Day.

ଈ   ଈ   ଈ   ଈ

Some of my clients had expressed an interest in the fiftieth anniversary D-Day observances in Europe. In order to get tickets to the ceremonies, I made arrangements with a company that specialized in tours for veterans. There were about four hundred passengers on the tour and our bus had thirty-six people, fifteen of whom were my clients, including two who had participated in the original invasion. Tom was a pilot who dropped the first wave of paratroopers behind enemy lines, and Charles, a retired doctor, landed in the second wave to take care of the wounded. Also on our bus were three veterans from Louisiana who had operated a half-track on the third wave and were successful in taking out the last German pillbox, enabling the American troops to continue up the beach. The nearby French village had placed a plaque on this structure to honor their achievement.

We began our tour in London and, after a city tour, started down the "path of the troops" to the English shore. En route we stopped at prehistoric Stonehenge and the ancient Salisbury cathedral before arriving at Bournemouth, the site of the allied crossing of the English Channel. Cold rain and wind lashed the tent where a special World War II party was held that evening and the veterans remarked that this was pretty much the same kind of weather they had endured fifty years ago. We were served that soldier's favorite, "S.O.S.," as a band played Glenn Miller tunes.

We then ferried across the channel to Cherbourg in Normandy. The D-Day invasion was centered on two beaches, code-named Omaha and Utah. The mission began with the dropping of some thirteen thousand paratroopers south and west of Utah Beach in the first hours of June 6, 1944. As the men landed in the dark, they were able to recognize each other and regroup by using a special toy "cricket," a clicking device. At 4:30 a.m. on June 6, the American flag was unfurled at the town hall of Sainte Mere Eglise. Charles, of my group, was anxious to return to this little village church where he had helped set up a hospital for the wounded. Today there is a replica of the soldier whose parachute hung on the church steeple when he landed.

Monday, June 6, 1994 – D-Day plus fifty years! Our schedule called for an early morning departure to go to the Normandy American Military Cemetery for a special veterans' memorial service honoring the soldiers in the tour company's group. We started in our motor coach and were stopped along the road because the route had been closed to all traffic until President Clinton's convoy passed. There we cooled our heels for over an hour until, finally, his limousine zipped by. By this time, we had missed the memorial service and had to go straight to Utah Beach were we had reserved seats for the speeches of President Clinton, French President Francois Mitterand, and French Prime Minister Edouard Balladur. We made it just in time to find our seats before President and Mrs. Clinton arrived. It was rather embarrassing when many of the veterans booed his entrance.

Afterwards, we were bussed to a two-hour French lunch. We were supposed to be at Colleville on Omaha Beach at 3:30 p.m. for a special ceremony. This is the American Military Cemetery. This is where the 1st U.S. Infantry Division fought such a bloody battle to secure a foothold on D-Day, 1944. Here the rows and rows of white crosses mark the graves of 9,386 Americans who died in the Normandy campaign and another 1,557 names of the missing are inscribed on a memorial. It is a highly emotional experience to walk through those crosses and read the names, hometowns, and ages of the men who died so young that we might have freedom today. President Clinton and the French Minister of State made brief memorial speeches.

Somewhere in this area of Omaha Beach was the location of the pillbox where the three Louisianans had taken down the Nazis. The tour company brochure stated that if any veterans had a "special place" they wanted to visit, every effort would be made to see that they got there. The three men wanted to drive along the beach to locate the bunker with their names on it. As it had rained, the bus could not drive along the beachfront without getting stuck. Our guide told them they could have twenty minutes to find their memorial. There was no way they could locate it in such a short time. I felt so sorry for them. Here they had come all this way, at great expense, for the sole purpose of seeing this bunker, and they were not allowed to. They appealed to me to talk to the guide. I tried, but he was emphatic that we could not waste time trying to find one little concrete fortress. If they had been my clients, we would have found it come hell or high water. It is hard to see grown men cry, but that is exactly what they did. The only thing that made their trip bearable was that Peter Jennings of ABC saw them wandering along the beach and interviewed them on national television.

At least they got to tell their story to America. But because of the callousness of our guide, a military historian who should have known better, they were denied an opportunity to relive that touchstone moment of their youth and see how their bravery had been immortalized by a grateful French village. Surely that is the least they were owed.

ꝫ ꝫ ꝫ ꝫ

It is impossible to describe the awesome sight of hundreds of hot air balloons simultaneously rising into the clear blue New Mexico sky. I took a small group of twenty-two to the twentieth anniversary of the Albuquerque International Balloon Fiesta in 1991 and had one of those serendipitous experiences that make a tour group ecstatic and a group leader look like a hero.

The morning of the big fiesta, we had to leave the hotel at 4:30 a.m. in order to be out at our reserved place for viewing the big lift-off around seven. It was dark when we arrived at the balloon field and because the minibus we were traveling in looked a lot like those used by the balloon crews, the security guard directed us right out onto the ascension field. Our driver commented that we were in the wrong place, but there was nowhere for him to turn around, so we continued right along with the balloon crews and sponsors. When we reached the end of the road, he tried to turn around but got stuck in the sand.

"The group is going to get out here and, if you get unstuck, you can come back and get us at noon," I said and unloaded everyone right there.

Here we were in the middle of the VIP area, right among the scores of balloons stretched out on the ground as their crews worked furiously to get them inflated for flight. At the edge of the field were rows of food tents provided by the fiesta's sponsors for the crews and officials. No one questioned our presence, for only those who were supposed to be there were allowed in this area and, since we were a small group, I guess we just blended in. We had the time of our lives. We sampled complimentary treats from the various booths and took advantage of the chairs around the area for viewing. Some sponsors even gave us gifts!

As each balloon rose in the sky, we had an up close and personal "take off view." The balloons were a riot of colors. There were balloons shaped like a piggy bank, a tennis shoe, a cow, and a Coke bottle, but most were the traditional multicolored balloons with a basket below for the pilot and assistants. What a magnificent sight as the hot air giants glided silently through the early morning skies. Around noon, after all the balloons had made their way into the wild blue yonder, we found our bus right where we had left it. The driver had managed to get it unstuck, but by that time, he just decided to wait where he was and take advantage of the great view.

As we left our VIP area, we saw, way down at the other end of the field, the place where we had reservations with the other regular spectators. Food vendors of all kinds were selling their wares, and nothing near as good as what we had had for free. And this location certainly did not offer the excitement of being where the balloons were inflated and launched. That was one mistake that turned out great for my group. Some people thought I'd planned it that way, and I just let them think so.

That evening at dusk, we returned to the field for the "Balloon Glow." The balloons are inflated but anchored to the ground. A dramatic effect is produced as the balloons are illuminated from the fires that create the hot air. The balloons remain in place, side by side, shining in various colored hues in the dark. From there we took the tram up Sandia Crest Mountain from which we could still see the brilliant display below. On top we had a delicious dinner at the High Finance Restaurant as we drank in the great view of the city and surrounding area.

Three of my ladies wanted to take a hot air balloon ride. I set up the appointment for early the next morning. Keith and I were at breakfast in the hotel dining room when they returned.

"Have you already been on your balloon ride?" I inquired.

"No, he would not take us up because we were too old!" one said despondently.

"Surely, that is not the case. You ladies are very active."

"He said that the weather was not right, but we saw other balloons in the air, so we know it was just that he thought we were too old."

I felt so sorry for them, for one especially said that all her life she had wanted to take a hot air balloon ride.

る   る   る   る

Serendipity played an unexpected part in another of my tours, one that should have been very ordinary, one millions of people have taken before and since. Our group flew to Philadelphia where we had a brief city tour of Independence Hall and the Liberty Bell. Then we bussed on to Wilmington, Delaware, to overnight at the grand old Du Pont Hotel, owned by the family of the same name. It was very elegant, with fresh flowers everywhere. Even the bellmen wore white gloves.

The next day we went to the Hagley Museum and Library, where a machine shop and a restored worker's community depicted nineteenth century life as it was when the Du Ponts settled there from France. Our guide said that one day Du Pont went hunting with a neighbor who remarked that what America needed was some really good gunpowder. This gave H. F. Du Pont the idea and, on the banks of the Brandywine River, he built a powder factory and home. The business was an instant success. In 1803, he built his 196-room Georgian-style mansion which he filled with furniture and collectibles from all over the world. I was sorry there were only 16 rooms open to the public. The spacious grounds were most impressive and, as it happened, we were there on Mr. Du Pont's birthday, May 27. He lived to be eighty-eight, and the tour guide said that we were doing just what he would have wanted us to do, admiring his treasures and beautiful grounds.

We toured the elegant Longwood Gardens, once the estate of Pierre S. Du Pont, with its vast conservatory, formal gardens, fountains, lakes, and woodlands. We stopped at the Brandywine River Museum that exhibits numerous Wyeth originals and an extensive collection of eighteenth and nineteenth century antiques.

Then it was on to Washington, DC. We stayed at the Washington Hotel where, from the rooftop restaurant, you can look right down on the White House and its grounds. Our room had a direct view of the Washington Monument, which resembled a picture postcard when illuminated at night.

That evening we went to a performance at Ford's Theatre. I questioned why they had a picture of President Washington on the box where President Lincoln was sitting when he was assassinated. I was told that this way people would think of it as the President's box, and that it wouldn't be remembered simply as where Lincoln had received the fatal shot. Seemed strange to me, since that is what Ford's Theatre is known for.

As we returned to the hotel, limos were lined up to go into the White House driveway. We were told that this was part of Soviet President Mikhail Gorbachev's entourage and that he was to arrive two days later, on Thursday.

Early Wednesday morning we walked the two blocks to the White House where I had arranged through Texas Representative Jake Pickle for a private tour. We were lucky that we had chosen this day for the tour, as the White House was closed the next day because of the summit meeting with the Soviets. (I was unaware of the summit meeting when I made the reservations months before.) As we approached the White House, there was a long line waiting to go in. I told the guard who we were, and we were admitted immediately. We were especially thrilled to see the room where President and Mrs. George Bush would host a dinner party for President Gorbachev on Thursday night.

Afterwards, we continued to the Capital for another private tour arranged by Representative Pickle. Our guide was the curator for the National Heritage Society. He took us all over the place, in back corridors and stairways to avoid the crowds. He pointed out in the House chamber the two big paintings of Washington and Lafayette displayed on either side of the Speaker's platform. He said the Lafayette painting had been covered up with a wall and was discovered only when they were recently redecorating. We met Chaplain Ford who opens each Senate session with a prayer and he spoke to us briefly.

Thursday we cruised on the Potomac River to Mount Vernon, the estate home of George and Martha Washington. As we returned to the hotel, we noticed crowds of people gathered around the White House fence, and policemen everywhere. We decided to join the group to see what was going on. About that time a motorcade of ten limos was heading for the White House. In the middle of the procession, one limo stopped right in front of us. Out stepped Gorbachev who started shaking hands with the people on the side of the street. The Soviet Secret Police and the local men in blue had conniptions. They managed to get him back into the car as quickly as they could and it continued on to the White House for his dinner with President and Mrs. Bush. But not before we were treated to an impromptu audience with the President of our Cold War enemy.

A Peruvian girl speaks the universal language of friendship

Everyone is friendly at the Dani village in Irian Jaya, Indonesia

THE NATIVES ARE FRIENDLY

11

One evening after dinner, Conrad, one of my passengers, was sitting on a bench outside our hotel, the Burlington in Dublin, Ireland, enjoying his cigar. His wife, Kathleen, always insists that he go outside to smoke, and he continues this practice even away from home. As he was sitting there, enjoying the solitude and his cigar, a young lady approached him.

"Lonely, laddie?" she inquired.

Being past retirement age, he said that he was so taken aback he couldn't think of a snappy comeback. So he just shook his head no. Later he said he was pleased to be called a laddie, even if it was by a "lady of the evening."

Australians have to be the friendliest people in the world. I can truly say I've never met an Aussie I didn't like. Australians seem to have such a happy-go-lucky view of life, they are fun to be around. I admit, I have a little trouble understanding their accent, but they have the same problem with my Texas brogue.

In 1977, Keith and I were on a solo trip to New Zealand and Australia. One of our stops was Heron Island, one of the most southerly of the Barrier Reef islands, just off the east coast of Australia. As the name implies, Heron Island is a bird island, and we fully realized this at mealtime. The restaurant at the Heron Island Inn where we stayed was a covered open-air facility, allowing the birds freedom of entrance. The birds liked the food more than we did. Somehow I lost my appetite when we had to wipe bird crap off the plate and salt and pepper shakers before eating. The staff kept chasing them out, but to no avail, so while you were eating birds were all around you — on the table, on the floor, everywhere — eating and pooping.

The island is less than a mile long, and about the only accessible Australian island where you can simply walk right out onto the reef at low tide. The Inn provided "viewing boxes," square wooden frames with glass bottoms that you could place on the surface of the tide pools to view the many multicolored creatures, plants, and coral. For this activity, you needed heavy rubber-soled shoes which fortunately the Inn provided. The most outstanding thing we saw on our reef walks were the up to three-foot giant clams, wedged in the coral, their bright colored "lips" in tints ranging from exotic purple to hot pink. We would touch a clam with a stick, and immediately it would slam shut. We were warned not to try it with our foot, or good-bye toes.

We returned to Gladstone on the mainland coast via helicopter, which was great as we flew low enough to see the vibrant coral reefs in the clear Pacific water. When we arrived at the small airport, the only person around was a heavy-set man in his fifties asleep on one of the lounge benches. I remembered seeing him on Heron Island with a group of the fishermen. After going to the ladies room, I returned, to find Keith talking to him. He said his name was Ray and he was flying to Brisbane and then driving to his home in Coffs Harbour, located on the coast about halfway between Brisbane and Sydney.

"Where are you going and what do you plan to do?" he inquired.

"I have always wanted to hold a koala bear," I told him. "I read that there's a zoo in Brisbane where you can do that. And Keith is a rancher so we want to go out to a sheep station. We heard we could get a tour out of Sydney."

"Tell you what! I know a bloke who has a small zoo and you can hold all the koalas you want. Then there's another bloke who has a sheep station not far from where I live. Come with me and I will show you all around."

About this time, the plane arrived and, before we could respond, everyone had to get in line for boarding passes.

"What do you think?" Keith said to me. "Do we chance going off with a complete stranger?"

"I think if we watch him closely we'll be okay. He's not very big and between the two of us, I think we can handle him," I said, always ready for a new adventure. And what an adventure it was.

When we boarded the plane, we told him we would accept his offer. He was sitting at the rear of the plane and we were near the front, so we couldn't make any plans during the thirty-minute flight. After we arrived in Brisbane and collected our luggage, Ray said to me, "Stay with the luggage. Keith, you call the hotel where you're staying and get me a room. I'll go get a rental car." He was obviously in control, just like a good group leader, and we followed orders.

He soon returned and led us out to the car.

"Put the luggage in the boot," he commanded. It took me a moment to remember that "boot" is the Aussie term for "trunk." We complied and got into the car, Keith up front and me in the back. He started the car, then suddenly jumped out saying, "I need to do something with the fish! I'll give it to the Avis girl." From the "boot" he extracted his suitcase, opened it, and there among his clothes, loosely wrapped in a newspaper, was a whole fish over two feet long. I don't know how thrilled the Avis girl was with that "present."

Back in the car, he threw me a map and instructed me to find the way to the hotel. Here I am in a city I have never been in before, it's dark, and I've been appointed navigator. With my flashlight I did manage to locate the street the hotel was on and he seemed to know the way.

We came up to a red light and Ray bailed out once again, this time to run back to the car behind us.

"Damn fool had his headlights on bright," he mumbled when he returned.

Arriving at the hotel, he threw the car keys to Keith and said, "Bang on my door at seven in the morning." And off he went.

In the privacy of our room, Keith and I wondered what kind of character we had attached ourselves to, but so far everything seemed to be okay. At least he had trusted us with the keys to his rental car.

Next morning, promptly at seven, we knocked on Ray's door, and he was ready to go. We drove south of Brisbane to the zoo he had mentioned. It was small, and seemed to have seen better days, but the owner was pleased to see Ray and in no time, I was holding a little furry gray creature that was clinging to my shoulder with his sharp claws for dear life. I don't blame the poor little koala. We had awakened him from his day's sleep. However, he was very gentle and posed for pictures like a star. The zoo had many colorful birds and we were able to feed some emus and kangaroos.

Ray announced that we would go to his home for "tea," and he apologized that we could not spend the night at his house, because his mother-in-law was occupying the guest bedroom at the moment. Since we still didn't know quite what to make of Ray, we were kind of relieved and quickly said that we could stay in a nearby motel. Around four that afternoon, we drove up to his house, a luxurious home perched on a cliff overlooking the Pacific. I assumed it must be tea time, but I learned that in Australia "tea" can be a full meal deal. His wife, Jean, was in the kitchen busily preparing the dinner when we arrived.

"Does Ray often pick up strangers at airports and bring them home?" I asked her.

"No, this is the first time," she replied, and she seemed as puzzled about it as we were. Later we figured out that he found us interesting because we were from Texas, plus, he seemed to have taken a shine to us and wanted to show us his country.

The next morning he arrived at our motel in his car, a Mercedes. I was getting curious about what he did to support this posh lifestyle. Ray explained that right out of high school he became a mechanic and started out working on cars and trucks before graduating to working on the electrical generators that supplied power for the many remote towns in Australia. As electrical lines were installed in the '60s to most of these areas, he bought the now-obsolete generator plants for next to nothing. He refurbished them, sold them to various Pacific Islands that did not have local electric plants, and became a millionaire in the process. He had invested in property along the coast between Brisbane and Sydney and the value had skyrocketed in recent years. At that time, he told us, there was no capital gains tax in Australia, so he was really raking in the dough.

As we drove west from Coffs Harbour that morning, we saw eucalyptus trees lining the road. To our delight, an occasional wallaby jumped in front of the car. We came to the "sheep station" around ten. The owner and his wife cordially welcomed us and insisted we have tea. This time it really was tea and cakes. Then the owner, John, said, "I want you to see me spread."

We were led to an ancient vehicle much like the old two-ton trucks back in the States. All four of us climbed in the cab, which left me to sit in Keith's lap, right up close to the windshield. We drove around and saw hundreds of sheep, but the grass was not nearly as good as it is in Central Texas.

John said with a sly grin, "I'll show you me gullies." I had no idea what he was talking about.

He accelerated the truck and all of a sudden we dropped down into a deep ditch, which nearly threw me through the windshield. He continued this mad drive up and down cavernous gorges. John laughed and laughed, but I failed to see the humor in being thrown around and driving up and down in deep ditches — pardon me, gullies.

We were then invited to stay for tea and this time around it was lunch consisting of lamb, potatoes, and carrots, all very, very tasty. But, in the Australian fashion, nothing to drink until the meal was completed. Then came the hot tea.

Leaving the sheep station, Ray asked if we would like to go to an opal mine. I was so excited! One of the items on my Australian shopping list was an opal ring.

"When we go in the gift shop," he warned me, "don't open your mouth. The instant they realize you're a tourist, the price will go up. Just look around and then point out the one you want to buy." I now have a fire opal ring that has been valued in the U.S. at twice what I paid for it.

Before our night flight to Sydney, Ray took us to the country club where Jean was participating in a "lawn balls" tournament. The ladies, all in white dresses, were out on the lawn rolling balls about the size of softballs. This sport is an English import and very popular in Australia.

When we said good-bye to Ray and were expressing our thanks for an unbelievable experience of Australia, we told him the only way we could really repay him was for him and his wife to come see us in America. That is exactly what they did. The next summer, we proudly showed Ray and Jean our Texas, taking them to an Astros game in Houston, the Alamo and Riverwalk in San Antonio, across the Mexican border at Laredo, our beautiful hill country, and the capital building and LBJ Library in Austin.

Ray had told us about how he loved to fish for marlin off the coast of Australia and about the large ones he had caught, and we expressed an interest. He invited us to return to Australia, saying he would make all the arrangements for us to go deep-sea fishing. In 1980, when we checked the airfare to Australia, we discovered that we could go around the world on Pan Am cheaper. And that is what we did. At the end of this five-week round-the-world trip, we arrived in Melbourne, Australia where the fishing boat was moored. Upon arrival, to our great disappointment, Ray said that the boat was "out of commission" and that we would not be able to go fishing. Here we had come all that way for the sole purpose of going marlin fishing, and couldn't go. We were tired from the long trip, and I was homesick and missed the children, so I immediately changed our tickets to return early from Sydney.

Ray and Jean insisted they at least show us some of Australia that we had not seen previously. The four of us drove from Melbourne to Sydney in his Mercedes, going through Canberra, the capitol, and enjoying the scenic drive through the Blue Dandenongs Mountains. We flew home five days early and to this day I am still waiting to go marlin fishing.

🐦 🐦 🐦 🐦

It was 1976 and we were staying at Munich's wonderful Hotel Konigshof. The 106-room hotel first opened in 1862 and it has retained its old world charm and traditions. With up-to-date facilities, it is perfectly located for touring Munich's old town.

Our first priority was to stroll down the Marienplatz and be positioned at the famed Glockenspiel in plenty of time for a good view of the 11 a.m. performance when the little enameled copper figures put on their show. Shortly before eleven, an elderly gentleman and young man asked if they could sit with us. The boy, age seventeen, spoke excellent English. He had lived in the U.S. with his family for three years, but they had to return to Germany because of his grandfather's failing health. It had been over two years since he had been in the United States, and he wanted to brush up on his English by offering to be our guide for the day.

His name was Siegfried and he gave us the grand tour. Up to the top of Town Hall for a great view of the city, over to the Frauenkirche (Cathedral of Our Lady) that had been bombed during the war and rebuilt, into the subway for a ride out to the Englischer Garten, an eighteenth century park with lovely flowers and trees. Here we had tea at the Chinese Pagoda. By now it was four in the afternoon and I was exhausted, but Siegfried was still going strong.

"I need to return to the hotel and rest," I said. It was July, and it was very hot and humid.

"Come with me to the cinema and you can rest and cool off there. I will translate," he pleaded.

I hated to disappoint him, but we needed to catch our breath at the hotel as we had planned to go out that evening. We went into a bookshop and I asked him to select something as a token of our appreciation. He took a small round crystal ball that reflected the light like a diamond. I told him that whenever he looked at it, he was to remember the day that he had shed extra light on Munich for two Americans.

After a rest at the hotel, we walked down to a sidewalk restaurant on the Marienplatz for dinner. The menu was totally in German, and our waiter did not speak English so we just pointed to "special of the day." Big mistake. It was horrible. As we sat there shuffling our food around the plate instead of eating, a well-dressed man, about Keith's age, approached our table and in German, asked to sit with us, as all the other tables were occupied.

At least, judging from his hand motions, I assumed that's what he said. I replied, "We would love to have you join us, but we speak only English."

"No, matter," he replied in perfect English. He introduced himself as Fritz, director of the German Dairy Association. He had traveled in the United States many times. His home was in Hamburg, and he was in Munich on business.

"What are you eating?" Fritz asked.

"We don't know. It was just the special of the day."

Fritz laughed. "You have yesterday's leftover venison and it was not good even the first day."

He called the waiter and ordered us some delicious sausages and potatoes. We had an enjoyable time during the meal and, as we rose to leave, he asked what we had planned for the remainder of the evening.

"We are going to the Hofbrauhaus, because I have heard so much about it and everyone says that you must see it when in Munich."

"Well, there are certainly better places to go, but if that is what you wish, I will gladly go there with you."

This was great! We had toured the city by day with a local guide, and now we had a night guide. The Hofbrauhaus is probably the most famous beer hall in the world. It became known in 1920 as the notorious meeting place of Hitler's newly launched German Workers Party. Today, forty-five hundred beer drinkers can squeeze into the place and consume three thousand gallons of beer at the same time in the large hall. The beer is served in large quart size mugs brought to the table six at a time by waitresses clad in traditional German dirndl costumes. I think all forty-five hundred were there that night, as we had difficulty locating a place to sit. Finally we found a table with room to slide in on the long bench. I went first and found myself next to a jolly gentleman, about seventy years old, dressed in the traditional German lederhosen, loden jacket, and felt hat complete with a jaunty feather. He looked like he should be on a poster advertising Bavaria. I had no idea people still dressed like that.

We ordered the big mugs of beer, as it appeared to be the correct thing to do, even though Keith and I don't drink beer. In fact, I can't stand the taste of the stuff. So I just let mine sit there, and Keith did a pretty good job of sipping his. Fritz drank two mugs full, and he had already had one that same size during dinner! Meanwhile, the little old German man on my left kept trying to talk to me in German and patting my leg under the table. Keith and Fritz were conversing with the other people at the long table, most of whom spoke English. When we were ready to leave, the little old man asked Fritz to ask me if he could kiss me in thanks for the Marshall Plan. I had been a teenager in the days of the Marshall Plan. I had heard of it but wasn't sure what it was. Fritz explained that the Marshall Plan was a United States program that helped rebuild Germany after the war. Feeling very patriotic, I leaned over (he was as short as he was old), and the little man kissed me on the cheek.

On the way to the hotel, Fritz laughingly said he thought the old geezer just wanted to kiss me, and the Marshall plan was just an excuse that he found would work on American women.

Fritz invited us to come see him if we were ever in Hamburg. Three years later, we realized that Hamburg would be on our route from the Scandinavian countries to the Netherlands where we were to meet our daughter who was on a band tour. We had a marvelous dinner at his apartment. His wife did not speak English, but she was certainly an excellent cook, and the evening was very special to all of us.

     презент ব ব ব

Our group had flown from Austin to Acapulco to board a Princess ship for a cruise through the Panama Canal. The Princess staff met us and instructed us to take our luggage from the airport carousel and leave the bags in the area marked for transfer to the ship. When we boarded the transfer buses, I asked if everyone in my group had moved their luggage to the appointed place and all assured me they had. It is about a thirty-minute drive from the Acapulco airport into the city and harbor where the Royal Princess was docked.

"You will need your cruise documents and proof of citizenship to board the ship," I announced to my clan. As I was assisting them off the bus, one lady came up to me in a dither. "I don't have my purse!" she cried.

"Where do you last remember having it?" I asked.

"When I came through immigration where I showed my passport — I don't remember anything after that."

It took some talking to the ship security to admit her on board. I showed them my confirmation from Princess, which showed that her name was on the manifest and that she had been assigned a room. That seemed to do the trick and I told her to go to her room while I notified the ship's purser of our problem.

"I had all my jewelry, plus my money and passport in my purse. You said not to pack any jewelry in our suitcases, so I had it in my purse," she wailed. In other words, it was all *my* fault.

By this time, after getting everyone else in my group settled, the ship had sailed. I ran to the Purser's Office to report the loss of the purse.

"Is it a black one?" the purser inquired.

"Yes!" I cried.

He reached under the counter and handed me the lost purse. A little Mexican boy who was helping load the luggage had found it on top of the pile of luggage to be transferred to the ship and he had turned it in to the ship officials. There was not one thing missing! She had left it there with her luggage. I know that boy certainly needed extra money, but he was honest and turned it in apparently unopened.

So, what looked to be a bleak cruise for my lady passenger turned out to be a wonderful lesson in human nature. I hope it also taught her to be more aware of her possessions in the future.

⁊ ⁊ ⁊ ⁊

In London, in 1980, we were entering the Victoria and Albert Museum. I was looking around at the art in the entryway and didn't notice the security checkpoint and x-ray machine.

"Miss," the guard stopped me. "I need your purse to go through x-ray."

"Y'all don't need to do that. I'm not carrying anything dangerous," I said in my regular Texas drawl as I placed my purse on the machine.

The guard grinned up at me and said: "Who shot JR?" The television series *Dallas* was the most popular show in England at that time, and the big cliffhanger of "who shot JR?" had just aired. I was from

Texas, but didn't know the "big secret" and so was unable to enlighten him.

We have found that, years after the hit television series went off the air in the United States, it was still shown abroad. Many people in third world countries don't know where Texas is, but if you say "Dallas" they immediately respond. At a market in Indonesia, I saw a little girl wearing a knit cap with the inscription "Dallas." I asked her if she knew where that was and she shook her head, "no."

ॐ ॐ ॐ ॐ

One of my group cruises stopped at Grand Cayman. Keith and I had been to the island several times, and loved the northern region called Cayman Kai about an hour's drive from the port. We had the afternoon free from the ship and decided to rent a car. To our dismay, they refused to rent a car to Keith because he was over sixty-five. I could qualify, but I hadn't thought I would be driving and had left my driver's license in the safe on board the ship. We were so disappointed that we couldn't visit our favorite place.

We had taken a taxi out to the rental agency and they did offer to have one of their staff drive us back to the ship. On the way, we explained our quandary and the driver said he knew another rental firm in town that would rent to us and took us there.

At this rental place we were able to get a car without any questions of age and enjoyed our afternoon renewing the many good times we had had up on the beautiful beaches at Cayman Kai. This would not have been possible if the young man had not cared enough to take us to a competitor so we could rent a car.

ॐ ॐ ॐ ॐ

In 1989, I was leading a group on a Princess cruise that stopped in Leningrad (before the name was changed back to St. Petersburg). Since Keith and I had taken an extensive tour of Leningrad just the previous year, we wanted to see some of the area outside the city. In checking my reference books, I discovered Nizhni Novgorod, the third largest city in Russia, about seventy miles south of Leningrad. Novgorod, a World Heritage Site and the site of the first Kremlin, is known for its historic architecture, icons, and an art museum that houses more than ten thousand of the finest works to be found in Russia.

Working with the Princess Excursion Staff, I arranged a private car and guide for our day in Novgorod. The ship was spending the night in the port of Leningrad, so we felt we could surely get back in twenty-four hours. I had the ship prepare four box lunches for the driver, guide, and us. I also brought fresh fruit, Kleenex, soap, cigarettes, and candy.

I had obtained visas since I did not want to get caught without the proper documents in what was still the Soviet Union. When we arrived on shore, Immigration checked our passports and visas. Then we met Scott of the Princess staff who informed us we could not go to Novgorod because, even though we had Russian visas, we needed a special permit, which he had been unable to obtain, to travel over thirty kilometers from the city. Novgorod was 120 kilometers away. He said that the guide and driver with car were available for the day if we still wanted them. We didn't want to keep them from a day's work, so we thought maybe we could see some things we hadn't seen before.

The guide was Eugenia, who asked to be called Genia. She was very attractive and smartly dressed in a black and aqua pants suit and high-heeled black sling pumps with rhinestone bows. Certainly not like the average Russian women in their tacky plain dresses and clunky shoes. She told us she was thirty-seven years old, divorced, with a fourteen-year-old daughter. She taught English and Russian art and culture at the equivalent of our high school. Although not a member of the Communist Party, she had been an Intourist guide for four years.

The first thing she said to us was, "I have just returned from a visit to Sweden and Italy and I am so depressed to be back here in drab Leningrad." I then realized her wardrobe had come from Italy.

As we drove through the streets of Leningrad, she couldn't seem to shake her disappointment at being home again. "Just look at our trucks! Even they are ugly."

I told Genia we had seen the standard tourist attractions and wanted to see new things. She took us to the Russian Museum housed in the Mikhailovsky Palace that Nicholas II converted into a museum in 1898. There was a long line to enter, but Genia talked to the gatekeeper and took us right in. We joined a Russian group and Genia translated for us, much to the annoyance of some Russian women who gave us hard looks. Here we saw many exquisite icons of the fourteenth and fifteenth centuries, painters of the World of Art Movement, and even examples of twentieth century Russian artists.

Genia explained that Princess Cruises had arranged for us to have lunch at a restaurant in the city, even though I had box lunches and wanted to go to a park to eat. She stressed that the lunch was included in our payment and we must eat there. It was a restaurant just for tourists. There was a table reserved for Keith and me and I asked that Genia sit with us, but the management refused. She had to sit in another part of the restaurant and I am sure she got a very basic lunch, while we had caviar, tomato and cucumber salad, potato soup, a tasty veal cutlet, some surprisingly good Russian champagne, and warm Pepsi. They chill the vodka and champagne, but not the Pepsi. We topped off the meal with terrible ice cream.

After lunch, we went to a Russian cemetery where artists and important citizens were buried and it was very attractive with its restored headstones. Then we stopped at an Orthodox church. Genia told us that Leningrad had eighteen active houses of worship. There was one Catholic church, one Lutheran church, one Jewish synagogue, and one Muslim mosque; the rest were Russian Orthodox. I remarked that the church had no pews.

"The worshipers stay on their knees during the service," she explained.

I insisted that we wanted to see some of the countryside, at least as far as we were permitted to go. So out from the city we drove. We saw dachas, summer country homes for the wealthy, but at this time, most were in a run-down condition. Genia said that it cost a great deal to maintain homes this far out of the city, as it was difficult to find labor to do this kind of work. It looked to me like the owners could take a hammer and paintbrush and do a lot of good in a weekend or two.

As we were driving along, the driver, who had hardly uttered a word the entire day, said something to Genia, indicating he was stopping for gas. The first station had no gas and neither did the second station, several miles away. I began to worry that we would be stranded in the Russian countryside and wouldn't be able to get back to the ship! Finally, at the third station, he was able to purchase gasoline.

Genia said that the driver had to turn in the car at four, but she wanted us to come to her apartment. Since we had planned to attend a folklore show in the evening and return with the Princess group to the ship afterwards, we eagerly agreed. When we left the driver, I gave him a ball cap, one of the box lunches, two packs of Marlboros, and some candy. He didn't seem to appreciate any of it. After he had departed, I asked Genia about his attitude.

"He is unhappy because he does not want to drive a car. He wants to be a doctor, but the government makes him be a driver."

"I want to stop and pick up some cakes to have with tea," she said as she went into a nearby shop. Soon she returned and said she was so sorry, but they did not have any cookies or cakes left. I told her we still had the three box lunches and that would be more than enough for us.

We walked a few blocks from the main street where the driver had left us. There were no sidewalks, just paths between the buildings. We were in an apartment complex of typical Russian design, rectangular gray concrete block buildings four to five stories high. When we reached Genia's building, she entered a code to unlock an outside door that immediately led to a flight of stairs.

"The building does not have an elevator, so we have to walk four flights up. Do not say anything until we are safely inside my apartment. It is against the rules for tour guides to bring clients to their home and I have some military personnel living here, so that might get me in trouble," she warned.

Silently we climbed the dark stairs to the fourth floor. We entered an even darker hallway and then stopped in front of her apartment door. She unlocked one door, and there was another locked door. When the last door was opened, we were greeted by a dog about three feet high, half German shepherd and half St. Bernard. He immediately jumped up on me. Even though he was friendly, I said "Down!"

"He doesn't understand English." Genia laughed, and called off the dog in Russian.

Genia explained that originally her family had had a three-room apartment, and she was the only child. They all lived together when she was married and had her baby. After her father had died and Genia was divorced, they traded for a one-room place for her mother and she and her daughter were awarded this two-room flat. It consisted of a living room about eight by ten feet, a small bedroom with two single beds and a tiny kitchen, which I guess doesn't count as a room. She said the apartment cost 23 rubles a month, at that time about $36. The living room had nice Scandinavian style furniture and there were many books in English on the shelves. The kitchen was pitiful by American standards, although I am sure it looked adequate to the average Russian. The appliances were a two-burner gas stove and an old refrigerator like the kind on the TV show, "The Honeymooners," with the cylinder contraption on top. She said that the refrigerator didn't work. I saw no sign of a sink. The bathroom consisted of a commode. That was all, just a small closet with a commode in it. I didn't dare ask where they took a bath.

As we munched on our box lunches in the living room, she told us of her desperation at not being able to travel outside Leningrad. The only way she could leave was by invitation and sponsorship by someone in another country. Then she could only take 200 rubles (about $320) out of the country. She had been able to go to Finland and Italy through such a sponsorship. She said she felt that Gorbachev might be helping the situation a little, but saw no chance of much improvement in her lifetime; she hoped things would get better for her daughter.

"I hate everything about Russia, even our ugly trucks," she proclaimed.

Then she wanted to know all about life in the United States, what things cost, and on and on.

From a cabinet, Genia brought out three lovely lacquer boxes that she wanted to sell to us. I so wanted to help her, but the ship's captain had strictly cautioned us about buying anything that was not from a government-sponsored store, as it was against the law and the customs officials could hold us. I was too afraid to take the chance, so we gave her a nice tip instead.

It was time for us to go to the folklore show, and Genia walked us down to the main street and showed us where to get the trolley. I told her I would rather take a cab, since we could not read the signs or speak the language. We stood by the curb and tried to hail a cab, but empty ones would go right past us.

"They don't want to work," she said. "Maybe a private car, some-one who needs the money, will come by." I took out a package of Marlboro cigarettes and held them up. A cab stopped instantly. We re-gretfully said good-bye to Genia and she instructed the driver to take us to the theatre.

When we returned to the ship, the customs officials didn't even check for purchases or ask any questions, so we could have bought the boxes, but better to be safe than sorry. I often think about our day with Genia and wonder how this lovely woman and her daughter are faring now that things have improved somewhat in Russia.

æ æ æ æ

Good things can happen right here at home, too. At the Kentucky Derby, in Louisville, one of the men on the trip had brought his video camera in a rather large carrying case and the security officers at the entrance gate asked him to open it. He complied, taking out the cam-era and all the attachments, showing them that everything was in or-der. They passed him on through.

When it was time for the first race to start, he walked up to the window to place his first bet. He reached into his hip pocket for his wallet, and nothing was there. When we reported the loss to the secu-rity personnel, they said that nothing could be done because of the time lapse. Apparently the wallet had been removed right before the security guard's eyes while he was checking the camera equipment. The man's wife had some money with her so they could get by for the day, but the theft certainly curtailed his betting on the horses.

When he got home, there was a message on his answering machine. It was from a man who lived near the Derby grounds. He said he had been sitting out on his front porch when a car drove by and tossed out a wallet on his front lawn. Inside the billfold were identification, credit cards, and other documents. Only the cash was missing.

A few days later, our gentleman received his billfold in the mail — with everything intact — from this kind Kentucky man who had found his wallet, called him, and then mailed it to him. So there are good guys out there.

ès ès ès ès

I thought it would be special to celebrate Thanksgiving in colonial style, so I planned a trip to Williamsburg, Virginia, and the surrounding area. We flew to Washington, DC, and then boarded our bus. The bus driver was a little guy about five foot five. He was so excited to be driving for Texans that he showed up in boots and a big Stetson hat. He seemed disappointed that Keith was the only man in the group dressed cowboy style.

We stayed at the Williamsburg Inn right on the grounds of Colonial Williamsburg. Thanksgiving Day we had a private tour of the buildings in Old Williamsburg, followed by, and this is a quote from the brochure, "a traditional Thanksgiving Dinner." The dinner was served in the banquet hall where they jammed about one thousand people into an area that should accommodate about eight hundred. Crunched together, we were served semi-warm frozen sliced turkey (I don't think the Pilgrims had turkey this way), terrible dressing, cranberries, candied yams and a poor excuse for pumpkin pie. There was not a mention of a prayer or blessing of any kind before the meal. I certainly believe in saying a blessing at Thanksgiving. Isn't that the reason for the day? So my group said our silent blessings, and we were thankful when we got out of that noisy, crowded room.

The tour included a visit to Jamestown, the first permanent English settlement in the New World, founded in 1607. One plaque intrigued me. "Captain James Smith ruled that you must work to eat, and several starved," it read. There were replicas of typical buildings of the time with docents dressed in colonial costume demonstrating various crafts. There were also some teepees with Indians depicting their way of life. In my group I had a mother and her thirty-year old son. When it was time for the bus to leave, everyone was there except the son. I walked the entire area and could find him nowhere.

"Let's go," his mother said, "he is big enough to find his way to the hotel and he certainly has enough money for cab fare."

I had never left a customer before, and was hesitant, but at her insistence, we drove off. Later I found out why I couldn't find him. He was inside one of the teepees with a young Indian maiden. So the natives were indeed friendly.

Another one of those friendly Aussies

A close encounter of the furry kind with an Amazon jaguar

A group leader gets to scale mountains (Machu Picchu) . . .

. . . and always gets the handsomest camel boy (Giza, Egypt)

12

So You Want To Be A Group Leader

Sounds great, doesn't it? Go to all these wonderful places and see and do so many exciting things. Yes it is, but being a successful group leader requires a lot of energy, patience, love of people, and hard work. Of course, by now, after reading about my trials and tribulations, you may have decided that this way of life is not for you. And it certainly is not for everyone. Above all, you must love to travel and have the desire to seek out new places and adventures. If you have high blood pressure, don't consider it, for the stress level can be overwhelming.

First, some definitions. A group leader is a person who organizes a tour, promotes it, and accompanies the members from the beginning of the trip to the return home. A tour guide is a professional who works for a tour company and handles all the details of a tour once the group arrives at the destination. When a professional tour guide is not available, the group leader may sometimes have to serve as the guide as well. A travel agent is employed at an agency and books tours and can occasionally be a group leader/tour guide.

Never consider being a group leader to get rich or even to make a living. You must have income from some other source: a spouse, a job, a pension, lottery winnings. The sole purpose of being a group leader is to travel, and if you are successful, you can make a little money on the side, either for the company where you work, if you are on a salary, or for yourself if you are on your own.

You must love to work with all kinds of people. A deaf couple took several tours with me and each morning of the tour I would give them a written schedule of the day's activities, which I normally announced to the others over the bus microphone. The couple's appreciation was so rewarding to me. I love to see people having fun, and if I can assist, then I am pleased.

Once, a couple at the bank for which I organized tours wanted to be my assistants. They thought all I did was "travel around the world free." I took them on a one-day bus trip, "A Bluebonnet Trail in the Hill Country." We had a full bus of senior citizens and spent the day serving them and helping them in and out of the bus. The next day the bank lady told me that she and her husband had decided they didn't want to be my assistants after all.

"Oh, what changed your minds?"

"We didn't like taking care of all of those old people," she admitted.

To me there is special gratification in knowing that I am helping others. I have had several of my regulars tell me that they would have never gone abroad or managed to see the many things they had if they had not gone with me.

Dottie and Monty, two of my most faithful followers, wrote the following when I retired: *"We want to say thanks for opening up the world for us. We went places we never dreamed we would ever go. We knew if we went with you we would be taken care of and everything would be okay. We will always cherish the wonderful times."*

Following the terrible Copper Canyon trip, Claude and Frances wrote, *"You did indeed perform yeoman service in fulfilling your duties as our tour guide. We both thoroughly enjoyed this trip and feel that you are a 'helluva' credit to you and your employer."*

Vivian wrote after an Alaska tour/cruise, *"No question, the enjoyment of the tour goes to you. You gave us all the peaceable feeling of security which certainly contributes to the wonderful time had by all."*

It was cheering to receive this note after I had been retired for some time. *"As I sat watching the Olympic Games from Australia on the TV, wearing my Olympic T-shirt from Sydney, I wanted to thank you again for the memories of my wonderful trip to Australia and New Zealand. Fondly, V.A."*

Hundreds of letters like these make all the problems and the bad experiences vanish and fill me with a quiet satisfaction. Looking back and knowing that I gave so many people a good time and fond memories tells me I've done something important with my twenty-odd years in the travel industry.

GETTING STARTED

Don't make the mistake so many beginners make and think you can put a group together from your friends and relatives. Many have discovered that their "friends" are not interested in traveling with them. It is best to be associated with an organization that has a mailing list, a bank, a travel agency, or a club. If your bank doesn't have a travel program, ask about setting one up for them. You can go to the local travel agency and see if they would be interested in having you promote and sell group tours. Many agencies are too short-handed to spend the time and effort to establish a successful group travel program. If you live in a small town and know a lot of people, you can probably just use the telephone book as a basis for a mailing list.

You need to schedule a tour itinerary *at least* six months in advance, and preferably one year. When you are planning your schedule, consider your mailing list. What type of people are they and what are their interests? As a rule, most group travelers are senior citizens, since they are the ones with the time and the money and they have reached an age when they prefer not to drive and take care of all the arrangements themselves. Consider what trips you think would appeal to them. Do not think that just because the destination is a place you always wanted to visit, it will sell. I personally love adventuresome and exotic places with lots of wildlife and unique cultures. I found out that I could not fill a bus for this type of trip and had to concentrate on cruises, historical and scenic places, and football games! After I had taken the troops on many of these trips, they were ready to venture out with me to more exciting destinations that were right down my alley.

So start out simple and inexpensive. Your passengers have to get to know you and gain confidence in your ability as a group leader. Plan short bus trips to interesting local areas, perhaps capitalizing on special events. Have a variety of interests included to reach as many people as possible. On the first mailing you could include a popular destination in the United States, such as Las Vegas, Branson, or, if you live in the south, a Fall Foliage tour to the northeast, or a trip to New York City. These were always popular for my group. You might also include a short cruise to see if that appeals to your clientele.

Put together an attractive brochure of your tours. To save postage (which gets more expensive each year), I sent out just two mailings a year, one at Christmas listing the trips for the coming year and another in July, re-listing the tours remaining for the year and the proposed schedule for the first six months of the next year. Be careful that the weight of the mailing does not exceed the first class limit. You sure don't want your customers to have to pay extra postage to receive your mailing. By using first class postage, I could receive returns and keep my mailing list updated. It is easy to prepare your own attractive brochures with today's computers. I completed the layout on the computer, added clip art, and had the brochures printed at a local "quick print" place. I then ran off individual itinerary sheets for each trip with my Xerox machine to send to customers when they requested additional information.

If you are with a small bank, the brochure can be placed in the customer's statement. This can be difficult these days with the large holding companies, and it may be best to just handle your own mailings to your segment of the bank customers.

If you have the resources, advertise in the local paper. My bank did not allocate funds for this, so I had to find "free" ways to spread the word. I put together a program on how to pack for a seven-day trip, and contacted all the local clubs. (I got a list from the local Chamber of Commerce.) You have no idea how many clubs (men's and women's) are urgently seeking speakers for their programs. I spoke to numerous organizations and, at the same time, handed out my brochures and left a pad at the door so people could sign up for my mailing list. This effort resulted in hundreds of new clients. Later, after I had been on foreign trips (like an African safari or to the European Tulip Festival), I presented slide shows that were also well-received.

Join as many local organizations as you can. This will automatically introduce you to new people and give you access to additional mailing lists. Have your brochures with you whenever you go to parties, meetings, etc. and hand them out at every opportunity. Find places where you can post them on bulletin boards and ask doctors' offices if you can leave them in the reception room. People are always looking for something interesting to read while they wait for their appointment, and anything is usually better than the ancient, tattered magazines found in most medical offices. Grocery bulletin boards are another good place to post your trip information. I never placed a paid ad during my entire career, and was able to fill buses with creative promotion. I found word of mouth was the best advertising. If people have a good experience on your trip, they will talk about it at their next bridge meeting, cocktail party, or any other gathering. Carry your brochures with you everywhere you go. Hand them out to people you meet at parties, grocery stores, sports events, and so forth. I found that people were more interested in reading the brochure when they had actually met me and talked to me.

SOMETHING SPECIAL

You have to offer customers something that they can not get from any other source. Otherwise, why should they go with you?

Food and drink always appeals to everyone and if you cater to their wishes and needs, you become what's known in the trade as a Pied Piper. On your local bus trips you will need a large cooler. Depending on the group, you need to have cold drinks (regular and diet) and, if it is not your local church trip, wine and beer. I always had a separate thermos with drinking water. When we left early in the morning, I had hot coffee and "donut holes." (I discovered they were much cheaper than regular donuts, are easier to eat in the bus, and people loved them.) When we had to leave extra early, I had a local café prepare breakfast tacos, which were always a big hit.

We always had a rest stop after about two hours, and I would check the route and find a place where we could get snacks and go to the restroom. (McDonald's or a truck stop are good places.) On our trips to Houston, we stopped at a restaurant known for its baked bread.

I ordered ahead some hot, sliced buttered bread. I served this with coffee, wine, or cold drinks as we continued on our way and everyone loved it. When we would be traveling by bus in the late afternoon, I would serve crackers, cheese, and grapes with the beverages for a "happy-hour on wheels." All during the trip people could help themselves to the drinks in the cooler, and at first I was amazed at how many of my Texans would "pop a top" at 8:30 in the morning! But I can a truthfully say I never had anyone get out of line from drinking too much. Maybe just a little overuse of the bus lavatory. I also carried wrapped candies to hand out periodically. I found that the big tins of popcorn disappeared quickly. All this extra food requires lots of paper cups and paper towels, which I found worked better than napkins. With all this food consumption, you will need several plastic garbage bags and it is your responsibility to keep the bus clean. You don't want to make a good bus driver angry with you and request that you not serve food because the bus was such a mess afterwards. After serving, I would go down the aisle with small garbage bags to collect the garbage and then put it in the larger bags. These can then be stored in the luggage compartment underneath the bus.

All the above applies if you are chartering the bus and operating the tour yourself. If you are leading a purchased tour, you need to contact the company and request permission to bring a cooler on the bus and ask if it is permissible to serve beverages. If this was approved (and it always was), I would wait until I arrived at the destination. Then I would purchase an inexpensive Styrofoam cooler and drinks on the spot to put on the bus. Keith and I were always responsible for icing down the drinks, as I didn't want to create any extra work for the tour guide. One word of advice: If you plan to buy your wine and beer in Canada, be prepared to pay about twice the price as in the United States.

As you will be serving the patrons while the bus is in motion, it is very important that you always make sure your body is secure before you start pouring coffee or wine. I use the "three point" system. Always have three parts of your body steadfastly positioned (i.e. your two feet, and one hand). If you need to use both hands, keep your butt firmly pressed against one of the seats. You certainly do not want to spill anything on your guests, and you definitely are no good to the group if you are injured from falling down in the bus. It helps to have a smooth-driving bus driver. My driver, Ben, did an excellent job of taking us down the road with hardly a bobble. I have ridden with some drivers who jolt everyone around just shifting the gears, which results in black and blue thighs the next day.

Little souvenir gifts of the trip are an extra-added touch (T-shirts on cruises, tote bags, and the like). I usually tried to take a group photo and send it to everyone with a thank you note upon return. On cruises, plan a group party at the end of the journey. I found that a morning party with coffee, tea, and cookies was not as expensive as a cocktail party in the evening, and it accomplished the same purpose.

Whenever possible, add something extra to a regular tour. These little things will give people a reason to want to go with you instead of the "tour off the rack" and you can always build the cost into the tour price.

When I was in charge of fund raising for the Austin public television station, I conducted several wine tastings. This enabled me to become friends with the Jack Daniels distributor (who also distributed wines). He offered to arrange a free private tour of the distillery in Lynchburg, Tennessee, if I wanted to take a group. So I planned a bus trip to include it on a tour to Nashville.

The Jack Daniels Distillery has been making fine whiskey for over one hundred years in a hollow just outside Lynchburg. A guide instructed us on how this popular liquid is made. They start by making their own charcoal from hard sugar maple wood. Then they take corn, rye and barley malt, ground and mixed up with pure spring water (from a source right there in the hollow), and use the same recipe that Jack Daniels created in 1866. Once the mash is cooked and cooled, it is transferred to big open tanks to ferment, and you can get drunk just from the fumes. When it is just right, it goes through Jack Daniels' special "Charcoal Mellowing" in large vats. Then, when the tasters have determined that the whiskey is to their standards, it is put in brand new barrels that, when full, hold about fifty gallons and weigh about four hundred pounds. The next stop is the aging warehouse where the barrels are marked and dated. They store up to twenty thousand barrels in the warehouse at one time. When it is mature whiskey, the women of Lynchburg come for "Bottling Day." It is said that this is the best way to catch up on community gossip.

After the tour, we went to the "party cabin" where several employees had formed a band of fiddles, banjos, and guitars. Good old foot-stomping music was played; we danced and the Jack Daniels elixir flowed freely. The distillery is in a "dry conty" and they cannot sell their product there, but they can give it away. My group certainly accepted their hospitality generously, and I had to practically pour them back into the bus, but we all had a great time.

In Nashville, we went to the Grand Ole Opry. Liz, one of my passengers, had invested in a recording company, so she had a "back stage pass" and she invited Keith and me to join her. You certainly get a different perspective on the show from the benches at the back of the stage, but the biggest thrill of all was going back to the dressing rooms, where Roy Acuff invited us into his dressing room and posed with us for a picture.

I had another trick up my sleeve on this tour. I had the local operator arrange for the group to have dinner at the home of country music star, Tom T. Hall. His wife, Dixie, raised basset hounds and was a patron of the Humane Society. She opens their home for dinner to groups, with the revenue benefiting the Humane Society.

When our bus pulled up to Fox Hollow, the Hall's large, comfortable home about five miles outside Nashville, Dixie and Tom T. were on the porch to greet us. Dixie and some of her neighbors had prepared a delicious traditional southern buffet of fried chicken, grits, pecan pie, the works, for us. Afterwards, we gathered in the living room. Tom T. got out his guitar and entertained us with some of his favorite hits such as "Watermelon Wine" and "I Love." They even had autographed pictures of Tom T. for each of us. We went out back of the house to see her kennel of several basset hounds, looking sad with their big brown eyes. This was one of the most pleasant events in all our travels.

The same Jack Daniels distributor arranged for my group to have a private tour and free reception at the headquarters of the Bols Liqueur Company when we were in Amsterdam. After seeing how the many liqueurs were made there, we were treated to a generous tasting party with sumptuous snacks. My Texans, who had never sampled this brand, had the time of their lives and became Bols enthusiasts. Our local guide, Willie, had lived his entire life in Holland and had never had the opportunity to visit the distillery, much less have a party there.

When we were going to be in Rio de Janeiro, Brazil, I contacted H. Stern Jewelers, which is headquartered there. I had been impressed with their lovely shops at so many cruise ship ports of call in the Caribbean, and since Brazil is known for its jewels, I requested a private tour of the Stern facility. To my shock, I received a letter back stating that Mr. and Mrs. H. Stern would like to invite my entire group of twenty-five to be guests at their home for dinner. I was overwhelmed. I accepted, and we went to their residence, a huge apartment in an exclusive part of Rio. From their balcony you could see the brilliant lights of the city with the mountains in the background. We were served a lavish buffet, complete with wines and even cigars for the men at the conclusion of the evening. I never knew if Mr. Stern thought that, since we were a bank group from Texas, we would buy large pieces of jewelry, or if he was just being nice. But we all had a delightful time and the next day when we toured the jewelry factory, we probably did buy more than usual.

During my brief stint as a travel agent in 1980, Pan Am inaugurated a flight from Austin, Texas, to London, England. To mark the occasion, Pan Am brought over the Tower of London's Chief Yeoman Warder and his wife, "Pop" and Dot Davis. As I was the new kid on the block at the travel agency (and thus was not too busy) and personally knew the Pan Am representative, Donna, I was selected to host the dignitaries.

Pop and Dot Davis were the most congenial folks and a delight to be with. From them I learned that there have been Tower of London guards, known as Yeoman Waiters or Warders of the Tower, since 1485. Their duties throughout the ages have been guarding the tower, and in olden days they had to provide an executioner or headsman when the death penalty was decreed. Today they still carry the axe in parades, but in modern times, the Warders, in their bright red uniform with gold braid, complete with black felt hat (called a Tudor) and white gloves, serve as guards and receptionists for the tourists at the Tower. Pop said that no one actually knows for sure where the nickname "Beefeater" originated. Legend is that during times of famine in London, the Warders were given extra rations of meat to ensure their loyalty to the throne. Thus the jealous Londoners started calling them "Beefeaters."

As hostess for the Davises, I asked what they would like to see and do while in Texas. They immediately said that they wanted to see the "cowboys and Indians." I regretfully informed them that we were fresh out of Indians in the Austin area, but that we could certainly show them some cattle and modern day cowboys, just minus the six-shooters they had seen in the movies. Keith drove them out to tour ranches in the hill country and they were continuously looking for an Indian to appear in the rolling countryside.

Pop and Dot insisted that I contact them the next time I was in London, so I took them up on the invitation in 1985, when I had a group on a British Isles cruise that originated in London. They invited the group to witness the "Ceremony of the Keys" at the Tower. We were told to be at the Tower gate at 9 p.m. sharp. Dot met us at the gate and then Pop gave us a brief tour of the grounds before he had to be in place for the formal procedure.

The "Ceremony of the Keys" has remained the same each night for the last seven hundred years. At exactly seven minutes to ten o'clock, the Chief Warder (this time Pop) emerged from the Byward Tower with a candle lantern in one hand and the Queen's Keys in the other. Slowly he moved along to Traitors' Gate where one of the Foot Guards awaited him. Pop handed him the lantern and they continued side by side to the outer gate. He locked the outer gate first, then the Middle and Byward Tower gates. Afterwards, the two approached the sentry who challenged, "Who goes there?"

Pop replied: "The Keys."

"Whose Keys?" the sentry asked.

"Queen Elizabeth's Keys."

"Pass Queen Elizabeth's Keys. All's well," the sentry instructed.

Then Pop and the escort proceeded through the Bloody Tower archway and up the steps where the main guard soldiers were in formation with arms presented. The Chief Warder raised his Tudor bonnet high and cried: "God preserve Queen Elizabeth." The guard answered "Amen" just as the tower clock chimed ten o'clock and the bugler sounded the Last Post. Pop then dismissed the guard and took the keys to the Queen's House where they remained until the following night.

We stood in silence and awe during this impressive ritual in the cold dark night. Afterwards, Pop and Dot invited us to their cozy apartment in the Tower for tea. Warders originally were appointed for life, but since 1952 they are required to retire at age sixty-five. Pop told us he had one more year to serve. He and Dot were looking forward to moving to the south of England afterwards.

If you are in London and wish to attend the special "Ceremony of the Keys," the tickets are free, but you need to contact the Ceremony of the Keys Office at the Tower of London well in advance.

These are just a few of the "little extras" I arranged for my groups over the years. Some were possible because I was lucky enough to know the "right people," but many of them happened simply because I had a clever idea and the nerve to ask. So investigate where you are taking the group and see what special events you can provide. Your clients will talk about it for ages.

INSTILL CONFIDENCE

Your passengers must have confidence that you will take care of them in any situation. Take a First Aid course. Acquaint yourself with medical procedures in whatever country you are touring. I found that when an emergency arises, if you immediately start doing everything possible to help, the patient will respond accordingly. Your people will feel safe traveling with you.

In these days of lawsuits at the drop of a hat, you have to be careful that you do everything in your power to assist or get proper care for people who are the slightest bit injured. Go to the hospital with them or call a doctor immediately even if they insist you don't bother.

In your brochure, be sure to include a general disclaimer stating that you are not liable for anything that might go wrong on a tour. Check other companies' brochures to see about wording your disclaimer. This may not hold up in court, but at least you will have something in writing if necessary.

I always try to paint a worse picture than things really are when I know a sticky situation is approaching. For instance, if the hotel is not as great as you would like, tell your people to be prepared for an unpleasant experience and you will be surprised how many will tell you later that things weren't near as bad as they thought they would be. If they are thinking they are getting a luxury suite and the room is the size of a closet, they are going to be very unhappy chickens.

On many tours in the United States, I was tour guide/group leader. This entails reconfirming everything — the airlines, the hotels, the meals, the local guides, counting the luggage, handling the tips, the whole works. If you are on a tour with a professional guide, this is all handled for you.

Have your personal special colored tags to identify your group's luggage. I used bright yellow which was easy to spot. This will save a lot of time and worry at airports and hotels. It also helps identify your passengers' baggage if you join other travelers on a group tour.

It is standard procedure to tip professional guides, and companies usually request that this be handled individually. I always advise tour members as to the appropriate tip so they will be prepared. Personally, I *never* accepted any tips, whether I was the guide or not. I found that this created more respect and admiration for the professionalism of my position and me as the leader, and not as a hired hand who would expect a tip. I received many gifts from grateful followers, which I cordially accepted.

Smile when all around you is caving in. This is the hardest part. When the hotel does not have your rooms ready and your group is exhausted from an all-night flight or a long bus ride, you have to keep relations good with both the hotel and your people. I have found that clerks will respond more favorably if you keep your cool and don't raise your voice with angry demands.

How To Handle the "Complainer"

Most tours have a "lemon," someone who complains about everything. I usually just agree with these folks and, when they find that they can't get a rise out of me, they usually quit. Also, the other members of the tour are the best cure for someone who complains or who is always late. They will usually gang up on the culprit and that takes care of the situation.

I have found that, as a rule, most married couples *must* sit together on the airplane and must have *two* beds at the hotel. I always sent out a form with the final payment bill asking for "any special requests." When this was returned to me, I made every effort to comply. If they did not request anything, I had a leg to stand on when they started complaining, for I could always say that they had not told me of this before the tour.

One incident with a "problem member" comes to mind:

On a tour to Alaska, I had an elderly man and his wife who were a constant source of irritation. She walked with a cane and, for days, I helped her in and out of the bus, stayed back with them while they delayed the group, secured her cane on the bus. You name it, I was there to assist. When the tour guide would be explaining something, the old man would always interrupt with a totally unrelated question. The couple had just been a pain during the whole trip, but I kept quiet. The last night aboard the ship we had a farewell party in the ballroom. Just as the party was over, the band came on stage and started playing. My complainer grabbed his "invalid" wife, and you would have thought they were Fred Astaire and Ginger Rogers on the floor. They were dancing as if they had not a physical problem in the world, and the cane was left at her chair. This just infuriated me! The next morning I went around to my group at breakfast reminding everyone that we needed to be on the first departure bus as we had a short time to get to the airport to catch our plane.

"We may not be able to make it on time," the old complainer said.

"That's fine with me. Just plan to get home by yourselves," I replied and walked away. You know who was sitting on the front seat of the departure bus when I boarded. But I can assure you whenever they called to sign up for another tour, I was "fully booked" and had no room at all.

On one cruise to the Hawaiian Islands were two little ladies who were traveling with me for the first time. One of them, whom I will call SP (for sourpuss), looked like she had never smiled in her life. I thought if a cruise to Hawaii and my tender loving care didn't coax a smile from her, there was no hope. I decided to make it my mission to get SP to smile before we returned home.

When we arrived in Honolulu we were transferred to the SS Constitution in the nearby harbor. On board, I started my usual check of everyone's cabin to make sure they had their luggage, and the flowers I had ordered, and that everything was generally ship-shape. I made my rounds and all was in order, except when I went to Cabin #62 where SP and her roommate were supposed to be. There was their luggage, but no ladies. I assumed they were just looking around the ship. I kept checking back at the room numerous times, and no sight of them. I met one of their friends in the hallway and asked if she knew their whereabouts.

"They are in 362," she stated.

I had the group room assignments, and knew they were supposed to be in 62. I rushed up to 362 and there they were.

"When we got here, we noticed the dining room assignment was wrong. It says 362 and we are in 62. We didn't want to bother you, so we went to the maitre d' and had it changed. And where are our suitcases?"

Before I could explain they were in the wrong room, in walked the real owners of cabin 362. They were not too pleased that strangers were in their cabin and the bathroom had been used, etc. I quickly showed my ladies their mistake, and apologized to the couple. We hurriedly gathered up their belongings and trudged down to 62. During all this SP certainly was not smiling!

As the week passed, I just saw SP in passing in the dining room. Since she was not complaining to me, I did not want to muddy the waters, so I left her alone.

The final night on ship the entertainment was by passengers who had taken the hula classes offered on the cruise. I watched as a group of little old ladies paraded up on stage in their bright flowered muumuus and leis around their necks. They began swaying to the rhythm of the Hawaiian music and I couldn't believe my eyes. There was SP, all decked out in her colorful native dress, wildly dancing the hula and SMILING! She would have been the last person on earth I would have thought would take hula lessons. So, mission accomplished — not through my efforts, but the magic of the Hawaiian Islands.

COUNT AND COUNT AGAIN

You must be extremely careful in counting your people on the bus, especially if you do not have a busload. If the bus is totally full, all you have to do is just check to see that every seat is occupied. But even this can backfire.

We were at a Dallas Cowboys football game. Finding your way back to the bus after the game, in a parking lot loaded with hundreds of buses, was always a mad house. I had carefully told my people the parking lot number location of the bus. I had a full bus, so I checked to see that there were no empty seats and I told Ben to take off. The traffic was so jammed, he could not move at that moment. I started down the bus aisle, chatting with folks, when I came to a couple I did not recognize.

"Are you with the RepublicBank group?" I asked.

"Don't say a word," the wife whispered to the man.

"What are your names, please?" I continued.

Then the man broke down and confessed that they were also staying at the Adolphus Hotel, had seen our bus, and wanted to ride back with us.

"I would gladly accommodate you if I had the room, but every seat is full with my group, and you nearly caused me to leave two of my customers!"

I was so upset that we nearly drove off and left two people. I found them wandering between the buses trying to find us. So please, check all your people carefully. You may have a hitchhiker and not even know it.

SELECTING SUPPLIERS

In planning your local bus trips, try to find a bus company and driver you like and use them all the time. It is so important to have a rapport with the driver, someone you feel comfortable with to get you to your destination safely and on time. He or she should willingly assist with the luggage and help the people descend the bus steps, something that can be difficult for elderly travelers. You also need someone with a good sense of humor to help you through difficult situations.

If possible, go check out the hotels and restaurants you will be using on the tour. When I was booking within the United States, I always contacted a local tour operator to make the arrangements. They are best qualified to know about the accommodations, dining, and attractions available.

When I took my groups to New York City, I had a local company make special arrangements for us such as a Champagne Twilight Tour of the city before the Broadway show (they were also able to obtain excellent seats for us). They arranged a "high tea at Trump Tower" that was greatly received, plus a tour to an "artist's loft in SoHo."

I found it best to work solely with one wholesale tour company and one cruise company. This gives you clout. You get to know the personnel, and if anything goes wrong, you know whom to call to correct the problem. You also will have more offers to go on their fam trips. After using several companies, I concentrated on Collette Tours (now called Collette Vacations) and Princess Cruises. In my opinion Collette offered the best value for the money, selected the most centrally located hotels, and had the best tour guides. I selected Princess because of its name recognition at the time and the fact that it had an excellent reputation. In choosing tour companies, compare what you get for dollar spent in hotels, meals included, and optional tours. Try to take a tour yourself with the company to see how it is operated before you book a group .

Pick a tour company in the price range of your clientele. If your mailing list consists of "high rollers," then you will want to choose a more expensive product. But I have found that, as a rule, even if people have lots of money, they like good value for the price. Check to see if the company has a record of always operating the tour, or if they have a high ratio of cancellations. It is terrible to get twelve or so people signed up for your tour and have the company cancel because they do not see a profit in operating it.

Be sure that the company is a member of the United States Tour Operators Association, USTOA, which provides tour operator's insurance (similar to FDIC for banks) offering five million dollars in consumer protection if a member company goes bankrupt. I know one bank travel program that had a trip to Ireland booked with a company that went bankrupt two weeks prior to departure. The company did not have USTOA insurance, and the customers lost the $1,200 per person paid to the company, and had no tour. In this case, the bank came to the rescue, but you might not be that lucky. You certainly do not want to get caught in this situation so, regardless of the company, make sure they belong to USTOA.

Check out what kind of cancellation policy the company offers. I can guarantee that you will have cancellations, and it is a hassle with many companies to collect refunds. This is the primary reason I settled with Collette Tours as my provider. A sensible, easy-to-use cancellation policy is just as important for a group leader as it is for the individual traveler.

Pricing The Tour

This is a very important factor in being a successful group tour leader. If you are putting the trip together yourself, this is my recommendation:

Standard tour buses have a capacity of forty-four people, leaving the back seat unoccupied. This is the ideal number for profit.

When you are planning and pricing a tour, calculate on twenty-five paying passengers to get the price you will charge for the tour. This means that when you reach twenty-five paying passengers, you start making a profit. The trick is making sure you know the total cost ahead of time and don't have any unpleasant surprises. Take the cost of the bus and divide by twenty-five. Take the hotel room rate, including taxes (very important today) and divide in half for twin rate, or use the full price for single rate. Add the cost that each hotel will charge for luggage handling per bag. Then determine the cost per person for any included meals, entertainment, or special activities. Figure what the drinks and snacks you provide will cost and divide by twenty-five. Add all the results together to get price per person, double occupancy. Then add $10 per person for any unforeseen expenses. You now have a *preliminary* cost per person.

To make sure you travel for "free," take the preliminary cost per person and divide by twenty-five. Add this to the preliminary per-person total; add it twice if you want to bring along a companion. This way, the first twenty-five paying passengers also pay for your trip. Often, the hotel will give one complimentary room, restaurants a free meal, and airlines a free ticket with a group booking. In this case, the extra amount you have built into the price will be "gravy."

If you follow this system, you will arrive at a realistic cost per person and you will be just fine if you have at least twenty-five paying customers. If you do not reach this number, you have to make the decision to cancel the tour or take the loss and hope to make it up on the next trip.

When booking a tour with a wholesale supplier, the price per person is usually already set and published in a brochure, covering lodging, listed meals and activities, and tour guide. You will need to negotiate with the supplier how many free places will be awarded with how many paid passengers and what, if any, commission will be offered you. This is another reason to always use the same company. The more you book with a supplier, the better rate of commission you will receive. You will have to budget your "extras" for the passengers (drinks, T-shirts, etc.) from the commission received. As I said earlier, the object of this exercise is not to make money, but to travel "free."

BEFORE THE TRIP

After you have sent out your brochures you should receive reservations with deposits. You need to spell out the last date by which the deposit is refundable. Standard procedure is that the deposit is refundable up to ninety days prior to departure, at which time the balance is due. This varies with tour companies, so be sure to check each restriction. Upon receipt of the deposit, I send the passenger a copy of the trip's itinerary and notation of monies received. About three weeks prior to ninety days before departure I send out a letter listing the airline schedule and a billing form indicating the amount due. If payment has not been received by one week before it's due to the supplier, I call the person to see what the problem is. I had such wonderful customers that I rarely had to make such a call. Then you have to make sure that payment is received by the supplier on time.

The tour company will send the entire group's documents to you prior to the trip. Check each voucher and airline ticket thoroughly. It is amazing how many times there will be a flight coupon missing, or the wrong date on a voucher or ticket, or a complete set of documents omitted. This is time-consuming if you have a very big group, but it is vital. Today boarding passes are issued at check-in, which takes a lot of pressure off you for being responsible for their seating on the plane.

I never send airline tickets out with the final documents. This way I know that they won't be lost in the mail and that the customer won't leave them on the dresser at home. (I actually had that happen once.) In the final document packet I include: airline schedule (if going abroad stress that passports must be easily accessible and not packed in suitcase), phone numbers of hotels, when and where to meet you for departure, clothes suggestions, things to take for the trip (for example, sun tan lotion, insect repellent, coat and tie for men, plenty of film), maps marked with the tour itinerary, important information about the destination, and a list of tour participants. My clients always would call me and ask what the weather would be like on the trip.

To this I would reply: "If I knew that, I certainly would not be a group leader but on TV telling everyone what the weather conditions are." I advised them to watch the Weather Channel or check the Internet.

If you are traveling with a tour company, find out who will be the tour guide. If possible, talk to him or her and go over any particular problems or requests your group may have. But remember, the tour guide is in charge. No successful tour has two chiefs. Your job is to assist the guide any way they request and to take care of the special needs of your clients. I usually chose to bring up the rear when the group toured a site. This way I could see if my clients needed any help and when I showed up, the guide knew we were all there. Many guides expressed to me how much this helped.

You must set rules and stick with them. If you have a full bus, you must rotate the seats. You will be surprised how many people get "car sickness" if they have to sit in the back. If I have a guide, Keith and I always sit on the back seat. That way, I can see if there is any problem in the bus and be the last off to see if anyone left anything. You can also monitor the condition of the restroom. Also this means that no customer will be forced to use the back seat.

I learned the hard way how important it was to have me lead the group and Keith bring up the rear when we traveled without a guide. On our first trip to Hawaii, we arrived at a remote gate in the enormous Honolulu Airport. Keith and I led the group down to the baggage claim, which had to be at least half a mile away. When we got there, I noticed I was missing one lady. No one knew what had happened to her. I had to get a security officer in a cart to retrace our tracks. We found her sitting on a bench.

"What are you doing here?" I asked.

"I got tired and wanted to sit down and rest," she replied.

"Why didn't you let someone in the group know?"

"They were all ahead of me, and besides, I knew you'd come get me."

From that time on, I was in front and Keith in back. This paid off on a transfer between gates in Atlanta. One of our men had a slight heart attack, and if Keith had not been bringing up the rear and on hand to get assistance immediately, things might have been disastrous.

I am a stickler for being "on time." (Remember, I left my boss behind when he was late for a tour.) But I stressed the importance of being on time and I always set a good example. My regulars liked to say, "If you are fifteen minutes early on Joyce's tour, you are late."

FINAL ANSWER

Learn to accept things that you cannot change and work harder on those you can. In other words, concentrate on the controllables. It took me a long time to not let the weather, plane delays, or schedule changes do me in. When these occurred, I tried to divert people's attention with candy, food or drink, card games, or whatever else I could think of. For me, the worst thing is when you ask information from someone and you are given the wrong instructions. It just killed me to stand up and tell my group something that I had just been told, and then find out it was incorrect.

Even if you have a tour guide, research your destination carefully. Your clients expect you to know about where you are going, so don't disappoint them.

It is your responsibility to listen very carefully to the tour guide's instructions. You will always have a few who can't hear well, or do not pay attention and have no idea where they should be when doing what. And they will always come to you for the answers instead of asking the guide again.

Most of all, have fun and enjoy what you are doing. If you are happy, you will have happy followers. Also, it certainly helps to have a traveling companion, someone to help with the luggage while you take care of the people and someone to spout off to in the privacy of your room about the day's problems. But, mostly, someone to share the wonderful and exciting places you visit. I was lucky to be married to the "best luggage handler in the world."

So, go for it. The whole world is waiting for you.

Take a hat, but not this many (market in Ho Chi Minh City, Vietnam)

It's a bird, it's a plane . . . no, it's a kid in the Amazon, holding a giant gourd

13

READY, PACK, GO!

What has travel taught me? Many things.

That God created a beautiful world filled with a wealth of land-scapes, animals, birds, fishes, and people for us to appreciate. That I am truly blessed to have been born in the United States. That, basically, people are pretty much the same the world over and will respond to a friendly smile, even though you speak a different language. That every trip is a learning experience — about history, culture, flora, fauna, and human nature. That every country offers you something unique to see and learn if you will simply allow yourself to be open to the experience.

PLANNING THE TRIP

If you want someone else to do all the planning, there are many dependable and dedicated travel agents out there who will gladly assist you. If you are the independent sort and want to do it all yourself, there are excellent guidebooks and there is a wealth of travel information on the Internet to turn to. I think it makes the most sense to do a bit of both. Even if you turn yourself over to some latter-day Joyce Brooks, who is designing and leading tours for a local bank, you should still make the effort to educate yourself about the trip you are going to take, the places you are going to visit, and the sights you are going to see.

If you are considering taking an escorted tour (which means you will be traveling with a group even if it's just you and your spouse going on the trip), here's a good way to do some preliminary research. Go to the nearest travel agency and pick up brochures from several tour companies that serve your selected destination. Read the itineraries carefully. Compare what is included in each brochure. List the number of nights and number of meals included. If many of the sights you wish to see are not included and have to be purchased as "optional tours," the tour that looked like such bargain may end up being your most expensive choice.

See where the hotels are located and note the ratings (3-, 4-, or 5-star). You can check them out on the Internet or in a good guidebook. If you have just one or two days in a city, and the hotel is located miles from the city center, then you will not be able to walk around and see anything in your free time, and a cab ride to where you want to go may be very expensive, especially in Europe. Take the number of days of the tour and divide it into the total cost to get the price per day; that will serve as a valuable tool for comparison. If you are going abroad, notice how many days are used up by air travel.

Check the itinerary to determine the pace of the activity. Do you want to be on the go continuously, or do you prefer to have some free time to rest or see exactly what you want to see? Evaluate each company's tour to find the one just right for you.

Read the fine print. Pay very close attention to the cancellation policies, penalties, and any cancellation insurance offered. So many cancellation insurance policies have restrictions on refunds. Many require two doctors' letters and will not reimburse if the cause for canceling is due to illness or death of anyone not of the immediate family. Then there is the "prior conditions" clause, the classic way insurance companies weasel out of paying what you thought you were due. If you have a history of heart trouble and need to cancel due to chest pains, many insurance companies will not issue a refund and point to the "prior conditions" clause. I sometimes think that to avoid the "prior conditions" clause, you'd have to get run over by a truck.

This is the primary reason I almost always selected Collette Vacations for my group tours. If you have to cancel, for any reason, makes no difference what, all you have to do is to notify Collette headquarters and within about two weeks you will receive full reimbursement for the cost of the tour. No doctors' letters, no forms to fill out. That's it! I know it works, because I have collected many, many times for my clients.

The other reason I book Collette Vacations is that, after working with several very reputable companies, I personally think Collette offers the best value for the money. You will frequently stay in the same hotels used by Collette competitors, yet pay considerably less. Also, the company's tour guides are top notch. I have taken thirty-five Collette tours all around the world and can heartily recommend them. The toll-free number is 800-832-4656. Tell 'em Joyce sent you!

WHAT TO TAKE

I have seen some people take one carry-on on a tour, while others would drag along three large bags on the same trip.

If possible, pack everything in the popular roller bags that fit in the overhead bins of the airplane. That way, you won't have to worry about the airline misplacing your luggage. If you need to check your bag, be sure that you have identification on the inside *and* outside of the bag. That way, if the outside tag gets ripped off, they can still return your bag from the address in the inside. It is helpful to add a colorful ribbon or decal to your luggage to help you spot it when it comes around on the baggage carousel.

When you get ready to pack, look at your itinerary and count the days. Consider the type of tour it is and the activities planned. Then lay out on your bed all the clothes you plan to take, putting together items that will go together, according to colors. Dark colors are best because they do not show dirt as easily as lighter colors. Then determine the number of days you can dress using the same pants/skirts with various tops, jackets, or whatever. Put everything you don't need back in the closet. There's an old saying that contains more than a grain of truth: "Take half the amount of clothes and twice the amount of money."

Place shoes (*always* bring an extra pair) in the bag first, lining them up at the end that will be the bottom when the bag is lifted. Stuff shoes with socks. Then, again consulting the itinerary, place the items you plan to wear last in the suitcase first. After the clothing is in place, push underwear in the corners and around the edges. Remember, when traveling abroad in coach class, your baggage weight limit is 44 pounds per person.

In your carry-on bag pack:

- All medications and toiletries necessary for your daily maintenance.
- A change of underwear. I take an oversize T-shirt that can serve as a nightshirt, cover-up, or extra shirt if necessary. This comes in handy if the airline loses your checked bag.
- Water bottle, snacks, and reading material.
- Notebook and pen to jot down instructions. And it's always a good idea to keep a travel diary. This helps when you are trying to identify pictures and is great fun to read when you return home, or even (perhaps especially) years later.
- Camera and plenty of film, plus spare camera batteries.
- Binoculars if you are going on a nature tour.
- A travel alarm clock. If traveling abroad, pack a hand calculator for converting the foreign currency.
- A small flashlight. This can be especially useful abroad, where some tourist sites are poorly lit, or not lit at all. In some remote places, there is no electricity late at night.
- Duct tape. This is my "secret weapon." You can use it to repair suitcases, hem a skirt, or even patch a mosquito net.
- Ziploc or other plastic, resealable baggies. Use them for wet bathing suits, leftover food, that rock you picked up, or even as an emergency air sickness bag.
- Antibacterial Wet Ones in the "Travel Pack." Keep one in your purse for immediate use. If going to a remote location, take Purell Sanitizer and a can of Lysol spray.
- Small first-aid kit.
- Small sewing kit, the kind that nicer hotels will put among the bathroom amenities.
- Washcloth. Most foreign hotels do not furnish them. I bring a sponge that will dry quickly and store in a baggie.

- A flat rubber stopper. For some reason, in many hotels, the sink stopper is gone or won't hold water in the basin, which is a problem if you plan to do hand washing.
- Outside North America, the electrical outlets vary. I have purchased the adapters and burned out several hair dryers, for it is hard to always have the right one. I have found the best curling iron is a butane model that can be used anywhere, regardless of the current.
- Earplugs, if noise disturbs your sleep. And if you need to get up during the night and are in North America, take a small night-light to plug into the bathroom socket.
- If you wear eyeglasses, bring an extra pair if you have them. Get a glasses repair kit at Wal-Mart or a pharmacy because those little screws always seem to come loose on vacation.
- Small plastic tube of Prell shampoo to hand wash clothes. This concentrated soap is wonderful for your small laundry.
- Check to see if insect repellent is needed for your destination and, if so, bring it. It may be hard to find (or very expensive) when you get there.
- Many one-dollar bills for tips the world over. They are especially useful abroad. I bring at least $50 in crisp new singles for trips of two weeks or more. When you are getting your other travel money, make sure that the bills are in excellent condition. We have had trouble in foreign countries changing U.S. bills with a slight tear or even a mark on the face. The best solution for cash abroad is to use the ATM machines. The credit card was always my choice in a foreign country, because you usually received a better rate of exchange. But now, some card companies charge extra for using their cards abroad, so check with your card company regarding this before you go. Travelers checks are another form of carrying money, but obtain them in at least $50 denominations, for you are charged per exchange transaction, and it is rather a blow to be socked with $3 to cash a $10 travelers check. Figure how much is included

on your tour to determine the amount of cash you will need. Count the meals and tours that are not included in the package and then allow for souvenirs you might wish to purchase. If husband and wife are traveling together, separate the cash between you. I also stash some money in the tote bag that I keep with me all the time.

- Have a secure place for your airline tickets and passport and always keep them in your possession. The only time you should separate yourself from these items is when you have access to a safety deposit box. Be sure to have photocopies of the page in your passport that has your personal ID information. Carry it with you if you lock your passport in the hotel safe. You may need it to use a credit card or cash a Travelers Check. I usually make several copies of our passports and put one in each piece of luggage. If you ever lose your passport, a photocopy will be invaluable in obtaining a new one quickly. Bring extra passport photos if needed for immigration and especially when traveling in the third world.

- Tuck a foldable tote bag in your large bag to bring home all those souvenirs.

- If you enjoy a cocktail, remember that liquor can be very expensive abroad. And you might not be able to get your favorite brand. We always take our vodka with us in a plastic bottle.

BEFORE YOU LEAVE

If you are traveling outside the United States, make sure your passport is up to date. Many countries require that the expiration date in your passport be at least six months from your date of entry. Check into any other travel requirements, such as visas or tourist cards. Some you can get on arrival, others must be obtained before you leave.

Look over your travel documents carefully, making sure all the dates are correct and all items present.

Check to see if any shots are required or if you will need medications such as anti-malaria tablets. If we are going to a third world country, we always have our doctor prescribe an antibiotic and anti-diarrhea medications.

Reconfirm your airline schedule and seat assignments about two days before departure. If you belong to a Frequent Flyer program, be sure to have your airline card to show at check-in.

Research your destination. I have had so many people who had no idea what they were going to see. I had one couple that went on a Bermuda cruise with me thinking they were going to the Bahamas! You will find your trip much more gratifying if you know something about the place before you go.

Leave an itinerary with locator phone numbers with your relatives or neighbors.

If you plan to buy an item overseas, check out the price locally before you leave. You may be surprised to find that you can buy the item cheaper right here at home. I found this to be true with Lancome beauty products in France.

DURING THE TRIP

When a problem arises, go immediately to the source that can do something about it — the airline, hotel, or tour guide. Many times things can be handled right away, but the longer you wait to inform the authorities, the more difficult the solution may become. Document any troubles in writing so you can speak with authority when filing a claim later.

When traveling abroad, always assume a "low profile." Do not wear any valuable jewelry or splashy clothes to draw attention to the fact that you are a "wealthy American." Not only is this asking for trouble, but it puts you in an unfavorable light. Many people overseas will assume that, if you have enough money to travel to their country, you must be rich.

Don't expect everything to be the same "as it is at home." The reason you travel is to experience new things, so don't complain if you do not have all the conveniences to which you are accustomed.

Travel with an open mind and have a good time! Look to each new day as an opportunity to see new sights, meet new people, and learn new things. See and do as many things that interest you as possible, for many times you only pass this way once. (I have had some people with me who could not tell you anything about the tour except the food.) Flow with the little travel complications. Life is short, so go and see this wonderful world we live in while you can. Enjoy the moment!

If you have any questions, as a group leader or an individual traveler, contact me by e-mail at jbrooks@centex.net or by snail-mail at P.O. Box 280, Evant, TX 76525. I would love to hear from you and I'm eager to assist you in any way possible.

Drop by my web site, www.joycebrookstravel.com, to see colorful pictures from my travels and the latest news about my personal appearances and forthcoming books.

Happy Tours to You!

14

PLACES VISITED

NORTH AMERICA

Canada (9 provinces)
United States (all 50 states)
St. Pierre et Miquelon (Fr.)

CENTRAL AMERICA & CARIBBEAN

Antigua
Aruba
Bahamas
Barbados
Belize
Bermuda
British Virgin Islands
Bonaire
Cayman Islands
Costa Rica
Curaçao
Dominican Republic

El Salvador
Grenada
The Grenadines
Guatemala
Haiti
Honduras
Jamaica
Martinique
Mexico
Nicaragua
Panama
Puerto Rico
St. Barts
St. Maarten
Trinidad
U.S. Virgin Islands

SOUTH AMERICA

Argentina
Bolivia

Brazil
Chile
Colombia
Ecuador
French Guiana
Galapagos Islands
Guyana (Devil's Island)
Paraguay
Peru
Uruguay
Venezuela

EUROPE

Andorra
Austria
Belgium
Bulgaria
Czech Republic
Denmark
Finland
France
England
Germany
Greece
Hungary
Iceland
Ireland
Italy
Lichtenstein
Luxembourg
Monaco
Netherlands
Norway
Poland
Portugal

Romania
Russia
Scotland
Sicily
Slovakia
Spain
Sweden
Switzerland
Turkey
Ukraine
Vatican City
Wales
Yugoslavia

ASIA

Brunei
Cambodia
China
India
Indonesia (Kalimantan, Sumatra,
    Java, Sulawesi, Irian Jaya, Bali)
Hong Kong
Japan
Macau
Malaysia
Nepal
Philippines
Sabah
Sarawak
Singapore
Thailand
Vietnam

AFRICA

Cape Verde Islands
Canary Islands
Comoros Islands
Egypt
Kenya
Madagascar
Mauritius
Morocco
Reunion Island
Seychelles
South Africa
Tanzania
Zimbabwe

PACIFIC AREA

Australia
Easter Island
Fiji
Guam
New Zealand
Papua New Guinea
Tahiti

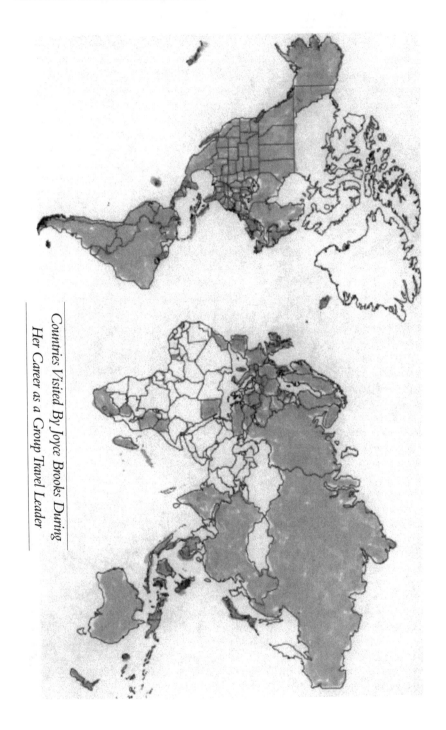

*Countries Visited By Joyce Brooks During
Her Career as a Group Travel Leader*

15

CHRONOLOGY

*Joyce and Keith on FAM Trip

1981

	Started work at Bank – Became Group Tour Leader
May	Kentucky Derby - Louisville, KY
August	Oilers–Saints Football - New Orleans
August	Oilers–Cowboys Football - Dallas
September	Fall Foliage in New England & Canada
November	Redskins–Cowboys Football - Dallas
December	Eagles–Cowboys Football - Dallas

1982

February	Washington's Birthday Celebration - Laredo
March	Spring Pilgrimage - Natchez, MS
April	Texas Bluebonnet Trail & LBJ Ranch
June	San Francisco - Tahoe - Reno
June	Astros Baseball - Houston
July	Texas Dude Ranch
July	Cayman Island
September	Cowboys–Oilers Football - Dallas
October	Renaissance Festival - Houston
October	Cowboys–Giants Football - Dallas

October	UT–OU & Cowboys–Redskins Football – Dallas
November	Hawaiian Islands Cruise
December	Candlelight Tour – Fredricksburg, TX

1983

*January	Banff & Lake Louise, Canada
*February	Jamaica
February	Las Vegas, NV
March	Mississippi River Cruise: New Orleans to Natchez
April	Bird Watching – Rockport, TX
April	Tulip Time in Holland – Belgium – France – Switzerland & Rhine Cruise
May	YO Ranch & Big Bend National Park, TX
June	Big Thicket Indian Reservation, TX
July	Rafting on Guadalupe River, TX
July	Jack Tar Resort – Montego Bay, Jamaica
August	Alaska Cruise & Interior Bus Tour
August	Cowboys–Oilers Football – Dallas
September	Cowboys Football plus Billy Bob's – Ft. Worth, TX
October	OU–UT & Cowboys Football – Dallas
October	Tyler, TX Rose Festival
November	Horseracing – Laredo, TX
December	Christmas on the Strand – Galveston, TX

1984

February	Caribbean Cruise: Puerto Rico – Curacao – Caracas, Venezuela – Grenadines – Martinique – St. Thomas
March	Dogwood Time in East Texas
April	Mississippi – Arkansas – Tennessee
May	"Carmen" Opera in San Antonio
June	New Orleans & Lafayette, LA
June	Jack Tar Resort – Bahamas
July	San Francisco – Tahoe – Reno
July	Texas Dude Ranch
August	South Africa – Zimbabwe – Kenya Safari – Egypt & Nile Cruise

September	New York City & New England Fall Foliage
October	OU-UT-Cowboys Football – Dallas
October	Renaissance Festival – Houston
November	Laredo, TX
November	Thanksgiving in Williamsburg & Washington, DC
December	Cowboys-Redskins Football – Dallas

1985

January	Mexican Riviera Cruise
February	Mardi Gras in Lafayette, LA
March	Azalea Trail – Houston
April	Vanishing River Cruise – Hill Country, TX
April	San Francisco – Tahoe – Reno
June	Galveston, TX Historical Tour
June	Canyonlands – Arizona – Utah – Nevada
July	Jack Tar Resort – Puerto Plata, Dominican Republic
August	King Ranch – Corpus Christi, TX
August	Shakespeare Festival – Winedale, TX
August	British Isles Cruise: London – Ireland – Isle of Man – Isle of Skye – Orkney Islands – Scotland & Hamburg, Germany
September	New York City & New England Fall Foliage
October	Laredo, TX
October	OU-UT-Cowboys Football – Dallas
November	South America Tour – Peru – Chile – Argentina – Brazil

1986

January	Tahiti Island Cruise
★January	Sea Cloud Cruise: Mexico & Honduras
February	Caribbean Cruise: Puerto Rico – Barbados – Martinique – St. Maarten – St. Thomas
March	Audubon Pilgrimage – St. Francisville, LA
April	Texas Bluebonnet Trail
April	Easter Time at New York City – Williamsburg – Amish Country Pennsylvania

May	YO Ranch & Kerrville Craft Show, TX
May	Kentucky Derby - Louisville, KY
May	Reno, NV
June	Alaska Cruise
July	Statue of Liberty Celebration, NYC & Cruise New England Islands
August	Mt. Rushmore - Yellowstone Park - Grand Tetons - Utah - Las Vegas
August	Shakespeare Festival - Winedale, TX
August	Cowboys-Oilers Football - Dallas
September	Banff - Lake Louise - Calgary, Canada
October	OU-UT-Cowboys Football - Dallas
October	Ozark Fall Festival - Eureka Springs, AR
October	Cowboys-St. Louis Cardinals Football - Dallas
October	Texas State Fair - Dallas
November	Laredo, TX
November	Thanksgiving at Cowboys Football - Dallas
December	Nashville Country Christmas - Tennessee

1987

*January	Whale Watching, Baja, Mexico - Cruise
January	Panama Canal Cruise: Acapulco - Cartagena, Colombia - Aruba - Martinique - Antigua - St. Thomas - Puerto Rico
February	Las Vegas, NV
February	Wildlife Expedition - Kerrville, TX
March	South Cruise: Savannah, GA - Hilton Head, SC - St. Simons Island, SC - St. Augustine, FL - Disney World, FL - Okeechobee Waterway, FL - Ft. Myers, FL
March	King Ranch & Whooping Crane Adventure - Rockport, TX
April	Cunard Cruise: Grand Cayman - Cozumel & Cancun, Mexico - Galveston
April	Bluebonnet Trail & Vanishing River Cruise, Texas
May	Galveston Historical Tour

May	Up California Coast – Los Angeles to San Francisco Bridge Celebration
June	Scandinavia – Russia Cruise
June	Louisiana Races & East Texas Train
June	Hawaiian Islands Cruise
July	Paradise Island – Bahamas
August	Idaho State Tour
September	Cruise: St. Louis, MO to Nashville, TN
September	Cowboys–Buffalo Bills Football – Dallas
October	New York City & Nova Scotia, Canada
October	Mexican Riviera Cruise
November	Australia – New Zealand – Fiji
December	San Antonio Christmas Celebration

1988

January	Citrus Festival – McAllen, TX
February	Caribbean Cruise: Miami – St. Maarten – St. Thomas – Dominican Republic
February	Las Vegas, NV
March	Brenham Home Tour, Texas
April	Texas Bluebonnet Trail
April	Copper Canyon, Mexico
May	Cruise to Bermuda
June	Cruise Alaska plus Midnight Sun Express Train
July	Canadian Rockies & Calgary Stampede
August	Eastern Europe: Russia – Czechoslovakia – Hungary – Romania – Bulgaria – Poland
September	Michigan & Great Lakes
October	Texas State Fair & Cowboys Football – Dallas
October	Laredo Races & Shopping – TX
November	Long Beach, CA – Stay on Queen Mary
November	Cowboys–Oilers Thanksgiving Game – Dallas
December	Chocolate Festival – Hershey Hotel – Corpus Christi, TX
December	Nashville Country Christmas – TN
December	New Year's Eve in New York City

1989

January	Texas Gambling Cruise & Valley Tour
February	Broadway Plays in Houston
February	Caribbean Cruise: Puerto Rico – St. Maarten – Martinique – St. Thomas
February	Las Vegas, NV
March	St. Patrick's Day in Ireland
April	Texas Bluebonnets & Wine Festival
April	Natchez, Mississippi Spring Pilgrimage
April	Bahamas Islands Cruise
May	Cinco de Mayo Festival in San Antonio
*May	Costa Rica
May	San Francisco – Tahoe – Reno
June	Indian Plays in Texas & Oklahoma
July	Sea World in San Antonio
July	Northern Europe Cruise: London – Netherlands – Russia – Finland – Sweden – Denmark
August	YO Ranch & Kerrville, TX
September	European Cruise: Spain – France – Italy – Greece – Yugoslavia
October	Fall Foliage Cruise: RI – NY up Hudson – Erie Canal – St. Lawrence Seaway – Montreal – Quebec City – Bus back through NH & VT
October	Guadalajara, Mexico
November	Christmas at Mansions in Brenham, TX
November	San Diego Faberge Art Exhibit
November	Laredo, TX
November	Cowboys Thanksgiving Game – Dallas

1990

January	Cruise: Spain's Costa Del Sol – Morocco – Canary Islands – Tangier – Rock of Gibraltar
February	Las Vegas, NV
February	Costa Rica
March	Bob Hope Show in Port Arthur, TX
March	Cruise: Puerto Rico – Martinique – Barbados –

	Devil's Island – French Guiana – Amazon River to Manaus, Brazil
April	Bluebonnet Trail & Wine Festival, TX
April	Easter in New York City plus Atlantic City
April	Atlanta, GA
May	Cruise: Ft. Lauderdale, FL – Cozumel, Mexico – Grand Cayman – Cartagena, Columbia – Panama Canal – Acapulco, Mexico
May	Brandywine Country – Pennsylvania – Delaware – Washington, DC
June	Galveston Gambling Cruise
July	Hawaiian Islands Cruise
August	San Antonio Broadway Show & Sea World
August	Ruidoso & Santa Fe, NM – Indian Market – Pala Duro Canyon Show, TX
September	Oberammergau Passion Play in Germany – Italy – Switzerland
October	Black Sea Cruise – Rome, Italy – Sicily – Izimir, Ephesus & Istanbul, Turkey – Yalta & Odessa, Russia – Yugoslavia – Venice, Italy
November	Ecuador & Galapagos Islands Cruise
November	Disney World, FL
December	Nashville Country Christmas, TN
December	Rose Parade in Los Angeles

1991

January	Belize & Tikal, Guatemala
February	Caribbean Cruise: Ft. Lauderdale, FL – Nassau, Bahamas – Jamaica – Grand Cayman – Cozumel
February	Las Vegas, NV
March	Corpus Christi, TX
April	San Francisco – Tahoe – Yosemite Park
April	Bob Hope Show in Port Arthur, TX
May	Branson, MO & Eureka Springs, AR
May	Tulip Time in Michigan
June	Retired from NationsBank – Moved to Ranch

July   Started Own Travel Business
October   Albuquerque Balloon Festival & Santa Fe, NM
December   Nashville Country Christmas, TN
December   Week in London, England

1992

February   Las Vegas
June   Train from Vancouver to Jasper – Motorcoach to
                Calgary, Canada
August   Vienna, Austria – Budapest, Hungary – Prague,
                Czechoslovakia – Elbe River Cruise through East
                Germany – Motorcoach to Berlin
September   Seattle, WA through Oregon to San Francisco, CA
October   New England Fall Foliage
October   St. Louis & Branson, MO
November   China – Hong Kong – Macau

1993

January   Amazon River Cruise: Manaus, Brazil – Trinidad –
                Martinique – St. Bart's – St. Maarten – St. Thomas –
                Miami, FL
February   Argentina – Chile – Brazil
March   A week in Paris, France
April   Las Vegas, NV – AZ – NM
May   Ottawa, Canada Tulip Festival – Montreal – Quebec
                City
July   Chicago – Train to Glacier National Park – Sun
                Valley, ID
August   Nova Scotia – Prince Edward Island – Newfound-
                land, Canada
September   England – Ireland – Scotland – Wales
November   Australia – New Zealand – Fiji
December   Nashville Country Christmas, TN
December   Rose Parade in Los Angeles

1994

February	Costa Rica
March	Amazon River Cruise: Iquitos, Peru to Manaus, Brazil
April	Georgia & South Carolina
May	50th Anniversary D-Day Celebration in England & France
July	Cruise: Alaska & Yukon Land/Rail Tour
September	Denmark - Norway - Sweden - Finland
October	Boston, MA - Maine - Gaspé Trail & Quebec City - VT - NH
November	Hong Kong - Bangkok - Singapore - Bali
November	Thanksgiving in New York City

1995

January	Chile & Easter Island
February	Las Vegas, NV
March	Portugal & Spain
May	Cruise from New Orleans to Chicago
June	National Parks - AZ - UT - WY - SD
July	Newfoundland - Labrador - St. Pierre

1996

	Became Texas Sales Representative for Collette Tours and did not escort any group tours
★July	Papua New Guinea Land & Cruise - Singapore - Malaysia

1997

	Resumed escorting a few group trips
January	Las Vegas, NV
★April	Vietnam - Cambodia
July	Washington State & San Juan Islands
September	Tanzania with group - Madagascar - Reunion Island - Mauritius - Seychelles on own

1998

January	Peru & Bolivia
April	France – Monaco – London via Chunnel
★August	Salmon Fishing in Alaska
★November	Indonesia (Bali – Sulawesi – Irian Jaya – Java – Sumatra)
★December	Argentina – Uruguay – Paraguay

1999

January	Costa Rica
February	Snowmobiling in Jackson Hole, WY
March	Retired from escorting groups and as Collette Representative
★July	Philippines – Borneo (Sabah – Sawawak – Brunei – Kalimantan) – Indonesia (Sulawesi & Bali)

The author, still in the middle seat

Visit

Family of Web Sites

http://www.IntrepidTraveler.com

Our main site with a complete catalog of money-saving, horizon-expanding books, plus our online travel magazine.

http://www.BeatTheAirlines.com

Learn how to beat the airlines at their own game on a site that helps make sure you never pay full fare again.

http://www.HomeTravelAgency.com

Join the thousands of people who are earning good money and free travel as home-based travel agents.

http://www.TheOtherOrlando.com

The site devoted to the wonderful world outside the Magic Kingdom.